COUNSELING AND THERAPY WITH CLIENTS WHO ABUSE ALCOHOL OR OTHER DRUGS

An Integrative Approach

COUNSELING AND THERAPY WITH CLIENTS WHO ABUSE ALCOHOL OR OTHER DRUGS

An Integrative Approach

Cynthia Glidden-Tracey
Arizona State University

LEA LAWRENCE ERLBAUM ASSOCIATES, PUBLISHERS
2005   Mahwah, New Jersey   London

Lawrence Erlbaum Associates, Inc., Publishers
10 Industrial Avenue
Mahwah, New Jersey 07430

Cover design by Kathryn Houghtaling Lacey

Library of Congress Cataloging-in-Publication Data

Glidden-Tracey, Cynthia.
   Counseling and therapy with clients who abuse alcohol or other drugs :
      an integrative approach / Cynthia Glidden-Tracey.
         p.   cm.
   Includes bibliographical references and index.
   ISBN 0-8058-4550-X (c. : alk. paper)
   ISBN 0-8058-4551-8 (pbk. : alk. paper)
   1. Substance abuse—Treatment.   2. Psychotherapy.   3. Counseling.   I. Title.

RC564.G54   2005
616.86'06—dc22   2004053323
                                                             CIP

Books published by Lawrence Erlbaum Associates are printed on acid-free paper,
and their bindings are chosen for strength and durability.

Printed in the United States of America
10   9   8   7   6   5   4   3   2   1

Dedicated to
Terence John Glidden Tracey

Contents

Preface

Do you know anyone who has engaged in risky use of psychoactive substances? If so (as I expect will be true for most readers), are any of those people clients with whom you have worked professionally? If you answered yes to either question, you probably already know that substance use concerns do not always come up in a clear or straightforward manner. Nor are complications linked to a person's substance use or abuse easy to unravel and resolve. Still indications are that substance use disorders are among the most frequently occurring human disorders, and they are often tangled up with other physical and mental health problems. The high prevalence of substance use disorders virtually guarantees that most therapists and health care professionals will encounter clients who engage in risky substance use.

The association among substance abuse, mental health issues, and social problems has been extensively documented and debated. Even so, addictions specialists and other interested parties continue to point out the scant training many health care professionals receive to prepare them to treat problematic substance use. Concentrating on psychological therapies, in this book I explore some of the barriers contributing to the disturbing discrepancy between the vast need and limited supply of thorough treatments for substance use disorders. In addition, I offer strategies for interweaving a focus on a client's risky substance use with an understanding of the therapy process.

In particular, my emphasis is on points in the therapy transaction when therapists need to make choices about how to proceed in light of concerns raised about the client's substance use. Crucial assumptions are that such concerns may emerge at any point in a course of therapy, and that the most effective therapists will be able to detect and address substance abuse issues however they arise. Additionally, the interpersonal dynamics of therapy relationships are assumed to shape the exploration and modification of substance use behaviors, with the therapist's feelings, attitudes, and responses as essential as the client's. From this perspective, the reciprocal impact of the therapist's and client's behaviors in session largely determines the therapeutic potential of their interactions regarding the client's substance use. The ethnocultural backgrounds of the therapy participants, including attitudes and practices regarding substance use, also influence the process of this interaction.

The first four chapters of the book present contextual knowledge to prepare therapists to work with clients who abuse psychoactive substances. Chapter 1 explores themes and patterns that are likely to characterize therapy with clients involved in risky substance use. Chapter 2 elaborates on the therapist's potential use of these themes and patterns within a therapeutic model. In chapter 3, factors contributing to the changing relationship of the substance abuse and mental health treatment fields are considered. Chapter 4 summarizes the actions and effects of psychoactive substances on the human brain and body.

The rest of the chapters address the tasks that therapists undertake to specifically address a client's substance use issues over the course of therapy. In chapter 5, the assessment of a client's substance use history and current behavior is detailed, with concentration on differential diagnosis of substance use disorders and corresponding treatment recommendations. Chapter 6 describes important considerations in developing and implementing workable treatment plans to address a client's substance abuse and related concerns. Chapter 7 focuses on psychoeducation as an intervention for enriching a client's appreciation of the personal significance of substance abuse, the process of personal change, and the nature of psychotherapy. In chapter 8, the critical value of relapse prevention strategies is emphasized, along with practical applications. Interventions for addressing medical, emotional, interpersonal, occupational, and legal difficulties that may be associated with a client's substance use are enumerated in chapter 9. Finally, chapter 10 addresses the particular issues that can arise in the termination of therapy, incorporating a focus on a client's problematic substance use.

On the one hand, these chapters attempt to track the evolving process of therapy, but they also acknowledge the ongoing relevance of each of these therapeutic tasks across a course of therapy. I further provide numerous clinical examples to illustrate the multifaceted and diverse nature of substance use issues that may surface among clients in therapy, although comprehensive treatment of culturally specific factors is beyond the scope of this work. (All clients described in the book are based on fictional composites, and no real names of actual people are used.) By examining the complexities of process and content in therapy to address substance use concerns, I hope this book helps motivate and equip therapists and health care professionals to improve services to this huge and difficult population. With increasing facility to provide compassionate care integrated with shared accountability for change, therapy and associated treatments for substance use disorders in all their manifestations hold great potential for tremendous impact on responsible decision making at important choice points.

Many wonderful people deserve my deep thanks for their contributions to my completion of this manuscript. First, I am grateful for the insightful feedback from Jamie Bludworth, Nancy Farber, Christy Hofsess, John Horan, Susan LeClair, Terry Tracey, and Bruce Wampold, each of whom reviewed drafts of chapters in progress. Thanks also to Susan Milmoe for her editorial input throughout this project, to Elsie Moore for helping me free some time to write, and to Sharon Zygowicz for indexing the book with me.

Second, I have been blessed with incredible guidance from my clinical supervisors across many sites, including Don Bybee, Lynda Birckhead, Mark Combs, Deb Freund, Jim Hannum, Judy Homer, Juli Kartel, Cheryl Kurash, Doug Lamb, Don Mullison, David Reardon, Pamela Spearman, and Terry Tracey, all of whom have expanded my understanding of therapy in general and substance abuse issues in particular. I gained much, too, from my formal, trial-by-fire introduction to full-time substance abuse treatment with my professional colleagues at Prairie Center Health Systems.

Third, I only wish I could adequately acknowledge the impact of each client with whom I have shared the struggles, insights, and outcomes of attempts to deal with substance use concerns because I carry their memories and stories with me every day. Fourth, my students and supervisees over many years have taught me so much about the mechanisms of therapy and the processes by which they are learned.

Fifth, I count myself lucky to have great friends and family who have given terrific moral support in the long process of writing this book. In addition to friends already mentioned, I want to thank Marilyn and Bill Boyle, David Bower, Bob Glidden, Sandy Stokes Goff, Maria Hafford, Betty and Curtis Hall, Sue Labott, Fu-Lin Lee, Melissa and Bruce Richardson, Marilyn Thompson, Tim and Mary Tracey, Fran Venegas, Tina and Brian Westmoreland, and, most especially, my parents, Ted and Dorie Glidden, and my mother-in-law, Ginny Tracey. Finally, and most important, my work infinitely benefits from the patience, love, and inspiration provided by my husband, Terry, and the kids (some grown up already!) whom I adore: Trevor, Beilee, Erin, Cameron, and Kendra.

—*Cynthia Glidden-Tracey*

Chapter 1

Might as Well Face It, There's Addiction Among Your Clients*

Every day huge numbers of people use drugs or alcohol for recreation, medication, celebration, stress management, worship, social lubrication, or escape. Although some substance use is considered normal, it is no secret that drug and alcohol consumption can become excessive or compulsive to the point where it disrupts normal human functions. The use and abuse of psychoactive chemicals bombard our society with controversies and complications, which eventually lead some individuals to seek professional psychotherapy or counseling. In therapy and treatment settings, evidence (to be considered shortly) points to rampant rates of disordered substance use among clients, even when substance abuse is not presented as the problem of interest.

Sometimes clients initiate therapy specifically to address their problematic substance use because they are considering a change. Many other clients are responding to pressure from third parties when they show up for a therapy session to talk about substance use issues. Still other clients discuss substance use with their therapists not as a presenting problem, but only after many sessions have transpired. Drug or alcohol use may come up as a topic when the client gets ready or concerned enough to address it, or perhaps only when the attentive therapist probes for more information based on the client's hints about substance use. Whenever and however the issue of substance abuse emerges in therapy among the issues the client is struggling to handle, a competent therapist is prepared to intervene.

---

*The title for chapter 1 is loosely derived from lyrics of the song "Addicted to Love," with apologies (and thanks!) to the late Robert Palmer.

The purpose of this book is to help prepare therapists to effectively assess, treat, and, when necessary, refer clients who abuse psychoactive substances. Hopefully the book will also persuade therapists and counselors to consider skills for treating substance use disorders as necessary compositions in our repertoire. In this chapter, I demonstrate that the likelihood of encountering substance abusing clients is high and the spectrum of substance use disorders is multifaceted. To adequately treat the frequent and varied presentations of substance abuse issues in therapy, the practitioner deliberately tailors therapeutic strategies to the expressed and assessed needs of each client. This process, in many respects, parallels the course of therapy for other psychological disorders, but treating or appropriately referring clients with substance use disorders also confronts the therapist with distinctive features and barriers to the therapy process.

When discussing substance use, clients are stereotypically more withholding, deceptive, manipulative, hostile, or uncooperative in sessions. Such behaviors can make sense in the context of the strong reinforcing effects of substance use combined with the probable presence of either the need to hide illegal or otherwise sanctioned behavior, or external pressure to attend therapy sessions (if not both). These factors, along with the concomitant negative consequences of frequent or heavy substance use, create strong ambivalence about change in the substance user. The substance abuse treatment field is paying increasing attention to the importance of addressing client ambivalence about continuing drug or alcohol use (Miller & Rollnick, 1991, 2002).

The convention of distinguishing psychoactive substance use disorders from psychological problems and mental health disorders has historically resulted in treatments for substance use disorders that are relatively isolated from psychotherapeutic approaches. In recent years, however, the literature increasingly notes both the potential applicability of psychological models for treating problematic substance use (Miller & Brown, 1997) and the dearth of adequate training for psychologists and other mental health professionals to treat substance use disorders among their clients (Carey, Bradizza, Stasiewicz, & Maisto, 1999; Cheirt, Gold, & Taylor, 1994). Psychotherapy is promoted here as an appropriate and effective form of treatment to reduce problematic consumption of drugs or alcohol.

In the chapters to follow, I assume a model of therapy in which the therapist intentionally aims to create conditions of interaction in therapy that are conducive to the client's behavioral change, including changes in substance use behaviors. With careful adaptations cognizant of the nature of substance use disorders, therapists can attempt to influence the quality of their relationships with substance abusing clients, the degree of structure in their therapy interactions, and the choice of personal growth goals. These three domains of relationship, level of structure, and specification of goals are described by Moos (2003) as common factors of the contexts in which personal change occurs. Psychotherapy has the greatest potential to promote beneficial change in substance use behaviors when the quality of the relationship is high, the structure of therapy is planful but flexible, and the choice of goals is collaborative, directly involving the client.

GENERAL THEMES IN SUBSTANCE ABUSE THERAPY

Therapists choose their approaches for particular clients by attending to the topical themes and behavioral patterns evident in the transaction between the therapist and client. Therapists track and interpret such patterns with most any material the client brings to therapy sessions to help detect problems and shape new options. In therapy for substance use disorders, the therapist tries to develop the core conditions for behavioral change by specifically considering the following likely themes in the patterns of content and in sequences of events emerging across conversations between members of the therapy relationship.

Detecting Patterns in Client Behavior

First, the therapist watches and listens for an identifiable pattern suggesting that the client has used psychoactive substances in a manner that invites or produces problematic consequences. A pattern is quickly obvious in some cases, like that of Karina, who enters therapy based on a medical referral (and her mother's insistence) after an alcohol poisoning incident that resulted in Karina's hospitalization. During intake, Karina admits that she drinks heavily several nights per week, stating with a mixture of pride and chagrin that she can drink twelve beers in two hours. She suspects her drinking is problematic, although she would rather not think about it.

With other clients, evidence of a pattern indicating substance abuse is more subtle, like with Andre, who presented with a sharp increase in obsessive thoughts and compulsive behavior since his father's death last year. Over many therapy sessions, Andre gradually reveals that his father was an alcoholic who died of lung cancer after years of smoking cigarettes. Andre also mentions in passing that he uses marijuana to help him sleep because he has been plagued with nightmares since his dad's funeral, and that he sometimes gets into fights with his fiancée after Andre has been drinking.

Many clients presenting for therapy exhibit no indications of substance use concerns. But when the therapist detects a pattern of topics and behaviors that suggest possible substance abuse, the next consideration comes into play.

Conceptualizing the Client's Substance Use Behavior

Second, the therapist formulates an evolving conceptualization of the meanings the client attributes to personal substance use and the significance of those observed patterns in discussions of substance use with the therapist. Specific answers can be as diverse as the gamut of psychoactive substances and individuals who use them. The client's cultural background certainly influences the client's attitudes, beliefs, behaviors, and feelings with respect to the use of alcohol and drugs (Straussner, 2001). Conceptualizations shift over time as the therapist gets better acquainted with the client. I offer ideas in this book about how therapists can use the therapeutic tasks of assessment, treatment planning, psychoeducation, intervention, relapse prevention, and termination to develop and utilize their understandings of their clients' substance use or abstinence in the context of their clients' lives.

Choosing Interventions

Third, the therapist makes choices about how to communicate with the client regarding observed patterns of substance use and related issues. Therapists decide how and when to share perceptions of the meanings and consequences associated with these patterns in a manner that potentially increases the client's motivation to reduce involvement in risky substance use behaviors. Appropriate therapeutic suggestions and responses depend on the cultural sensitivity of the therapist (Council of National Psychological Associations for the Advancement of Ethnic Minority Interests, 2003; Straussner, 2001). In this book, I emphasize important choice points linked with the interrelated tasks of therapy addressing substance abuse concerns. Furthermore, I encourage therapists to expand their clinical judgment skills to make effective decisions in interventions with clients who abuse substances.

Selecting Terminology

A few words about terminology are in order. A slew of terms are used to describe psychoactive substance use disorders, ranging from the concise but vague *addiction* to the more precise but cumbersome *chemical abuse, misuse, and dependence*. Terminology differences result in part from the reality that substance use disorders can affect many aspects of an individual's well-being, including medical, psychological, social, occupational, and spiritual ramifications. Professionals from a broad array of fields are involved in addressing substance abuse and related problems, so debates (often heated) about appropriate terminology to characterize those problems quickly arise in discussions between interested professionals. Medically trained professionals speak of *treatments*, whereas psychologically trained providers describe their services as *therapy*. Ambiguity about the distinction between the use and abuse of chemical substances further pervades society in general, making clear communication about the benefits and dangers of consuming alcohol and other drugs challenging at best.

The following terminology is employed in this book. *Substance* refers to a nonfood chemical that alters psychological and neurological functions when consumed by a human being. In the context of this book, *substances* include alcohol, other licit drugs, and illicit drugs. *Substance use* refers to the consumption of psychoactive substances without evidence of a connection between that consumption and clinically significant problems or symptoms, whereas *substance abuse* implies evidence that consumption is problematic. (Note that the evidence specified earlier may be available to one but not both, or some but not all, members of a therapeutic relationship.) The general terms *substance abuse* and *disordered substance use* are used interchangeably to encompass chemical abuse, misuse, and dependence unless otherwise specified, on the basis that all persons who meet the more restrictive diagnostic criteria for substance dependence will also meet the first criterion for substance abuse, although by no means are all substance abusers chemically dependent. (It is furthermore acknowledged that some experts in the field view substance abuse and dependence as exclusive rather than overlapping terms. Diagnosis is discussed in detail in chapter 5.)

The term *addictions* is also widely used to refer to disordered substance use. The term has been extensively criticized, however, both for being too specific (when used to describe chronic disease processes that exclude less severe or obvious cases of substance abuse or misuse without dependence) and for being too general (when used to refer to habitual or compulsive behaviors other than substance abuse, such as disordered eating, Internet use, gambling, shopping, hairpulling, or sexual activity, to name a few). The equation of addiction with chemical dependence is a frequent definition, but such references to addiction and the treatment of addictions imply either that nondependent abuse of substances is outside the scope of interest or that all substance use is unhealthy or abnormal. Many psychologists and others who study or treat addictions are also interested not only in physiological disease processes and psychological disorders associated with chemical dependence, but also in addressing substance use behavior that puts the user at risk of encountering problems linked to their substance use. Because of ambiguities of definition, some experts recommend avoiding use of the term *addiction* even while acknowledging that common usage and convenience of the term virtually ensure continuing use of the word (Grilly, 2002). For purposes of this book, the term *addiction* is used to signify repetitive use of psychoactive chemicals in the face of resulting personal or interpersonal problems.

Psychotherapy and *therapy* are employed as interchangeable terms to refer to psychologically based treatment methods, applied here to substance use disorders. I view therapy as one subset among a larger set of treatments for substance abuse, including medical, pharmacological, educational, religious, and self-help treatment efforts. Therapy for substance abuse may be conducted independently or in concert with related treatments. However, I join ranks with those who dispute the common assumption that substance abuse needs to be treated in specialized programs separated from therapy as it is usually conducted. Outcome research consistently supports the relative efficacy of psychological treatments for addictions (Miller & Brown, 1997).

Creating Meaningful Therapy Relationships

In the treatment of substance abuse, therapy can make an impact insofar as the participants actualize the potential for a meaningful human interaction to occur between them (Kell & Mueller, 1966). Therapists can use their culturally sensitive understanding of the sequences of dynamic events occurring in sessions to guide interactions with clients in therapeutic directions. Furthermore, a course of therapy can be most beneficial when the client actively collaborates in choosing and implementing the goals and strategies of therapy. Clients engaged in substance abuse often display interpersonal preferences, interaction patterns, and personal goals that look different from those of clients seeking help for other types of problems. Yet as cogently argued by Miller and Brown (1997), substance abuse involves types of behavior that are influenced by the same psychological principles that shape behavioral problems in general. The basic process of therapy can be undertaken with substance abusers even if the therapy relationship starts off on a different basis of initial rapport or follows a different motivational trajectory than with clients who voluntarily seek help for symptoms they acknowledge as problems.

My goal in this book is to further examine how therapists can intentionally influence the structure, relationship, and goals of therapy to promote change with clients who abuse substances. I aim to explore how a therapist integrates knowledge of (a) substance use disorders, (b) the self in the role of therapist, and (c) the process of substance abuse therapy with an individualized, culturally relevant conceptualization of each client in efforts to form a high-quality relationship with the client characterized by flexible structure directed toward negotiated client goals. Each area of knowledge listed earlier is elaborated in the present chapter. In later chapters, I attempt to demonstrate the integration of these components across the course of therapy with substance abuse disorders.

THE NATURE AND PREVALENCE
OF SUBSTANCE USE DISORDERS

Substance use often starts when a person is still young. In the general population, survey data indicate that 48% of high school seniors have used illicit drugs at least once, with 51% of them reporting use of alcohol in the past thirty days and 33% of those to the point of intoxication (O'Malley, Johnston, & Bachman, 1999). Many experimenters use psychoactive substances without encountering substantial detrimental consequences. However, of the large numbers of people who experiment with substance use, some will go on to develop significant emotional, interpersonal, occupational, health, or legal problems associated with their substance use. The National Household Survey on Drug Abuse (SAMHSA, 1999) estimated that, from 1979 to 1998, lifetime use of any illicit drug ranged in prevalence from 31.3% to 35.8% of the U.S. population ages twelve and older. For alcohol, prevalence of lifetime use in the same sample ranged from 81.3% to 88.5%. Of those respondents who reported use of any illicit drug in the past year, 8.2% reported related health problems, 14.8% indicated emotional or psychological problems due to substance use, and 17.5% reported substance dependence. (Only 4.1% of this subsample reported receiving treatment for substance abuse in the past year.)

By adulthood, the mean probability of developing any substance use disorder during any year of adulthood is estimated at 1.8% (approximately 1 in 55) for alcohol and 1.1% (1 in 90) for other drugs, with two to three times higher rates of risk for young adults. Higher rates of prevalence are also reported for men than women across all categories of substance use disorders (Anthony, 1999; Ott, Tarter, & Ammerman, 1999). Lifetime prevalence estimates range from 8% to 13% for drug dependence (Anthony, 1999) and 14% for alcohol dependence (Kessler et al., 1994). Galanter and Kleber (1999) estimated that 18% of the U.S. population will experience a substance use disorder in their lifetimes. Based on results of the National Comorbidity Survey, Kessler et al. (1994) placed that estimate at 26.6% of the general population between ages 15 and 54 exhibiting any substance use disorder in their lifetimes, with 11.3% prevalence within a given year.

Compared with other psychological problems, substance abuse is one of the most frequently occurring forms of mental health disorder in the general population. Anxiety disorders are the other most prevalent psychological disorders, with an estimated 14.6% of the population experiencing an anxiety disorder in their lifetime (Ordorica & Nace, 1998). These same authors further reported 13.3% estimated lifetime prevalence rates for alcohol use disorders and 3% to 7% lifetime prevalence rates of mood disorders.

Incidence Among Clients Seeking Therapy

Among client populations, rates of substance abuse and dependence are considerably higher than in the general population for at least two reasons. Persons with psychological disorders frequently try to relieve or escape from their symptoms of anxiety, depression, or other distress by using psychoactive substances. Furthermore, many habitual substance abusers develop psychological symptoms of depression, anxiety, or psychosis among the consequences of heavy drug or alcohol use. Galanter and Kleber (1999) estimated that 20% of patients in general medical facilities and 35% in general psychiatric units present with substance use disorders. These authors further stated that in some treatment settings the proportions of clients who abuse substances are even higher. Celluci and Vik (2001) found that their sample of licensed psychologists reported on average that 24% of their caseloads had substance abuse problems.

Client issues regarding substance use, abuse, and dependence arise in therapy in many different ways. A client may voluntarily seek therapy specifically to address drug and/or alcohol use that the client admittedly cannot control. Good examples are Barry, who was upset by his child's reaction to Barry's chaotic behavior under the influence of alcohol; and Kenisha, who got scared by confrontation with negative health outcomes of her smoking. In many voluntary cases where substance abuse is among the presenting problems, the client has been strongly urged to seek help by a concerned friend, family member, or other party with personal interest. Under such circumstances, the externally encouraged client may present the other person's concerns or pressures as the actual problem, and if the client acknowledges other problems, they may be defined in terms other than drug or alcohol use. Examples include the client who enters therapy in response to a spouse's vow to end the marriage, or an employer's threat to fire the client if the client does not change problematic substance use. Such clients may express either ambivalence or outright denial of considering their substance use as problematic, and they are likely to view themselves to some degree as coerced rather than voluntary clients. Treatment providers working with clients like these need to know how to motivate clients to invest in therapy and internalize their focus.

Substance abuse issues also appear as problems presented by clients who have troubles with legal or other formal consequences, in addition to more private ones. For example, when a judge, probation or parole officer, or child protective service agency has mandated treatment for drug or alcohol problems, the client often views participation in therapy as voluntary only to the extent that compliance with the treatment mandate helps the client avoid less desirable sanctions, such as returning to jail or prison, or losing custody of or parental rights to one's children. Clients who present the mandate to obtain treatment as their reason for seeking therapy are often convinced that their substance use is not genuinely problematic or that they do not really need substance abuse therapy, or both.

In contrast to the presentation of substance use issues in the initial phases of assessment and therapy, self-referring clients who first presented with mood, anxiety, career, or various other problems may bring up substance abuse concerns only in the middle or later phases of the therapy process. Sometimes substance use is addressed at the client's initiation, like with Jerica, who confided to her therapist that she had been drinking a lot more since they discussed the possibility of revisiting memories of sexual abuse that Jerica endured as a child. In other cases, the issue is raised by the therapist, such as the previously mentioned case of Andre, whose therapist commented on Andre's frequent hints about using marijuana to cope with bad dreams about his father in the months since his dad's death.

The later emergence of substance use issues may be attributable to any number of factors, such as the client's need to establish trust in the therapist before discussing sensitive issues, or the increasing acknowledgment over the course of therapy of the contribution of the client's substance use to the original presenting problem. The client's substance use may also emerge as a topic of concern if the presenting problem has been resolved to the extent that the client feels ready and able to tackle problems that were initially assigned lower priority or dismissed as irrelevant, or if the client's substance use has changed or become associated with new problems that develop during the course of treatment. For examples, a client already in therapy for depression, anxiety, or grief may begin drinking or "drugging" more heavily in response to current stressors, or may be arrested for driving under the influence of drugs or alcohol. Clearly, the therapist's approach to addressing clients' stated issues regarding personal substance use will vary depending on how and when those issues come up in the therapy relationship. Tailoring the therapy approach to the client's expressed and assessed needs is examined in detail throughout this book.

Incidence Among Persons Not in Therapy

It is worth mentioning, too, that in addition to the relatively large proportion of clients experiencing substance abuse problems or disorders, there are also many more people who face the detrimental consequences of substance abuse without seeking or receiving therapeutic help. Anthony (1999) cited field survey estimates indicating that, for every treated case of drug dependence, at least three persons with similar symptoms go without treatment. Some of these individuals also do not consider their drug or alcohol use to be a problem (although other people around them might), nor do they see any personal need for therapy (although others affected by their substance use may seek services). However, many others recognize some problems associated with their use and still do not obtain treatment for a variety of reasons. They may be ashamed to ask for help in light of the stigma associated either with losing control over substance use or with engaging in psychotherapy, or both. Even if they are aware of treatment options, individuals with limited finances, possibly exacerbated by an expensive drinking or drug habit, may be unable or unwilling to pay for therapy. Furthermore, many users are highly ambivalent about their use, and a person's cognizance of a drug or alcohol problem can frequently be overridden by the pleasure, relief, and liberation that same person experiences, even temporarily, from continued substance use.

I focus in this book primarily on providing appropriate assessment and effective therapy to substance abusing clients and those at risk who have sought therapeutic services. Interested professionals may also be involved in extending information about the availability and desirability of services to potential clients. Furthermore, by consuming, translating, and adding to the research literature on substance use disorders and their treatment, mental health professionals and researchers are in a position to help reduce the high personal and social costs of drug and alcohol abuse and dependence.

Co-Morbid Disorders and Overlapping Problems

Whether treated or not, substance abuse issues occur within the broader context of an individual's life and culture. Considering the interrelationship between a person's substance use and other aspects of that person's life is crucial to understanding not only what maintains the disorder, but the factors that can maintain resolution of substance use disorders (Moos, 2003). Many substance abusers simultaneously struggle with other, usually related problems, such as marital difficulties or occupational concerns. Individuals who meet diagnostic criteria for a substance use disorder may also meet the criteria for one or more other psychological disorders at the same time. The determination that a person simultaneously exhibits symptoms of a substance use disorder and some other psychological disorder is sometimes referred to as *dual diagnosis,* but the term *co-morbidity* is preferred here for its ability to reflect the reality that a substantial number of clients suffer from more than two disorders at once. The National Co-Morbidity Study (1994; cited in Ordorica & Nace, 1998) estimated that one sixth of the U.S. population had a history of three or more disorders including alcohol dependence. A 1997 follow-up study (also cited in Ordorica & Nace, 1998) found that fully 86% of alcoholic women and 78% of alcoholic men had a lifetime co-occurrence of an additional mental disorder.

The substance abuse treatment field is increasingly recognizing that substance use disorders frequently co-exist with other diagnosable disorders (Westermeyer, 1998) and personal problems (Miller & Rollnick, 2002). In response, there is a major trend toward improving the quality and integration of treatment approaches for co-morbid disorders (Frances & Miller, 1998; Polcin, 1992). To address the full scope of a client's problems, a treatment provider needs to assess the presence and nature of concomitant difficulties, and plan treatment according to the findings of initial and ongoing assessments. Effective treatment planning and implementation for clients with co-morbid disorders and multiple problems require the practitioner to be adept at assessing, diagnosing, educating, motivating, and intervening with complex clients. Also the practitioner may need to coordinate efforts with other members of a treatment team. Continuing education about the causes, manifestations, pathophysiology, clinical course, and treatment outcomes of addictive disorders also helps practitioners to conduct appropriate treatment, referrals, and consultations regarding clients with co-morbid disorders. Certainly this need for enhanced information and communication among professionals trying to integrate treatment efforts also points to the essential role of researchers in translating their findings for practical application as well as generating new knowledge about addictive processes.

Anxiety Disorders. Aside from multiple substance use disorders, anxiety and mood disorders occur most frequently along with substance use disorders. However, virtually every *DSM–IV* Axis I and II disorder has been observed in combination with substance abuse or dependency (Ott & Tarter, 1998). Persons with anxiety disorders, compared with nonanxious controls, have a doubly high risk of substance use disorders, with alcohol users exhibiting higher rates of anxiety disorders than either cocaine or opiate users (Ott, Tarter, & Ammerman, 1999). Attempts to determine which disorder is primary are complicated, but research suggests that, among alcoholics, generalized anxiety tends to precede alcohol use disorders, whereas most other anxiety disorders among alcoholics are alcohol-induced (Ordorica & Nace, 1998).

Mood Disorders. Clinically significant depression also occurs approximately twice as frequently among substance abusers. Evidence indicates that secondary depression is substantially more common than primary depression, particularly among men (Ott et al., 1999). Among women, however, depression leads to excessive alcohol consumption in about 66% of cases. Gender differences in the risk of mania have also been observed, with alcoholic men three times more likely than the general population and alcoholic women ten times more likely to develop manic symptoms over a lifetime (Ordorica & Nace, 1998).

Personality Disorders.   Personality disorders also frequently co-occur among substance abusing populations, especially antisocial and borderline personality disorders. Engaging in interpersonal violence or behavior that violates social norms has been found to predict illegal drug use (Ott et al., 1999). Among alcoholic client populations, men were four times more likely and women twelve times more likely to meet the criteria for one of these two personality disorders compared with the general population (Ordorica & Nace, 1998). Family history studies suggest a genetic link: The children of parents with substance abuse disorders often exhibit externalizing behavior disorders as early as age three, whereas the adopted out children of biological parents with antisocial personality disorders show greater than average tendencies to develop conduct disorders, attention deficit disorders, and substance abuse disorders (Ott et al., 1999).

Psychotic Disorders.   High co-morbidity rates have also been documented between substance use disorders and psychotic disorders—namely, schizophrenia. Clients with one of these disorders are four times more likely to also meet the criteria for the other (Ordorica & Nace, 1998; Ott et al., 1999). Some evidence suggests that alcoholism is likely to develop after the onset of schizophrenia (Ordorica & Nace, 1998). With stimulants and hallucinogens, however, chronic use by vulnerable persons preceding the development of psychotic symptoms predicts the earlier onset of schizophrenia (Ott et al., 1999).

Implications of Co-Morbid Disorders.   Most cases of co-morbid disorders, with the exception of anxiety, have been associated with higher morbidity and poorer prognosis for clients (Ott et al., 1999). Aside from that observation, there is little agreement about the meaning, relevance, and implications of co-morbid disorders. Hyman (2000) argued that society has systematically underestimated the extent of co-morbidity and the significance of associated problems. Evidence of the high rates of substance abuse among client populations and the frequent incidence of co-morbid disorders suggest it is likely that substance abuse concerns will emerge in many therapy relationships.

THE IMPORTANCE OF THERAPIST SELF-KNOWLEDGE IN SUBSTANCE ABUSE THERAPY

Many psychotherapists and trainees are quick to acknowledge the far-ranging extent to which their clients' lives have been touched by substance use. Even so, at least anecdotally, many mental health counselors and psychotherapists consider substance abuse treatment as a separate treatment modality, further expressing low interest in addressing a client's substance use issues in therapy. Such therapists may claim insufficient training or lack of motivation for working with clients exhibiting substance use disorders.

A major problem with this state of affairs is that, regardless of whether a practitioner has the skills or interests to counsel clients with substance use problems, many clients will be using substances, some in a problematic manner. The potential consequences of substance abuse, whether sporadic or continuous, can range from annoying to life-threatening, and can certainly exacerbate other complications the client is addressing in therapy. Thus, it is important for a therapist to detect and respond to indications of a client's possible substance abuse or dependence. Even if a therapist's specialty lies elsewhere, when substance abuse concerns are evident, the therapist should be able to facilitate appropriate treatment or referral.

The Therapist's Perspective on Substance Use and Abuse

Therapists are wise to develop adequate knowledge about their own feelings and attitudes toward people who use drugs and alcohol, most likely including people the therapist knows personally as well as users in the abstract sense. Personal experience with substance use or abstinence will also undoubtedly influence the therapist's own beliefs about drug or alcohol consumption as well as opinions about people who drink or use drugs. Therapists' feelings, attitudes, and experiences in turn shape the approaches they take with clients who admit substance use.

Not only will the therapist's perspective on substance use mold the treatment options the therapist is willing to consider with the client; it will also contribute to the responses evoked in the therapist during the therapy interaction. The more therapists are attentive to their own beliefs about and responses to persons who abuse substances, the better they will be able to utilize that awareness to track the therapy process. Among other cues, therapists can use their own reactions to each client to determine what facilitates and what hinders the interactions between them, and what needs to happen to mobilize therapists' effectiveness at points of impasse (Kell & Mueller, 1966).

The therapist who holds avoidant, condescending, or other negative attitudes toward persons who drink or take drugs will be challenged to maintain or rekindle a therapeutic alliance when such therapist attitudes are elicited in sessions. Examples of difficulties that therapists may need to address in themselves include feelings of responsibility for clients' substance use or sobriety, or countertransference reactions associated with the therapist's own experience with an addicted parent, relative, or friend. Biases may also be created by a therapist's positive attitudes toward substance use. Therapists who view drug or alcohol use in favorable terms may be tempted to minimize or normalize a client's substance use concerns, perhaps even joking with clients about use. In each case, the therapist will do well to consider how the client's interests would best be served in response to such therapist inclinations.

At many points in a course of therapy, the therapist is in a position to make choices about how to intervene in that moment, about whether and how to initiate a topic or respond to something the client has said or done. Therapists' awareness of their own feelings and intentions toward the client, both in that moment and over time, provides cues and criteria for deciding on an approach. The effective therapist uses knowledge of personal beliefs and values regarding substance use and abuse to weigh intervention strategies. The potential barriers posed by inadequate therapist self-knowledge regarding therapy with substance abusers need to be addressed.

The Role of Supervision and Training

Because this aspect of therapist self-awareness can be complicated by the therapist's own mixed, biased, or unclear cognitions about substance abuse, supervision and consultation can be crucial in the therapist's development of substance abuse treatment skills. Supervision and specialized training aim toward helping trainees recognize and surmount obstacles to progress in therapy (Powell, 2004). I contend that whether an impasse in the therapeutic relationship is attributed to the client's resistance, the therapist's countertransference, or the interpersonal dynamics unfolding between them, the therapist's effectiveness in reactivating momentum depends in large measure on the therapist's deliberate use of self-awareness in choosing interventions. Supervision that balances support, structure, and challenge for the trainee can foster these complex skills in the diffuse area of substance use disorders.

THE THERAPIST'S USE OF EMERGING PATTERNS IN THERAPY FOR SUBSTANCE ABUSE

As already mentioned, the therapist tracks patterns in the therapy interaction to generate change in the client's behavior. Then based on these observed patterns, the therapist makes predictions about how the client will respond to selected interventions, which the therapist then implements. The client's actual responses give the therapist more information that can be used to assess progress and formulate additional hypotheses to guide further intervention. Therapists addressing clients' substance abuse issues are encouraged to monitor three types of patterns that are likely to evolve, including: (a) the meaning of psychoactive substance use in the client's narrative, (b) the predictable dynamic phases of therapy relationships in general, and (c) the individualized interpersonal style exhibited by each client, particularly how that style is expressed and modified through substance use behaviors. Together an understanding of these interwoven patterns can guide choices of intervention.

The first type of pattern becomes relevant when concerns about the client's substance use arise, whether generated by the client or therapist, early in therapy or later. Therapy is unlikely to rectify those concerns without examining the significance the client attributes to personal substance use. Knowledge of the second pattern, expressed through assessing and anticipating the therapy process as it unfolds, helps the therapist gauge the progression of therapy. Thus, as client ambivalence and relationship tensions emerge, therapists perceive these as useful and predictable phenomena, rather than barriers to change. The third type of pattern becomes evident as the therapist and client interact. Through direct observations and experiences of the client, along with material the client shares in session, the therapist develops a conceptualization of the role of the client's substance use in self-expression and interpersonal transaction. Each of these types of patterns is described in more detail in chapter 2. Then I consider how to integrate utilization of all three in the course of therapy to address problems associated with substance use.

A Model for Therapy When Clients Indicate Substance Abuse

Clients who use psychoactive substances present therapists with many choice points in the course of therapy. In this chapter, a model for substance abuse therapy is presented based on the assumption that predictable, useful patterns emerge in therapy transactions. As outlined in chapter 1, these patterns include the meanings the client attributes to personal substance use, the dynamic nature of the therapy process, and the interpersonal messages the client communicates through substance-related behaviors. The significance of each of these three types of patterns is discussed in turn.

Furthermore, these patterns can be used by the therapist to interpret the contribution of substance use behaviors to the concerns that brought the client to therapy, as well as the client's degree of interest in addressing those interconnected issues. At many points in therapy, therapists use their best understanding of patterns occurring in sessions to choose interventions intended to elicit productive responses and therapeutic outcomes. Additionally, the therapist pays close attention to the client's actual reactions to the former's interventions to evaluate outcomes and adjust approaches accordingly. The client's responses and the therapist's own internal reactions become parts of the patterns the therapist is tracking. As patterns emerge and clarify, therapists continue to make decisions about how to interpret and intervene when clients exhibit substance use disorders.

PATTERNS EMERGING IN THERAPY WITH SUBSTANCE ABUSERS

The Meaning of Substance Use in the Client's Narrative

At any point in therapy, concerns raised about a client's substance use indicate that alcohol or other drugs, or both, have most likely already played some significant role in the client's past. That role may be perceived by the client as positive, negative, or mixed. The nature and significance of substance use in the client's life is usually revealed gradually in therapy over the course of multiple sessions as the therapy relationship develops. The client may explicitly name concerns or hint at them only vaguely. Difficulties may be associated with acute episodes, such as alcohol poisoning in a novice drinker who greatly overestimated his limits, or with chronic consumption, typified by the chemically dependent client who uses her intoxicant of choice whenever she has the chance.

Therapists working with such clients need to thoroughly explore the meaning of substance use in the client's life from the client's cultural perspective to maximize the quality of their collaboration, better comprehend the therapy transactions, and structure effective interventions. This joint exploration can be fascinating. Alert therapists will notice patterns of content and sequences of process elements. Therapists may also be aware of generalized assumptions or stereotypical characteristics of substance abusers. Although general knowledge of the array of substance use issues can definitely aid therapeutic efforts, the skillful therapist takes care to keep preconceived ideas about substance abuse from leading to premature conclusions about a particular client.

In addition to information about the client's substance use behavior and its consequences, the therapist can probe for details about the client's associated thoughts and feelings. Therapists can further investigate the client's impression of cultural practices and messages regarding substance use in the cultural context(s) within which the client operates. The therapist's sincere, nonjudgmental interest in the client's own story increases the therapist's credibility as a source of beneficial interaction. It also encourages the client to continue talking, thus disclosing richer personally and culturally relevant information. Even if the therapist intends to refer the client elsewhere for treatment of substance abuse concerns, taking the time and showing empathic interest in hearing what substance use means to the client helps target the referral. It also probably increases the likelihood the client will follow through with the referral.

When the therapist is alerted to the possibility of substance usage problems, assessment of the nature and intensity of the client's substance use follows, expanding as needed over the course of subsequent sessions. Substance use assessment is covered in chapter 5, but for now emphasis is on the therapist's use of the therapy process to search for themes and patterns in the client's report of experiences with substance use.

Elaborating Themes and Their Meanings.   As clients talk about their own use of psychoactive chemicals, therapists learn more about past and current behaviors, future plans and expectations, and cultural options and constraints. Therapists request more detail when client accounts are sketchy. They respond empathically to affect and attitudes the client shares as parts of the stories. Diagnostically, the therapist wants to know the nature, frequency, intensity, and duration of the client's typical and recent substance use. Also it is important to find out the client's pattern of use over the time span since the client began using substances. As these details get clarified, the therapist also invites the client to talk about the client's interpretations of the client's own substance use.

Table 2.1 lists a set of paired themes that contrast some of the many different meanings clients may attribute to their substance use. Clients may view their own experience at either extreme on each pair or anywhere in between. In other words, the paired themes represent continua of meaning rather than dichotomies. Therapists also find that, for some clients, the salience of different themes or specific meanings changes at various points in the client's life narrative or at different points in the therapy relationship. This list of potential themes in Table 2.1 is not exhaustive. It is intended to spark the therapist's awareness of what to listen for and what to ask.

The particular configuration and consistency of themes characterizing the client's narrative will help the therapist appreciate the meaning of substance use in the client's life. Each emerging theme also offers prompts the therapist can use to deepen shared exploration and understanding. For example, comments on consistency with family values or cultural norms allow the therapist to inquire about the nature of those norms and values. References to fluctuations in the client's frequency of substance use can be springboards to finding out whether frequency has increased or decreased and by how much. If the client says she uses to help cope with stresses on the job or at home, the therapist can ask about contexts or roles with which the client has trouble coping. The emphasis here is on the emergent nature

TABLE 2.1
Continua of Meanings That Clients May Attribute
to Their Substance Use

Clients may view their substance use as . . .

... a new behavior - an established habit.

... surprising - - - - - - - - - - - - - inevitable in light of personal or family values and history.

... consistent - - - - - - - - - - - - - - - - - - inconsistent with cultural norms and expectations.

... initiated under coercion - freely chosen.

... fun and desirable - miserable and repulsive.

... something of which to be proud - to be ashamed.

... a stable pattern over time - a changing pattern of use.

... primarily a social activity - something done in isolation.

... directly connected - - - - - - - - - - - - - - - - - - - totally unrelated to other life difficulties.

... a mechanism for coping - - - - - - - - - - - - - - - - - - - a factor interfering with life tasks.

... something they plan to continue - - - - - - - - - - - - something they want to stop doing.

... under their control - out of their control.

of this shared understanding because clients vary widely in their readiness to share the significance of their substance use with a therapist. The therapist's awareness and responsiveness to emerging themes help capture those meanings.

Often clients are protective or ambivalent about their substance use. Thus, they need time to establish trust in the therapist and the therapy process before they are willing to discuss or even acknowledge their substance use. Other clients are willing and able to reflect openly on the meaning of substance use in their lives or their cultures, but still the topic may be complex and require discussion across more than one session. This is especially true when the client has concerns to address in therapy in addition to (and maybe tangled up with) issues regarding substance use.

Therefore, once a potential concern about substance use is identified, the therapist not only listens and probes for the meanings the client attaches to substance use, but also watches for patterns of related messages evident across therapy sessions. Repeated messages about similar themes help clarify where interventions need to focus. The therapist may notice that themes associated with substance use change depending on the mood of the client, the time span in the client's life under discussion, the phase of the therapy relationship, the specific intervention of the therapist, and so forth. As therapists track these patterns and try to comprehend their significance, they gain information and insights that can be used to modify the patterns in the direction of therapeutic change.

Identifying and Responding to Emerging Patterns. The patterns of interest here are recurrent sequences of content or process elements in therapy sessions. Therapists listen for recurring messages about clients' perspectives on their own substance use for indications of important themes, such as those listed previously. Three or more repeated expressions of similar content regarding some topic—in this case, substance use—suggest a noteworthy pattern. For example, Darrion, a client in therapy for career concerns, comments during three out of four sessions that he "got trashed over the weekend, and it was so fun." Darrion brings this up each time in the context of intentions to get work done over the weekend.

As therapists notice repeated content, they start listening for further corroboration of a pattern. When accumulating evidence convinces the therapist that the pattern has therapeutic significance worth exploring, the therapist shares the observed evidence and asks the client what the apparent pattern means to the client. In the example given before, the therapist says, "I notice you've told me three different times now that you had a lot of fun getting 'trashed' over the weekend. Tell me more about that." The reader will notice that this therapist asks Darrion to elaborate before offering the therapist's own interpretation of the pattern. Like the reader, the therapist is probably already formulating hypotheses, but should choose carefully when to share those with the client. The client who agrees that a pattern exists and has potential significance is more likely to listen to the therapist's interpretation. If the therapist guesses too quickly, even if accurate, the therapist becomes the person narrating the story rather than the client. Using open-ended questions and nonpresumptive phrasing, the therapist can give the client opportunities to divulge perceptions and interpretations of the client's own behavior. Darrion, for instance, says, "It's good to throw caution to the wind on weekends and forget about all the stress I have to deal with during the week." Information like this from the client creates openings for the therapist to dig deeper, summarize, and offer timely interpretations when the pattern is becoming clearer to both participants.

In a sense, by commenting on an observed pattern in the client's behavior, the therapist is testing a hypothesis that the pattern of content has underlying meaning that is relevant to the goals of therapy. The client may confirm the hypothesis by elaborating with details and attributions of meaning. If the client instead dismisses the relevance of the therapist's observation, the therapist avoids argumentation the first time. However, the therapist can hold the hypothesis open to additional testing by listening for additional indications of thematic patterns and raising them for further discussion if they occur.

Continuing the earlier example, the therapist suggests they spend time in session talking more about the client's drinking on weekends, given the number of times the topic has been raised. Darrion could retort that it is true that he likes to get drunk on weekends, but everyone does it, it's not a problem, and it's unrelated to the concerns that brought him to therapy. The therapist may suspect otherwise, but trying to convince Darrion that excessive weekend drinking may be compromising educational efforts or career prospects is not compelling at this juncture. This is particularly true if the client makes it clear that he has other things he wants to discuss.

However, if the therapist in this case accepts the client's interpretation and then later hears additional evidence supporting a continuing pattern of content, the therapist brings attention to it again. When pointing out the repetition in content, the therapist also notes how the client reacts and may comment on the process of their discussions as well as the content. In this continuing example, the therapist could tell Darrion,

> Again I hear you talking about getting drunk on the weekend. I remember the last time I mentioned that you've talked about drinking several times in here, you said it was not a big deal and that we didn't need to talk about it. But since it keeps coming up, I'm still thinking it could be important to discuss, and I wonder what "getting trashed" means to you?

The nonjudgmental identification of a pattern that increasingly combines both repeated content and process becomes harder for a client to dismiss. It communicates that the therapist is listening, remembering, and connecting information revealed by the client with events transpiring between the therapy participants. The tolerant nature of the therapist's comments indicate that the therapist cares more about understanding the client's perspective than imposing the therapist's own.

Clients sometimes become willing to discuss topics like substance use that they previously minimized in session when they recognize that not only is the therapist pinpointing a pattern that is hard to ignore, but the therapist is also demonstrating ability to collaborate in addressing the topic. When the client comes to agree that in fact a pattern is evident and its significance is worth exploring, the therapist can help elaborate its meaning.

Sometimes when the therapist comments on patterns of content that recur after the client has already dismissed their relevance, the client remains resistant to exploring or even discussing particular content. This may be especially likely with the topic of substance use. Because of the desirable effects and other benefits clients typically associate with substance use, clients are reluctant to discuss their own use or even substance abuse in general terms with anyone who is likely to label substance use as a problem and possibly to press the client to abstain from further use. Because therapy involves attempts to change, a client may assume the therapist will rank among those who expect the client to give up drugs or alcohol. In fact a client like Darrion may perceive the therapist's repeated mention of the client's offhand comments about drinking, for example, as evidence that the therapist is going to harp on the client about the dangers and problems of drinking.

In such cases, the therapist works to modify the pattern to include explication of the process of their interaction regarding the topic. In addition to commenting on recurrent content, the therapist continues to reflect aloud the nature of in-session transactions about that content. This expanded, process-oriented pattern gradually incorporates increasing articulation of the therapist's approach. Each time the client makes reference to substance use, the therapist points out the recurrence, expresses interest in talking more about the topic, relays concerns where appropriate, and communicates respect for the client's decision about whether to talk about it. If the client continues to resist, the therapist agrees to pursue another topic, but only after clarifying that if substance use comes up again, the therapist will keep pointing it out. The therapist also lets the client know the therapist is interested in hearing the client's perspective if and when the client is ready to talk about it.

In this manner, the therapist expands an identified pattern of content to include focus on the process of talking about that pattern. The therapist builds in explanations of why the therapist is pursuing the topic and what the therapist plans to do if the pattern continues. Thus, if the client raises the topic of substance use again later, the therapist can do more than just say, "Here's that topic once again." The therapist can also, if needed, remind the client of past discussions that recurring content often has therapeutic significance, and that the therapist's concerns about the client and interest in the client's perspective can be used as a safe context for examining that significance, whatever it may be.

Novice therapists may worry that if they do not persist in investigating the client's mention of substance use despite resistance, they may miss their opportunity. With some experience, however, most therapists soon learn that if a topic is relevant to the client's problems or therapeutic goals, it will come up again. If the issue is significant, the client almost cannot help but bring it up later. If the therapist is able to engage the client in the meantime in talking about other issues that are important to the client, the client may increasingly want to bring it up. The therapist who has laid groundwork by clarifying the emerging patterns of content and process may not even need to remind the client of past discussions when the topic comes up again.

Thus, the therapist's deliberate attention to patterns of both the content and interaction in therapy sessions often brings the client to agree to further discussion of the client's experience of substance use. Once the client acquiesces that the topic is meaningful in the context of therapy, the therapist can help specify the underlying individual and cultural meanings of the client's substance use. The therapist's next steps, toward exploring those meanings within interventions aimed at therapy goals, can be determined according to the therapist's conception of the therapy process.

The Nature of the Therapy Process

The literature on the therapy process identifies tasks and transitions that characterize effective courses of therapy. The practicing therapist's understanding of the typical themes and patterns that emerge during a therapy relationship helps the therapist predict, guide, and interpret the process to fit the particular interests and needs of individual clients. Wampold (2001) argued for a contextual (as opposed to a medical) model of therapy in which therapeutic efficacy stems from the therapist's provision of a conceptual rationale that both explains the client's difficulties and also gives an interventional procedure for reducing the problems. Wampold based his definition of the contextual model on the work of Frank and Frank (1991), who postulated that the rationale for intervention becomes viable to the client in the context of an emotionally intense relationship with an expert who can address the client's "assumptive world" and directly involve the client in the treatment process.

Frank and Frank asserted that virtually all forms of psychotherapy and culturally based healing practices emphasize the importance of a confiding relationship, a healing setting, a compelling explanation for the client's symptoms, and a ritual for healing. The ritual component derives from the therapeutic rationale and collaboratively engages the client and therapist. Furthermore, Frank and Frank suggested that the ritual tends to incorporate six elements, which include counteracting alienation, connecting hope for progress to the therapy process, arousing emotions, providing new learning experiences, giving opportunities for practice, and improving the client's sense of mastery. Wampold (2001) presented extensive meta-analytical support for the assumption of a contextual (general factors) rather than a medical (specific ingredients) model of psychotherapy. It is assumed here that these contextual factors are highly relevant to successful outcomes of therapy for substance abuse disorders as well.

The therapy process has been described in terms of stages associated with the beginning, middle, and end of therapy (Tracey, 1993, 2002). At the *beginning stage*, it is crucial for the therapist to establish rapport and a working alliance. Therapists start to create a climate of trust and hope by clarifying what the client can expect while listening empathically and responding affirmatively to what the client has to say. As the therapist demonstrates interest and expertise, the client becomes more willing to elaborate on the problems that brought the client to therapy. The therapist in turn begins to notice and identify themes and patterns in session dialogue. In therapy for substance abuse, the nature and significance of the client's drug or alcohol use, as already discussed, typically emerge as central themes.

Together the therapist and client develop an increasingly shared understanding of the client's concerns and their intricacies, accounting also for cultural factors. This evolving conceptualization forms a base from which possible strategies can be identified for resolving the client's difficulties. This middle stage of therapy is often called the *working through* stage and involves choosing, rehearsing, implementing, and evaluating new strategies for coping with old problems. As they work through the therapy process, therapists typically help clients sort out what they can change from that over which they have no control. Therapists assist clients in accessing sources of support and addressing obstacles to progress toward the client's goals. During this stage, therapists also focus clients on clarifying their thoughts and feelings about personal history as well as current behavior and relationships.

It is common for clients to struggle and for therapy relationships to encounter tensions as troubling issues get explored in therapy. Differences in personal values or cultural backgrounds between the therapist and client can exacerbate tensions in their interactions. How the therapist interprets and responds to difficult moments and conflictual themes has tremendous bearing on the therapeutic potential of this intense stage (Glidden-Tracey, 2001). At any point in session, the therapist has options for responding to what is happening in session, and interventions can be built on the therapist's selections among response options. When clients exhibit the inevitable tensions and mixed feelings that accompany efforts to change, the therapist carefully chooses responses intended to support the client's struggle and correspondingly to challenge the client to try new things. Therapists' abilities to tolerate and utilize their own internal reactions to their clients are as essential to this process as the therapists' capacity to deal with clients' responses.

As clients begin to experiment with new options both in and out of therapy sessions, continuing discussion with the therapist helps define and refine progress. The collaborative focus of therapy provides a context within which clients learn to resolve their ambivalences and expand their behavioral repertoires. Emerging evidence of beneficial changes moves the therapy relationship into the final *termination* stage of therapy. In this stage, the therapy dyad (or group) emphasizes reinforcement of those changes and maintenance of gains accomplished in therapy. The meaning of closure to the therapy relationship is elaborated as participants share what they will take from the experience of working together.

This trajectory of the therapy process has been supported by both research and clinical experience. In therapy for most psychological issues, comprehension of this typical trajectory allows therapists to estimate the present stage of therapy with a particular client and anticipate the likely next steps in facilitating progress. With clients who abuse psychoactive substances in addition to any other concerns they raise in therapy, the general process evolves in a similar manner, although the amount of time spent in each stage may vary. Trusting this process to unfold with attentive effort can help the therapist maintain focus and choose immediate interventions when progress appears to be stalled. For example, if a client referred for therapy after being arrested for drunk and disorderly conduct (or after a positive drug screen at work) withholds information and willing participation, the therapist is alerted to the need for greater attention to building rapport and motivation before trying to work through problems.

The Initial Stage. One of the reasons therapists get discouraged from working with clients referred for substance abuse treatment is that establishing a therapeutic alliance often takes longer with persons who say they do not see their behavior as a problem and are not interested in changing it. Many substance abusers experience enough reinforcing effects of their drugs or drinks to muffle the less desirable consequences of use, at least for a while. Ambivalence about continuing use is not only common, but shifts in emphasis as the user cycles from promises of drug availability to present experience of desired effects, to suffering through negative consequences of use, to trying to maintain abstinence to avoid undesirable impacts, to seeking more drugs to blot out difficulties salient during abstinence. Even clients who are acutely aware of the negative variables in equations adding up to their substance abuse are often reluctant to label their use in exclusively problematic terms. They resent, perhaps understandably, anyone who tells them they must give up substance use. They may come to therapy in the early stages expecting, for any number of reasons, that the therapist will require or try to force them to stop drinking or taking drugs. Because there are at least two sides to their stories, they argue the other side of the ambivalence if the therapist appears to ignore it.

This starting point to therapy does not change the fact that, for the client to benefit, the therapist will need to work to establish an alliance with the client. The extensive work by Miller and Rollnick (1991, 2002) and their colleagues directly addressed the challenge of building rapport and generating motivation with clients who are reluctant or ambivalent regarding prospects for change. The beauty of their motivational interviewing approach is that, in the therapist's acknowledgment and exp. tion of all of the client's mixed feelings about behaviors that someone in the client's life has labeled as a problem, the client is invited to look in depth at the many dimensions of the issue so that the client articulates the argument for change.

The spirit of motivational interviewing communicates to the client that the therapist cares enough to directly involve the client in decisions about the client's treatment. Therapists can gradually establish good rapport even with initially resistant clients by revealing a caring, collaborative interest in the client's current stance.

The Middle Stage. Miller and Rollnick (2002) clarified that motivational concerns remain salient in later phases of therapy as well. Therapy moves into the middle stage when the client trusts the therapist enough to attempt discussion of troubling or conflictual issues with which the client wants help. Therapists will be best prepared to provide real help if they accept that working through this stage will involve moments of discomfort that must be faced and dealt with rather than avoided or minimized. In other words, therapists can remind themselves when things get tense in session that this is supposed to happen when a therapy relationship wrestles with difficult issues, and that working through the struggle can lead to learning, resolution, and inspiration. The inevitable mixed feelings about personal change can be therapeutic as long as the therapist stays open to maintaining both appropriate involvement in the struggle and hope for beneficial outcome. The therapist does more than watch and guide the client's exertions; the therapist also interpersonally enacts the client's struggles in their therapy sessions. Therapists must have a clear sense of purpose, value, and faith in the therapy process to engage so directly with clients and still maintain clear and appropriate therapeutic boundaries.

Why does the therapist get so involved? The rapport-building process focuses on establishing a trust that with this therapist the client can feel emotionally safe enough to talk about issues the client otherwise rarely talks about or maybe even thinks about. Or perhaps the client does converse about the issues, but only in superficial ways or in constrained contexts. Continuing the prior example of the reluctant mandated client, this individual may have had numerous arguments with the client's spouse over the client's drinking, especially since the recent arrest (or trouble at work). The client may also frequently joke with drinking buddies about the assets of alcohol. In fact the client made a point of drinking with friends not long after sitting through a lecture from the client's lawyer about the wisdom under the circumstances of refraining from drinking. The client in this example talks extensively about drinking alcohol, but hardly ever about the competing internal pulls to keep using versus quit using. When the client takes the plunge of verbalizing frustration and ambivalence about continuing alcohol use to the therapist, the words do not always flow freely and easily.

Clients in the middle stage of therapy can be like people unpacking boxes loaded into storage some time ago. They may uncover things they do not recognize, things they had forgotten about. They may be disgusted or amazed with themselves for still dragging these things around for so long. They may want to immediately discard some of the things they now expose, or they may worry what the therapist is going to do once the therapist has witnessed whatever the client uncovers. Clients may question how much they want to stay with the task of unpacking. In short, clients working through difficult material with therapists they have come to trust will encounter moments of discomfort in therapy sessions.

Seeing and hearing the client grapple with the discomfort of working through ambivalence can hardly fail to elicit some reaction in the therapist. Therapists may feel frustrated, sad, confused, troubled, angry, stuck, or exhausted, or they may have other emotional responses to the client's apparent struggle. Therapists learn to allow themselves to not only experience their own immediate reactions, but also to consult their own understanding of the therapy process unfolding with each client to decide how to authentically share their reactions with clients in a manner the clients are likely to hear and use. If therapists intellectualize or remove themselves from experience of feelings in those tense moments in session, clients will probably scale back their own emotional involvement and perhaps their trust as well. A therapist alert to such dynamics can alter ongoing intervention to reactivate therapeutic potential, but continual constraints on the therapist's genuine involvement in sessions will ultimately hinder the prospects of client change.

Keeping in mind that the therapy process aims toward eventual resolution and closure, the therapist carefully chooses how to express the therapist's own involvement with the client. Although it is important for therapists to allow themselves to experience the impact of interacting with each client and initiate responsive involvement, it is equally crucial for therapists to maintain clear boundaries on the role of therapist. They can do this through active awareness that whatever they are experiencing toward the client, there are various ways of communicating one's own response. Therapists can define the boundaries of their professional roles by asking themselves which among their options for responding to the client in that moment is most likely to produce a therapeutic outcome.

Therapeutic outcomes encompass client responses of feeling understood, supported, challenged, motivated, inspired, trusted, comforted, praised, changed, and so forth. The point is that, whenever possible, therapists intervene with intent to elicit a productive response from clients. This is particularly important in working with substance abusers (whose behavior may strike the therapist as irrational, destructive, unhealthy, etc.) because the therapist must consider how the client will react to hearing what the therapist is thinking and feeling. Not all interventions produce immediate therapeutic responses, nor do clients always respond as the therapist intended. That is the nature of working through the middle stage of therapy. Yet the therapist's actions and expressions are chosen according to the therapist's appreciation of the necessity of this stage and the corresponding role of the therapist in leading toward the final stage of therapeutic resolution.

The Termination Stage.   Through the therapy process, the client and therapist elaborate and address troubling issues to the point where new options can be identified, shared, rehearsed, and reinforced. A mutual goal is to bring the client to the point of coping satisfactorily with current concerns so that the client no longer needs therapy. Preparing the client for the termination of therapy comprises the important work of the last stage of the process.

During the last few sessions, the therapist guides review of the course of therapy from both the client's and therapist's perspectives. Looking back together helps consolidate memory of the experience for the client to take into the future. The therapist invites articulation of goals accomplished and lessons learned in therapy about meanings and options regarding personal substance use. Discussion focuses on how the client can use new insights and behaviors to deal with future challenges. Time may be spent on addressing specific concerns that the client anticipates, such as dealing with relapse triggers, along with plans for maintaining or advancing gains realized in therapy. The termination phase also involves talking about feelings toward ending therapy and the therapy relationship. With clients who have made some change in their substance use behavior, exploring memories and feelings about both former and current behavior is essential. In a relationship that has developed a strong working alliance through weathering heartfelt tensions, the discussions of the termination stage can be powerful indeed.

Chapter 10 further addresses the process of termination with clients who abuse substances. The emphasis here is on the predictability afforded by knowledge of the general process of therapy. The time spent in the termination phase provides the opportunities for resolution, consolidation, and closure, all of which make the struggle through the middle stage worthwhile. Termination discussions also involve identifying unfinished business (such as ongoing occupational or relationship issues) and future planning for those issues that still require the client's attention, such as relapse prevention strategies. When therapists recognize that their active involvement with therapeutic intentions during the earlier stages creates the potential for the powerful experience of the final stage, they can pace and choose their interventions more deliberately. Knowing that the termination discussions involve clarifying reflections on the therapy process and considerations of its impact on the client's future, the therapist can rekindle motivation to stay with the client's efforts to work through difficult or confusing material arising earlier in sessions. The therapist can better attend to signs of progress and readiness for termination while ensuring adequate time to talk about both the closure and the incomplete business of therapy.

The therapist's attention to the general pattern of therapy as it evolves with particular clients is thus a useful tool. The identifiable pattern of stages in the therapy relationship helps therapists predict, monitor, and utilize the consequences of specific interventions. As mentioned earlier, the therapist's efforts to interpret the sequence of events in sessions also suggest patterns unique to each individual client. An interpersonal framework for identifying, tracking, and (where appropriate) modifying the client's characteristic patterns of interaction is presented in the following section.

The Client's Interpersonal Style as Partially Shaped by Substance Use

Already it has been emphasized that as therapy progresses through the phases of building a working alliance and clarifying the focus of attention, skillful therapists notice themes and patterns evident in their clients' behaviors. In addition to meanings the client associates with substance use and patterns linked to the general progression of therapy, interactions between the therapist and client in session reveal patterns of behavior that characterize the client's style of dealing with relationships. The idea explored in this section is that in therapy sessions, the manner in which the client describes and discusses substance use tells the therapist much about how the client's substance use expresses aspects of the client's self-perception and relationship expectations.

Chemically altering one's state of mind can allow a person to experience emotions or engage in behaviors the client might otherwise suppress, which can create notable impacts on the client's interactions with other people in the client's life. Furthermore, as long as the individual wishes to continue using substances to permit particular forms of self-expression and interaction, the client may also exhibit interpersonal behaviors intended to protect the potential to continue using substances. Also once a client moves to change substance use behavior, it becomes important to develop alternative forms of self-expression and interpersonal interaction.

By examining the client's interpersonal messages communicated in terms of substance use themes as well as the therapist's own behavior in interactions with the client, therapists can assess the meaningfulness and test the utility of their conceptualizations of a client's dynamic patterns. I frame this discussion using interpersonal theory (Kiesler, 1982, 1996; Tracey, 1993) for its capacity to illuminate the common and distinguishing facets of therapy for substance abuse concerns. Interpersonal approaches to therapy additionally suggest specific, immediate, and individualized interventions toward therapeutic goals, which can be applied usefully in therapy with clients who abuse substances. The importance of attending to cultural factors shaping interpersonal transactions certainly also deserves mention.

Messages Communicated by the Client's Substance-Related Behavior.   Interpersonal theory assumes that everything we do or say communicates implicit messages to other people about how we view ourselves, how we expect to be treated in relationships and social interactions, and what we are (and are not) willing to offer to such interaction. Each person is postulated to have a preferred style characterized by relative dominance or submissiveness and by preferences for friendly (affiliative) or hostile behavior. A primary goal in interpersonal transactions is to get other people to respond in ways that validate the individual's sense of self in relationships. People are further presumed to vary in their ranges of interpersonal flexibility. Healthier people are presumed to be capable of exhibiting a broader range of interpersonal behaviors, displaying flexibility that allows them to adapt their behavior to meet the demands of various interpersonal transactions. People with rigid, narrower ranges of interpersonal behaviors attempt to constrain the behaviors of others to only those that fit the rigid individual's expectations and thus validate that individual's rigid view of himself or herself. In other words, persons with inflexible, limited interpersonal styles offer both themselves and others they interact with fewer options by which the course of a relationship can unfold.

Interpersonal theory thus suggests that we communicate to others not only how we see ourselves and how we expect to be regarded, but also roughly what we predict other people are going to do when they interact with us. It is as if our behavior says, "I need or want you to react a certain way with me in order to confirm my expectations so that I know how to proceed in this transaction." A rigidly dominant-hostile person, for example, lets others know she expects to take charge, does not mind doing so in a hostile manner, and probably does not expect to be liked by others. A person whose style is primarily submissive-affiliative will typically give in to get close even when circumstances suggest other possibilities are available or desirable. The other person's response (which of course communicates the other person's self-concept and interpersonal expectations) may or may not correspond to the first person's expectations. If not, and if the interactants do not sufficiently negotiate the interaction so that one or both alter their approaches to adapt to situational demands, the probability of continuing interaction is decreased, at least in that moment and to the extent the participants feel free to choose whether to continue the interaction.

Applying the general interpersonal model to substance abuse therapy prompts the therapist to consider if and how the client is using substances as a vehicle for interpersonal expression. From this perspective, the behaviors of drinking alcohol and consuming drugs carry messages about how clients see themselves, want to be treated, and tend to engage with other people. No uniform interpretation of the interpersonal impact of substance abuse is plausible, but I contend that it is fruitful to view an individual's substance use behavior, including discussions of the topic in therapy sessions, in terms of the interpersonal style the client displays corresponding to that and related topics.

The therapist may observe the client's interpersonal expression through substance use themes in at least three contexts. The primary context is a client's mention of how the client interacts with other people while participating in activities associated with substance use. The client's behavior in session while telling these stories of substance use episodes gives additional indication of the interpersonal functions of substance use for this client. The secondary context involves interpersonal behaviors in which the client engages to defend or protect the client's ability to continue using substances and thus maintaining access to the perceived benefits of use. To the extent that other people are affected by or concerned about the client's substance abuse, the client may report or demonstrate a style of interaction that serves to deter others from interfering with the client's continuing use potential. The tertiary context of interpersonal expression relevant to substance abuse discussions in therapy is echoed in the interactional style the client exhibits and elicits when undertaking efforts to reduce or eliminate disordered substance use. Both in terms of how the client describes transactions with other people and how the client interacts with the therapist in discussing the process and outcomes of therapy, the therapist will witness the client's corresponding interpersonal style in operation.

By tracking and interpreting the client's patterns of interpersonal behavior in each context, the therapist can hypothesize what messages the client's substance use communicates along with the extent to which the client is willing and able to engage in interpersonal processes to modify substance use behavior. Certainly the therapist will also need to consider relevant cultural vantage points for interpreting the client's substance use and associated interpersonal behaviors. To understand how the therapist can use such awareness, each of the contexts mentioned earlier is explored in more depth.

The primary context of interacting with others while participating in or talking about substance use activities yields indications of the interpersonal functions substance use may serve for the client. People often report initiating or resuming substance use because they expect the influence of the chemical will create or enhance their capacity to behave in certain ways, with desirable interpersonal consequences. Playing several variations on this theme, substance use may be perceived as allowing the user to be more fun, or sexy, or daring, relaxed, humorous, sophisticated, assertive, trendy, nasty, and so forth. People with more restrictive interpersonal styles may anticipate or discover that using alcohol or drugs appears to increase their flexibility of interpersonal response, temporarily removing inhibitions from saying or doing things from which they would otherwise refrain. More flexible (and presumably more healthy) individuals can find ways to express hostility (or friendliness, dominance, or submission) with or without the use of psychoactive chemicals. Less flexible people, in contrast, may find chemical alterations of their states of mind seem to permit them to exhibit qualities that are otherwise remote from their interpersonal styles.

A good example is Karina, the client described in chapter 1, who could drink twelve beers in two hours, and after one night of extremely heavy drinking ended up in the hospital. Karina reports to her therapist that in general she tries hard to be nice to everyone, except for when she is drunk, and then she feels free to be as mean as she pleases. She mentions that she often forgets the hateful things she says under the influence of alcohol and is later mortified when people report back to her the things she said when drunk. However, Karina also states that drinking is her favorite thing to do because it lets her express herself so genuinely.

It is not hard to imagine how such interpersonal expectations and behaviors regarding substance use can lead to both desirable and undesirable interpersonal consequences. Among the desirable outcomes is the substance user's perceived increase in interpersonal flexibility, which leads to expanded forms of interaction with others that in turn are among the reinforcers for continuing substance abuse. The social reinforcers in addition to the physiological and psychological effects of using substances combine to promote repeated use of substances to re-create the desired effects.

One of the possible undesirable outcomes, however, of using substances to expand interpersonal flexibility is that, for some persons, expression of interpersonal alternatives seems to become dependent on achieving a chemically altered state. Substance use to enhance interpersonal functioning becomes problematic when the user perceives or exhibits a lack of ability for flexible interactions without reliance on the drug. Although a substance may initially be sought and used to expand the user's range of interpersonal expression, coming to believe that one can only have fun, be liked, or face stressors when under the influence of substances can ultimately maintain interpersonal rigidity. In this manner, rigid interpersonal styles and reliance on substance use to facilitate interpersonal transactions can be mutually reinforcing.

Therapists can detect problematic use of substances for interpersonal communication by asking themselves what clients are attempting to say about themselves through their substance use, and what kinds of reactions they are trying or expecting to get from other people, including the therapist, by engaging in or discussing behaviors associated with substance use. The more narrow and rigid the client's messages are ("I can't have much fun without a few drinks" or "I'm better with women when I'm high") or the more inconsistent the client's interpersonal behaviors when discussing substance abuse compared with other topics, the more likely the client's substance abuse is performing a problematic interpersonal function. Other examples of substance use messages about self-perception and corresponding relationship messages in this primary context are listed in Table 2.2.

Therapists working with clients who exhibit disordered substance use can also ask themselves how the client's interpersonal expression through behaviors related to substance abuse both facilitates and inhibits the client's hypothesized interpersonal goals. As already mentioned, many substance abusers endeavor to continue using their favorite (or any available) substances to reproduce desirable social, physical, and mental effects. However, the detrimental results of some behaviors emitted under the influence of a chemically altered state of mind often lead to interpersonal consequences that consist of pressures to curtail such behavior.

For the client who wishes to maintain access to substance use and its desirable effects despite actual or anticipated interpersonal pressures to moderate problematic behavior, the second interpersonal context for disordered substance use comes into play. This context is secondary in the sense

TABLE 2.2
Interpersonal Messages That May Be Communicated
by Substance Use Behavior Among Persons With
Relatively Inflexible Interactional Styles

Messages . . . about perceptions of self	*. . . about relationship expectations*
Who I am is unsatisfactory to me, so I use substances (get high) to change who I am, or to express an alternative of who I am. I like who I am when I am high or drunk, so I get drunk or high a lot.	I expect you to react to me the way other people do when I am using substances, and when I am not. Deal with me (validate me) as I am when I am high because I don't like or even know who I am when I'm not.

that it reflects the client's responses to the interpersonal messages the client is receiving from other people in reaction to the client's substance use and problematic consequences. To protect substance use behaviors that sustain the client's self-perception in the face of interpersonal responses that fail to validate that self-concept, the substance abuser may employ defensive interpersonal strategies. A hostile style can be used to push other people away, or a deceptive style can be intended to appear to comply with others' expectations to convince the other persons to withdraw pressure. The perceived need to shield the possibility of future substance use may override the social contract to reciprocate with friendly, honest, and respectful behaviors.

With some clients, these tendencies may be less apparent in therapy sessions when the client is sober and/or under pressure to comply, but still evident in the stories the client tells. With other clients, interpersonal behaviors tied to substance abuse and its preservation may be quite apparent in the client's interactions with the therapist, requiring attention to rapport building and treatment motivation. An example of the latter is Charles, who has a long history of heroin use, but tells his therapist that he has not used any opiates or other illegal substances in the past year since he has been out of prison on parole. When the therapist says, "I am glad to hear that, and I support your efforts to stay 'clean,' " Charles asks the therapist, "How do you know I'm not lying to you?"

The therapist might interpret the message communicated by Charles' question, in concert with other knowledge about the client's incarceration history, as suggesting that Charles has experience manipulating the truth to hide illegal behavior as well as being suspected and accused of deception. In effect, Charles' question tells the therapist,

I expect other people not to trust me, and I don't trust them. So when you appear to give me the benefit of the doubt, I suspect that either you are trying to trick me into revealing a deception, or you are gullible enough for me to dupe you. So I'm going to show you how I am capable of making you doubt your own perceptions or defend your own sincerity, and by catching you off guard, see if you will reveal any information that will confirm one of my competing guesses about what you are up to.

The response elicited in the therapist hints at the interpersonal tensions that have evolved at least in part from Charles' persisting use of an illegal drug.

As the therapist comes to an understanding of the substance abusing client's interpersonal style in these primary and secondary contexts, an essential therapeutic goal is to provide the client with a response that declines to validate the client's maladaptive interpersonal expectations. For example, in response to Charles' apparent expectations of either deceit or insecurity, the therapist says, "I believe what you're telling me because I operate on the honor system, and so I take what you tell me at face value. I also want you to know that in addition I take into account all the other things I'm learning about you, and I expect you are giving me the truth until I have good reason to believe otherwise." Over the course of therapy, efforts to selectively counter problematic aspects of a client's substance use style incorporate attempts to elicit alternative behaviors from the client. The therapist tries to respond in ways that communicate appreciation of the roles of substance use and its protection in the client's sense of identity and relationship options while asking the client to consider the possibility that things could be different. If the client responds by experimenting with modes of self-expression and interaction that do not depend on substance use and its protection, the tertiary context of interpersonal expression through change in substance use behaviors becomes evident.

Tailoring a Response to the Client's Expression Through Substance Abuse Themes. How does the therapist choose to respond to client messages in the primary and secondary contexts to elicit transition into the tertiary context? The general interpersonal model not only describes personality types and behavioral styles; it also can be used to predict the outcomes of transactions between persons of particular styles or exhibiting specific behaviors. Dominant behavior predicts that the response will be submissive and vice versa; affiliation predicts an affiliative response, whereas hostility (the opposite of affiliation) predicts a hostile response. If the receiver of the initial message responds in a manner that is consistent with the relationship expectation communicated by the sender, the interaction is said to be complementary. If the receiver instead sends an alternate message, suggesting a different definition of the transaction or initiating another sequence, the transaction is noncomplementary.

In addition to the level of individual behavior exchanges (one message plus corresponding reply), complementarity can also be defined on the basis of proportions of complementary interactions (sequences of individual behavior exchanges) across a conversation or interaction. The pattern of complementary transactions proportional to noncomplementary ones over the course of a transaction or relationship may be conceptualized as characterizing the quality and stability of the relationship. The outcomes of a particular interaction can be predicted according to the interpersonal styles and flexibility exhibited by each participant as well as by the degree of complementarity reflected in their exchanges over time.

Interpersonal theory further postulates, then, that a relationship's character can be not only predicted, but also potentially shaped by careful attention to the patterns of interpersonal dynamics combined with reasoned choices of behavior intended to influence the complementarity ratio. With respect to therapy relationships, interpersonal models postulate that client change occurs in response to the therapist's selective deviation from the interpersonal expectations communicated by the client (Claiborn & Lichtenberg, 1989). Multicultural sensitivity and competence ideally inform and enhance a therapist's choice of noncomplementary responses intended to elicit therapeutic responses from the client. In substance abuse therapy, the therapist pays particular notice of interpersonal messages with problematic implications in the primary context of the client's substance use and in the secondary context of the client's efforts to preserve substance use potential. By clarifying implied messages in the client's substance-related behaviors and by using noncomplementary responses to selectively challenge those messages that contribute to the problems identified in therapy, the therapist can guide transactions in the therapy relationship toward altered or expanded behavior alternatives with respect to substance use or abstinence.

Research on the incidence of relative complementarity across the therapy process indicates predictable patterns and changes corresponding to the different stages of therapy. Consistent with predictions of the interpersonal model of psychotherapy, Tracey (1987, 2002; Tracey & Ray, 1984) demonstrated that, for mutually satisfactory therapy dyads, complementarity tended to be high in the initial stage, lower in the middle stage, and higher again during the termination stage.

In therapy, then, therapists can observe, track, and influence the course of interaction with their clients. Continually asking oneself what the client's substance abuse and related behavior appear to communicate and elicit helps the therapist identify the themes and patterns to be used in planning interventions to promote therapeutic outcomes according to the stage of the therapy process. For example, the task of developing a collaborative relationship with the client will probably be more difficult and lengthy with clients who primarily operate from a hostile perspective compared with those who exhibit a characteristic style of affiliation or flexibility on this dimension. Establishing goals and working through strategies for therapy will be a different experience and require different interventions with primarily dominant clients compared with those demonstrating more rigidly submissive styles of interaction.

Individual clients' different interpersonal styles require therapists to be flexible and deliberate in their interventions. Despite client variability, however, interpersonal therapists try to respond to clients in a manner that acknowledges the client's overt self-presentation while still holding out alternative possibilities for defining the present interaction and the emerging relationship. The therapist attempts to strike a balance between complementing the client's apparent and presumably rigid expectations, on the one hand, and offering another set of expectations that the client may choose to complement using new or atypical responses, on the other hand.

The point of balance between interventions that validate (complement) or challenge (decline to complement) the client shifts over the course of therapy. Theory and research both indicate that high proportions of complementary exchanges characterize the process of building rapport early in therapy, followed by lower rates of complementary exchanges in the middle stage of working through clients' difficulties. Therapists' high levels of complementary responding early in therapy contribute to positive alliance by communicating interest in understanding and effort to support the client's perspective. In addition, this early interventional emphasis permits the therapist to experience first hand what it feels like to interact according to the client's apparent definitions and expectations. By paying attention to when and how the therapist is inclined to complement or alter the client's definition of the interaction, the therapist formulates hypotheses about how the client's style benefits and hinders the client's interpersonal goals. In substance abuse therapy, this means responding to both the client's perceived social benefits and costs of using alcohol or other drugs.

The balance shifts as therapists test their hypotheses, deliberately declining to complement those client behaviors that appear to hinder therapeutic goals, and purposefully communicating interactional expectations intended to elicit client behaviors that potentially benefit the client's progress toward goals. The therapist makes predictions about how the client will react to the planned reduction in therapist complementarity. The client may be thrown off guard or frustrated, or may feel relieved or resigned. A mixture of reactions is also certainly possible and can be explored. The client's actual response compared to the therapist's prediction helps deepen understanding of the unfolding interpersonal process.

This enhanced conceptualization further guides subsequent interactions and interventions.

The key is for the therapist to maintain a reasonable degree of control over the shifting balance of complementarity. Naturally, some aspects of the interaction are beyond the therapist's influence. However, the therapist can exert choice over specific attempts both to initiate and respond to changes in the proportions of complementary exchanges in therapy sessions. The initial high degree of complementary responding needs to shift lower to evoke alternative behaviors from the client's usual style, but not so low or so fast that confidence in the therapeutic alliance is duly compromised. To the extent that the client's self-concept and interpersonal style revolve around substance use, the therapist especially needs to attend to relative complementarity of therapy transactions about the topics of substance use and abuse.

Thus, the therapist makes continual decisions, to the degree possible, about how to interpret the present interchange in light of the overall patterns evident in the interpersonal relationship with the client and inherent in the therapy process. At each point of intervention, the therapist uses these ongoing interpretations to make additional decisions about how to respond to the client in that moment. Ideally these interventional choices account for the competing needs to validate the client's extant views of self and relationships with the need to promote a wider range of possibilities for the client and the therapy transaction. If the therapist's intervention results in client resistance, the therapist moves the focus to complementary, supportive response as much as needed to maintain optimal complementarity for the present stage of therapy. If the client's response complements the therapist's alternative proposal for the exchange, the therapist continues to intervene from this position of challenge to the client's characteristic style, supporting and exploring new styles and flexibility in the client's response pattern. As the client engages with increasing consistency in behaviors consistent with therapy goals, the therapist reinforces these new behaviors with complementary responses, again shifting the complementarity ratio toward the higher levels characteristic of the termination stage.

CONCLUSIONS AND ASSUMPTIONS UNDERLYING
THE CHAPTERS TO FOLLOW

The issues, themes, and patterns described previously as relevant to therapy for substance abuse disorders are embedded throughout the chapters to follow. In chapter 3, the changing relationship between the substance abuse and mental health treatment fields is further explored. The types, actions, and effects of psychoactive substances are then summarized in chapter 4. In subsequent chapters, I examine the therapeutic tasks by which psychotherapists can construct conditions under which clients can become motivated and capable of modifying problematic substance use and related behaviors. Assessment and diagnosis of substance use disorders are covered in chapter 5, and the development and utility of treatment plans are demonstrated in chapter 6. Psychoeducational interventions especially pertinent in substance abuse treatment are described in chapter 7. In chapter 8, strategies for preventing and coping with relapse are identified. Interventions are considered in chapter 9 to address additional problems that may be associated with a client's substance abuse, including health and medical problems, emotional and behavioral difficulties, communication and relationship issues, educational and occupational concerns, and legal complications. Finally, issues in terminating therapy with clients whose work has addressed substance use concerns are dealt with in chapter 10.

Therapists working with their clients' substance use issues need to be cognizant that the client's culture influences the meanings a client attributes to psychoactive substance use. Differing cultural attitudes and norms regarding alcohol or drug use give rise to diverse expressions of feelings about substance use behaviors. Furthermore, therapists aim to attend and respond to ways in which cultural similarities and differences between the client and therapist shape the messages they communicate to each other and the interpretations they make of one another. As with all psychotherapy, the therapist's multicultural competence is presumed to be a crucial component of interpersonal flexibility and of therapy to effectively address the substance use concerns of a diverse clientele.

Underlying this approach to therapy for substance abuse is the assumption that the therapy process is a predictable sequence of dynamic events transpiring between the therapist and the client in discussions about substance use behaviors and concerns. Although some aspects of human transactions in therapy remain mysterious, uninterpretable, or capable of surprise, I contend that recurring themes and patterns can be detected in terms of the perceived significance of the client's substance use and the general progress of the therapy relationship. Clients who have histories of substance abuse are frequently ambivalent about confronting problems associated with their drug or alcohol use, but the therapist can choose appropriate interventions according to their expanding conceptualizations of the particular patterns and themes evident in an emerging therapy relationship.

Therapists will encounter many choice points throughout each course of therapy that addresses disordered substance use. It is important for the therapist to consider not only how the therapist wishes to intervene, but also why a particular intervention is chosen and how the therapist predicts the client will respond. The therapist working with substance use disorders also needs to be prepared to deal with any response the client actually produces, even if different from the therapist's predictions. In this book, I aim to articulate many of the choice points that are likely to occur when substance abuse is the focus of therapy. Furthermore, I hope the reader gains useful ideas about how to decide on interventions at such choice points to promote outcomes that both client and therapist agree are beneficial.

Chapter 3

The Changing Relationship of the Mental Health and Addictions Treatment Fields

Despite the extensive interplay of substance abuse and other psychological problems, the treatment of substance use disorders has historically been isolated from other mental health therapies. American society has interpreted excessive drinking and drug use quite differently than other behavioral indicators of mental health problems, at least partly in response to real and presumed differences that characterize the populations who exhibit addictions compared with other psychological disorders. (For example, contrast angry, risk-taking, defiant persons who deny personal responsibility for their actions with sad, anxious, insecure, or passive persons who voluntarily seek help to alleviate their problems.) Depending on their own interests and experiences, different types of professionals have been drawn to working with these stereotypically distinguished client populations. The addictions and substance abuse treatment field evolved separately from "mental health" treatment on the assumption of both fields that substance use disorders are distinct problems requiring a specialized form of treatment. Although the need for skills specific to substance use disorders is not in question here, I argue that the distinction has been greatly exaggerated to the point of neglecting significant overlap between addictions and other mental health disorders.

The problem, hinted at in chapter 1 and elaborated more fully in this chapter, is that the separation of the addictions and mental health treatment arenas has led to fragmented treatment efforts for the many individuals whose lives are complicated by multiple, interwoven disorders and problems. Some clients have been told they must address their substance abuse before their commitment to change is taken seriously and before any other concerns are addressed. Other clients have mentioned significant drug or alcohol use to therapists who gave the issue cursory attention because either the therapist considered the issue secondary or minimal, or did not know how to adequately assess or intervene with substance abuse concerns. Still other clients have been referred to additional professionals to deal with their "other" problems. Such referrals can be appropriate when treatment efforts are coordinated, but frequently the practitioner on the left hand has little knowledge of what the right-hand practitioner is doing. In any of these fractured attempts at treatment, the confounded problems of the client are more than likely to continue unabated.

Fortunately, recent developments in scientific understanding of the addictions, their connection to psychological concerns, and their effective treatments are changing the relationship between the substance abuse and mental health fields in the direction of increasing integration. There is still, however, much room for improvement. In hopes of stimulating further attention to promoting integration of the treatment fields, I first present several factors contributing to the historical and continuing isolation of the substance abuse treatment field, followed by discussion of several bases of growing integration of service delivery. Finally, I suggest some ideas for further enhancing the cross-pollination of psychological, mental health, and addictions treatments.

WHY HAS SUBSTANCE ABUSE TREATMENT REMAINED LARGELY ISOLATED?

Despite increasing recognition of the extent to which substance abuse co-occurs with other psychological symptoms, several sets of factors contribute to the continuing low interest and effort put forth by many therapists and mental heath practitioners toward addressing substance abuse concerns. This section explores social system factors, professional turf issues, client characteristics, and practitioner concerns that contribute to the segregation of substance abuse from other mental health treatment considerations.

Social Structural Factors

The social system in which addictions operate provides mixed messages to psychoactive substance users. A great many people drink alcohol or take drugs for purposes of recreation, celebration, ritual observance, temporary escape, or therapeutic intent. The high rates of "normal" social use of alcohol and medical use of drugs can make it difficult to distinguish between use and abuse. If "lots of other people are doing it," seemingly without adverse long-term consequences, then moderate and even heavy substance use can be more easily rationalized as unproblematic than, say, depression or anxiety, symptoms of which are rarely described as normal, common, and desirable for most people. The distressing and debilitating impact of mood or anxiety disorders not only defines the sufferer as different from normal, but also frequently motivates the individual to seek help to relieve the suffering. Compulsive substance use, in contrast, can be superficially equated with normal indulgence and additionally produces pleasurable immediate outcomes that reinforce continued use rather than problem identification. Thus, among society's mixed messages are that (a) people with mood or anxiety disorders need and deserve help (although not without a stigma that something is wrong or abnormal), but (b) people with substance use disorders are hard to pick out from normal substance users, and (c) once substance abuse clearly emerges as a problem, the person with the problem is "pretty far gone" and probably with limited hope for regaining normal status, considering the persistent nature of substance use disorders.

Mixed Messages About the Nature of Substance Use. The ambiguity of alcohol and drug abuse is further obscured by confusion deeply embedded in the social system about moral versus medical interpretations of the problems associated with substance abuse (Thombs, 1999). When alcohol or drug abuse is viewed as a moral issue, substance users are considered responsible for controlling their own behaviors. From this perspective, the user is presumed to have some ability to decide whether to take that drink or drug, and sympathy for the person's distress or dysfunction depends on the willingness the person exhibits to exercise that power. If viewed as a medical problem, substance abuse is thought to render the user unable to control his drinking or her drug use. Although at face value these two perspectives appear logically incompatible, social attitudes toward addictive behaviors often seem to imply that both are simultaneously true—that persons with substance use disorders are worthy of contempt for not exercising control over their excessive use even though they are presumably incapable of exerting that control.

Debate Over Appropriate Response to Substance Abuse. These mixed messages are reflected in the criminalization versus treatment debate over the appropriate means of responding to the problems associated with substance abuse. The moral view of addictions leads to decisions to punish substance abusers with stigmatizing attitudes, fines, and even incarceration. The medical perspective yields the conclusion that substance abusers need therapeutic treatment to reduce the deleterious impact of their drug or alcohol use. This debate is further complicated by the currently frequent stipulation of substance abuse treatment as a recompense for drug-related offenses, including driving a motor vehicle under the influence of alcohol or drugs. A major difficulty with allowing the courts to mandate treatment for substance abusers in legal trouble is that treatment under such conditions is understandably perceived as a punishment rather than as humane help. Mandated clients typically attend treatment grudgingly, if at all, and treatment providers for this population often encounter great difficulty motivating such clients to participate productively in mandated treatment. Some would argue that the decriminalization of drugs would permit greater provision of appropriate treatment to voluntary clients, who would presumably be more motivated to seek help if not required to reveal behavior deemed illegal to get treatment (Olson, Horan, & Polansky, 1992). Others maintain that decriminalization of drugs is a bad idea because it would remove some of the incentives available to promote the delivery of treatment to many who risk harm to self or others through their abuse of drugs or alcohol, but still deny a problem (Frances & Miller, 1998).

Economic Impact. In addition to philosophical and legal debates about the nature of substance abuse and its treatment, society is confronted with economic concerns. The estimated costs of substance abuse to society are staggering. Much has also been made of the relative costs of arresting, trying, and incarcerating drug offenders versus attempting to treat them therapeutically. Analyses clearly indicate that medical and psychological treatment is more effective and efficient in reducing the high costs associated with substance abuse (Ershoff, Radcliffe, & Gregory, 1996; Holder & Blose, 1992). Such results are leading to initiatives in a handful of states across the United States to reform drug sentencing laws, promoting mandatory treatment instead of prison time for nonviolent first-time offenders. Justifying and implementing these changes is also expensive, with proponents of different approaches competing for funds to support relevant research, training, and the provision of services.

In summary, society takes multifaceted and conflicting perspectives on the problems of substance abuse and chemical dependency, complicating the distinction between use and abuse. This confusion is further evident in the debate over whether substance abuse is by nature a moral or a medical problem, with controversial implications for how society should respond to the problem. Arguments about the relative merits of punishment versus compassionate care for persons who abuse psychoactive substances are alive, well, and unresolved in discussions of current drug policy and substance abuse treatment.

Professional Identity and Turf Issues

This complex societal backdrop sets the stage for the dialogue between mental health and substance abuse treatment providers. The attitudes, practices, and controversies mentioned earlier have defined *addiction* as a problem that emerges when a person loses or relinquishes control over an otherwise normal behavior, and the resolution of the problem presumably requires reestablishing behavioral control at least initially by the imposition of external means of control. The type of practitioner a client seeks out tends to vary according to how the client perceives the problem and the impetus for seeking help. Not surprisingly, different individual practitioners are also drawn toward different client presentations. Practitioners in the addictions field frequently see clients who present themselves for assessment and treatment at someone else's request or demand, be it an employer, doctor, caseworker, judge, exasperated spouse, scared parent, or worried family member. Mental health therapists, in contrast, more commonly see clients who present with complaints about subjective distress or dysfunction from which the client wants relief. These generalized differences in client styles and practitioner interests have shaped the evolution of different treatment philosophies in response to the needs of distinct populations as distinguished by presenting problems. The result has been the development of separate professional fields and different professional identities for practitioners who primarily treat addictions versus other mental health concerns.

With increasing awareness of the large degree of intersection of substance abuse behaviors and mental health symptoms, the philosophical differences between addiction treatment providers and other mental health therapists are easily polarized into competitive turf issues. Dialogue necessary for integrating treatment of complex disorders can break down in the face of discrepant assumptions. Substance abuse treatment providers frequently view mental health problems as symptoms or outcomes of addictive behaviors, whereas mental health therapists consider substance abuse to be a symptom or indicator of an underlying psychological disorder (Mee-Lee, 2001a). Addictions treatment practitioners tend to first address the client's chemical use on the assumption that no productive work can be done to deal with other issues until the substance use has been substantially reduced or eliminated. Mental health treatment providers typically concentrate initially on alleviating symptoms of emotional distress, attending to substance use concerns only if these fail to disappear in reaction to an affective treatment focus.

Although to some extent these differing approaches reflect appropriate responses to the manner in which the client's problem is presented, chapter 1 also demonstrated that the co-morbidity of substance abuse and other mental health disorders is both extensive and pervasive. Polarized treatment perspectives have at times resulted in some practitioners downplaying the significance of certain problems or the interactions among symptoms. The isolation of addictions from other mental health problems has led to the development of different treatment methods and terminologies that can inhibit communication between interested parties, which in turn leads to further isolation. Training programs and credentialing processes have emerged independently, to a large degree, with substance abuse treatment approaches emphasizing disease, denial, and practitioner detachment, while minimizing the utility of medication and the focus on process. Mental-health-oriented treatment approaches have tended toward the opposite emphases, focusing on psychological and behavioral factors, pharmacological interventions, and process factors in therapy (Mee-Lee, 2001a).

Client Factors

Three common characteristics of clients who seek treatment for substance abuse contribute to the isolation of the addictions treatment field, including low treatment motivation, interpersonal behaviors that inhibit relationship development, and ambivalence about changing substance use behavior.

Lack of Intrinsic Motivation for Treatment. The frequent absence of voluntary client participation in substance abuse treatment has already been mentioned, but further exploration of the implications of this first factor is warranted. A client who is showing up for sessions only to satisfy some third party and to avoid more undesirable consequences of nonattendance is likely initially to not take the therapist or therapy process too seriously. Resistance in the form of spotty attendance or reluctance to provide information, set goals, or engage in interventions all require the practitioner to employ interventions designed to motivate the client's attendance and participation.

Interpersonal Styles Not Conducive to Building Affiliative Relationships. Second, substance abuse clients also commonly exhibit interpersonal behaviors that interfere with the development of therapeutic bonds, regardless of how they were referred for treatment. Thus, in addition to knowing motivational strategies, addictions treatment providers must also be skilled at working through trust issues that arise when clients engage in subterfuge to disguise illegal or otherwise sanctioned behaviors. Substance abusing clients sometimes avoid straightforward communication with their therapists about the consequences of their substance use. Three commonly observed client maneuvers are expressions of open hostility (to get the therapist either to turn away or counter with hostility that justifies withholding trust), using charm and denial to mask manipulative or antisocial tendencies, and displaying perceptions of themselves as "out of control," often with stated preferences for operating from such a disinhibited state. To work effectively with such clients, the substance abuse treatment provider needs to be willing to work hard to develop rapport and be able to facilitate meaningful relationships in the presence of relationship conflict paired with the absence of trust.

Ambivalence About Substance Use.   A third client factor that helps distinguish the addictions treatment field is the high degree of ambivalence clients typically feel about giving up use of their substance(s) of choice. Although often by the time clients seek professional help many punishers are in place to discourage continuing substance use, and although the detrimental consequences and how to avoid or deal with them are articulated in treatment, clients still remain vividly aware of the strong, immediately reinforcing quality of drugs or alcohol. Substance abusing clients can benefit from guidance in acknowledging, confronting, and coping with ambivalent feelings and powerful impulses.

Therapeutic approaches to addressing these client factors are presented in subsequent chapters. Motivational interviewing to address client ambivalence about change (Miller, 1995; Miller & Rollnick, 1991, 2002), harm reduction strategies to minimize risk associated with substance use (Marlatt, 1998; Marlatt & Tapert, 1993), and relapse prevention methods to help clients maintain treatment gains (Marlatt & Donovan, in press; Marlatt & Gordon, 1985) are among the powerful therapeutic tools developed to work with clients who abuse drugs or alcohol and who exhibit the characteristics described earlier.

Individual Treatment Provider Concerns

To intervene with clients exhibiting any or all of the prior factors, addictions therapists clearly need to learn skills that differ in degree or even in kind from therapeutic skills developed by those who primarily treat other mental health disorders. These particular client factors and necessary therapy skills help separate the addictions field from other mental health care. Yet to more fully appreciate the isolation of substance abuse treatment, it is also instructive to consider individual therapist factors. Freimuth (2002) mentioned some of the attitudinal and emotional barriers that can interfere with therapists' efforts to address possible substance use among their clientele. Three categories of provider issues are discussed in this section, including stigmas associated with clients who abuse substances, stigmas associated with substance abuse treatment providers, and therapist ambivalence about personal substance use history.

Stigmas Associated With Clients Who Abuse Substances.   First, consider mental health therapists who are reluctant to work with clients who bear the stigma associated with the abuse of drugs or alcohol. Persons diagnosed with chemical dependencies or even less severe substance abuse disorders typically have poor prognoses, in part due to the conception of addiction as a lifelong disease. Its consequent problems are viewed as intractable, and expected progress is minimal. Therapists may anticipate that working with this population will be tedious, overwhelming, and frustrating at best, and hopeless at worst. Some therapists offer the following rationale for declining to work with substance use disorders: "I don't work with alcoholics (or addicts) because they don't really want to stop drinking (or using)." Some therapists also raise questions about how much expertise and how many resources should be invested in people with chronic problems and limited prognosis.

In addition to the expectation of a slow journey on a rocky road to the client's recovery from substance abuse, some therapists hesitate to wrestle along the way with the myriad factors that may impede treatment efforts. Legal entanglements, medical problems, occupational or educational difficulties, and symptoms of co-morbid psychological disorders are among the complications that substance abusers bring to discuss in treatment. Many therapists may be unwilling or feel unable to sort through these issues and address their ramifications.

Another stigmatizing concern about clients seeking addictions treatment relates to the likelihood of encountering volatile negative affect and hostile behavior. Even the anticipation of working with clients who openly express anger, provoke interpersonal conflict, deny responsibility for their behavior, or blame others for their problems can be daunting. The prospect of working with substance abusers who are referred for treatment because their drug and alcohol use has been associated with violence toward others or themselves, or occurred in consequence with other criminal activity, leads some therapists to reject work in the addictions field because of fears, insecurities, or sheer lack of desire to professionally tackle such difficult and troubling interactions.

Stigmas Associated With Substance Abuse Treatment Providers. A second individual provider factor that contributes to the isolation of addictions therapy is the extent to which therapists shy away from treating addictions due to stereotyped and real characteristics associated with substance abuse treatment providers and their job environments. Confrontation and the deliberate induction of crisis have historically been recommended (e.g., Bratter, 1975) to therapeutically engage clients exhibiting the characteristics described earlier, but some therapists view such confrontation as incompatible with their mental health training and philosophies, and perhaps their own professional styles.

Furthermore, historical and economic factors have contributed to treatment environments in which minimal credentials have been required of addictions treatment providers. Many agencies assign excessive caseloads to therapists with master's, bachelor's, or associate's degrees operating at low rates of pay, although it is questionable whether clients are being adequately treated under such circumstances. Although these job characteristics reflect some real constraints on the addictions treatment field, they also foster the perception of addictions treatment provider as a low-status occupation. Many aspiring therapists may be discouraged from working with addictions by this perceived imbalance between high job demands and low compensation and status.

Traditionally, the addictions treatment field has placed strong emphasis on the importance of spirituality in facilitating recovery from chemical dependency. This too may stigmatize addictions treatment and its providers in the eyes of more scientifically trained and oriented professionals. Good arguments can be made for the value of adding spiritual ingredients to the recipe for behavioral change, but some psychologists undoubtedly have ruled out work with addictions due to discomfort or disagreement with the treatment field's insistence on spirituality as a component of treatment.

One other stereotype of addictions treatment providers also certainly contributes to the isolation of the field from other mental health therapies. A high proportion of addictions therapists may well have been former substance abusers who became motivated to enter the field through their own process of recovery from a drug or alcohol abuse problem. Many who have traveled this career path are sincerely motivated to pass on what they have learned to help others in similar predicaments, and many are skilled, effective practitioners. However, some therapists may shun work with addictions to avoid being perceived as someone with a personal history of addiction. The stereotype is self-perpetuating: as if only a person who has lived through an addiction would be willing or able to work with other chronic substance abusers—besides, what other work would an ex-addict be qualified for anyway? The argument here is not that this stereotype is accurate, but that it may be pervasive enough to discourage interest in addictions among psychologists and mental health professionals who do not want to be thus stereotyped or do not want to work in environments populated by other practitioners who might fit the stereotype. This stigma is linked to a third therapist factor that contributes to the isolation of the substance abuse treatment field.

Therapist Ambivalence About Personal Substance Use History. So far this section has accounted for the likelihood that some psychologists and mental health professionals avoid the addictions field to rule out associating with the types of clients, practitioners, and job demands that characterize the field (accurately or otherwise). It is also crucial to explore the extent to which a therapist's interest in treating substance use disorders, however they arise in therapy, reflects the therapist's own feelings about his or her personal experience with substance use. It has already been noted that American society is one in which moderate consumption of alcohol and certain other drugs is widely practiced and largely condoned. Members of many other cultures also engage in regular use of psychoactive substances. Therapists, of course, are also social beings who participate to varying degrees in activities that involve the use of alcohol or other drugs (Good, Thoreson, & Shaughnessy, 1995).

The societal controversies surrounding the meaning of substance use and the response to substance abuse affect therapists in both their personal and professional lives. Observations and discussions with therapists and trainees frequently reveal considerable ambivalence and confusion about addressing client substance use in light of personal experience with substance use or with other users. Legitimate questions that arise include, "If I myself (now or in the past) drink or use drugs, even to excess on some occasions, how can I challenge another person's excessive use without being a hypocrite?", "Where does one draw the line between normal use and substance abuse?", and "If a client denies a problem or the need for treatment, who am I to impose my own values about substance use on this person? How can I be sure I'm not imposing my own conflicts about personal experience with use or with users?" Issues of countertransference and appropriate professional responsibility confront therapists working with clients involved in risky substance use.

Although these personal, professional, and societal factors constrict the provision of comprehensive help to people encountering trouble associated with their alcohol or drug use, there is much reason for optimism about the future potential of substance abuse treatment. Despite the difficulties, some people with substance abuse problems do succeed at reducing harmful behaviors and their consequences. Many do learn from working through their past problems to engage in more productive activity and to contribute responsibly to society. Regardless of the stigma and the barriers, many scientists and practitioners are so concerned about the detrimental impacts of substance abuse and drug policy on the mental, physical, and social health of the populace that they are dedicating their efforts to better understanding and treating the problem.

HOW ARE ADDICTIONS AND MENTAL HEALTH TREATMENT BECOMING MORE INTEGRATED?

As already described, substance abuse problems have been frequently treated in isolation from other types of psychological problems. Over the past two decades, the War on Drugs and related drug policies have resulted in large numbers of citizens being convicted and incarcerated for the possession and use of psychoactive substances (Anderson, 2003). Recognition of the limited successes or even, some would argue, the outright failure of prior efforts to reduce drug and alcohol abuse have stimulated new studies of addiction and new strategies for coping with it. Scientific investigation of the neurobiology of addictive behaviors has tremendously expanded our knowledge of how the brain, both structurally and functionally, is altered under the influence of alcohol and drugs (Wise, 1988, 1998). Not only does this research shed light on the basic nature of addiction, it also spotlights avenues leading toward enhanced understanding of the connections between substance abuse and other emotional, cognitive, and behavioral disorders.

Neurobiological Research Findings

Neurobiological research on addiction has focused on the mesolimbic dopamine pathway (MDP) to the nucleus accumbens region of the brain. Often referred to as the "reward center" of the brain, the nucleus accumbens provides pleasure when stimulated by specific actions of dopamine, serotonin, and other neurotransmitters. Both humans and animals will continue to engage in behaviors that stimulate the MDP and in turn the nucleus accumbens even if hard work is required to maintain the reward. Drugs, including nicotine and alcohol, stimulate the MDP either by rapid intensification of the effects of dopamine or indirectly by influencing the actions of other neurotransmitters that normally modulate or inhibit dopamine's role in MDP stimulation. Repeated drug use over long periods of time exposes this region of the brain to surplus levels of dopamine, which is thought to decrease the body's natural production of dopamine, causing a reduction in the number and sensitivity of dopamine receptors in the mesolimbic dopamine pathway (Thombs, 1999).

These neural mechanisms not only help explain compulsive behaviors involved in seeking and consuming drugs, they further suggest a neurochemical link between substance abuse and other psychological disorders, such as depression and eating disorders, in which abnormal neurotransmitter functions have also been implicated. Actions and effects of psychoactive substances are described in more detail in chapter 4. Research is also clarifying the learning and motivational factors that influence substance use (Baker et al., 2004).

Advances in Treatment

In addition to brain studies, addictions research has also made great strides in understanding the effective components of treatments of substance abuse (e.g., Annis, Schober, & Kelly, 1996; de Leon, 1993; Epstein et al.,

2003; Leshner, 1997; Miller, Meyers, & Tonigan, 1999; Rawson, Obert, McCann, & Marinelli-Casey, 1993; Witkiewitz & Marlatt, 2004). Treatment for substance use disorders tends to be most effective and lasting when the full scope of problems (emotional, social, occupational, medical, legal, etc.) can be addressed with the client. Also clients are more motivated to engage in treatments that acknowledge the client's definition and experience of their problems and permit the client to exercise choice in addressing those problems.

Taken together, these bodies of evidence support the conclusions that, although the treatment of substance abuse does require some specialized skills and knowledge, efforts at treating substance abuse hardly need to be independent from other psychotherapeutic approaches, and in fact can be usefully combined. Because both empirical and clinical findings point to the overlap in substance abuse, mood, anxiety, and other disorders, the arenas in which relevant therapy is provided are necessarily becoming more integrated.

Collaborative Professional Efforts

Increasing awareness of the confluence of substance abuse and mental health concerns is generating efforts to improve collaboration among researchers and practitioners from various perspectives. Some medical, psychological, and other substance abuse treatment providers are working toward establishing a common terminology to promote better communication among members of treatment teams. Active debates on controversial issues within the addictions knowledge base include attempts to address policy and program barriers to integrated substance abuse treatment.

Models of Behavior Change

Significant improvement in the ability to motivate client participation in therapy constitutes a crucial factor in integrating treatment efforts. Mee-Lee (2001a) noted traditional differences between the substance abuse treatment field's insistence on client accountability for change and the mental health treatment emphasis on supportive care. Confronting reluctant clients with personal responsibility for their behavior frequently yields anything but a sincerely motivated intention to change. Conversely, encouraging clients to return only when they are ready to receive compassionate care is likely to be equally unmotivating for some clients. Integrated approaches that balance care and accountability throughout treatment are proving to be better motivators.

Recent models for facilitating behavioral change describe the process of change as one of distinct stages. Identifiable transitions between stages can be promoted, according to such models, by a practitioner who can accurately identify and empathize with the client's present stage and who can help the client explore the meaning and implications of change in terms of the client's own experience. The transtheoretical model of change (Prochaska, DiClemente, & Norcross, 1992) is becoming widely used among substance abuse treatment providers (and the model is certainly applicable more broadly) in attempts to strike a balance between encouraging responsibility and expressing compassion for the client's change process.

The transtheoretical model of the change process fits well with the parallel development of motivational interviewing techniques. In summary, such interventions involve meeting the client at the place from which the client is willing to work and utilizing whatever the client brings to treatment to prod change in a (hopefully) positive direction. Interested readers may also wish to consult Miller and Rollnick (1991, 2002) and Rollnick and Morgan (1995).

WHY SHOULD THERAPISTS CARE?

Although some psychologists and mental health practitioners are interested and involved in working with substance abuse concerns among their clients or their research questions, many others are content to leave the study and treatment of substance abuse treatment to someone else's purview. As long as substance abuse could be defined as a separate entity and its treatment could be considered an independent specialty, psychotherapists could, if they chose to, fairly easily rule out or refer clients presenting substance abuse concerns. Some therapists, for example, have traditionally delineated their scope in terms of helping the motivated client and the "worried well." It is currently questionable whether a focus narrow enough to exclude substance abuse issues continues to be desirable or even possible in the future of therapy practice as well as related research and training.

As reviewed in chapter 1, data indicate that among psychotherapy clients and potential clients, high proportions have abused, do abuse, or will abuse alcohol or drugs in their lifetimes. Many other clients are indirectly affected by interpersonal contacts with substance abusers. Given the increasing documentation of connections between substance abuse and other concerns close to the hearts of many psychologists, therapists, and counselors (e.g., psychological disorders, occupational issues, lifespan development, and social justice), practitioners can no longer deny the need for at least basic knowledge and expertise regarding substance abuse treatment and effective referral. The populations that therapists aim to serve are likely to receive more appropriate treatment once therapists acknowledge the prevalence of substance abuse among their clientele and embrace the relevance of skills for treating addictions.

In addition to becoming better equipped to meet clients' multiple needs, the profession is likely to benefit in other ways from more extensively incorporating an addictions emphasis. As research and clinical experience continue to generate richer knowledge about addiction, substance abuse, and recovery processes, the scientific respectability of the addictions field is improving, and the trend toward empirically based, integrated therapy approaches is evident. Additionally, psychological and mental health specialties are uniquely poised to make cutting-edge contributions to the addictions treatment field. Diversity concerns, interpersonal processes, and supervision and training issues are exceedingly relevant, yet underaddressed in the substance abuse treatment literature.

Occupational and educational concerns are embedded in the stories so many substance abusers have to tell. Consider a client who reveals that now that she has started therapy, she is becoming convinced that her daily marijuana habit to combat boredom will subside once she can find a college major she truly enjoys, unlike her current major. Or how would a therapist work with another client who says he goes on drinking binges to avoid thinking about his grades and test scores, which are much lower than he knows he is capable of achieving? Or still another client, who just finished a term of incarceration for a drug selling offense and tells his therapist with all apparent sincerity that he wants to get a good job and be a good citizen and role model for his kids, but he also knows how much quicker and easier he could make money by returning to illegal activities? How might a therapist respond to the client who confesses that he has been drinking heavily and is planning to drop out of college because he is reluctantly starting to believe his alcoholic, physically abusive, working class father who keeps telling the client he will never be any better than his old man? Deficits in educational or occupational functioning are among the diagnostic criteria for substance use disorders, to be covered in chapter 5 on assessment and diagnosis. Chapters 6 (Planning Treatment), 8 (Relapse Prevention), 9 (Addressing Problems Associated With Substance Use), and 10 (Planning for Termination) are written in part to stimulate application of psychotherapeutic expertise to the educational and occupational problems confronting clients who abuse substances. Not only can such clients pose fascinating challenges, but therapists and counselors with an occupational specialization have a great deal to offer these clients and many more like them.

Considerations of diversity and social justice are crucial in the delivery of effective prevention and treatment to substance abusing populations. Substance use, for better and for worse, cuts across virtually all segments of society. Essential components of substance abuse treatment include the therapist's sensitivity to the sociocultural factors shaping a client's history and pattern of substance use. When the therapy participants differ in cultural or socioeconomic backgrounds, the therapist will need skills in utilizing multicultural interpersonal dynamics in the interaction between the therapist and the client. If social or institutional policy discriminates against a substance abusing client, the therapist may have a role to play as an advocate for social justice.

Psychologists interested in therapy practices and processes have developed a substantial research base addressing clinical supervision and training. However, the literature on therapy for substance abuse is only beginning to address appropriate training and supervision to address the particular needs of a substance abusing clientele (e.g., Powell, 2004). As substance abuse treatment is "mainstreamed" into mental health care, competent supervision and comprehensive training models are needed to disseminate and help integrate both empirically and clinically derived findings to trainees and clinicians working with addictions and co-morbid disorders. Psychologists have a potential role in developing and monitoring the skills of therapists who will be on the front lines of treatment.

*   *   *

In this chapter, I considered factors contributing to the historical isolation of treatments for chemical addictions from therapies for other mental health concerns. Despite the social, professional, and personal factors that may discourage some therapists from working with substance abusers, however, evidence of trends toward increasing integration of an addictions focus with mental health treatments is emerging. I reviewed the influence of accumulating neurobiological understanding of addictive processes, advancing development of relevant treatment models and methods, and increasing professional collaborations, all of which hold great promise for helping to more effectively address problems linked to the misuse of alcohol and other drugs.

Not only do clients and the field of therapy stand to profit from prioritizing attention to substance abuse, but individual therapists are likely to discover much professional satisfaction and personal reward from the gains in which they participate with substance abusing clients once biases against working with substance abusing clients are addressed and newly available knowledge is acquired, further developed, and applied. Considering the extent to which substance use disorders are intertwined with numerous social issues, work in the addictions specialty permits therapists to make substantial, lasting impact in areas of great social interest, concern, and need. The trends indicated earlier also point to a potentially expanded market for individuals who acquire specialized skills and knowledge in addictions research, prevention, and therapy. Many practitioner job descriptions include preferences for applicants with substance abuse treatment experience. The time is ripe for therapist training programs to include addictions and substance abuse treatment among the specializations they offer, and for both scholars and practitioners to explore the range of contributions they are specially equipped to make to the understanding of substance use disorders and their therapeutic treatment. This book contains some ideas and suggestions for those who would move farther in that direction.

The Types, Actions, and Effects of Psychoactive Substances

Therapists working with clients who abuse drugs or alcohol benefit from familiarity with the pharmacological actions and behavioral outcomes of substances with abuse potential, and they should be able to describe these to clients in terms clients can understand. Although the present chapter is not intended to provide comprehensive coverage of these topics, it is designed to provide an introduction to basic principles and concepts along with references for more extensive study. For some readers, parts or all of this material will be review. Other readers will have minimal background. Each reader is encouraged to consider that clients, too, will enter discussions about substances and their effects from a wide range of prior knowledge bases. Some clients have scarce idea how the substances they consume can and do affect their bodies. Other clients possess more sophisticated understanding of the actions of their favorite substances than do their therapists. Still others have partial or distorted information, or lots of questions and fears.

Thus, it is useful for therapists to comprehend models of drug actions and effects well enough to adapt presentation of the information to different clients' interests and abilities to digest it. Therapists are also recommended to admit the limits of their own knowledge and seek additional learning as the need arises. The following presentation covers information that is useful for the therapist to know when working with clients who engage in risky use of drugs or alcohol. Ideas about effectively using this information with clients are proposed in chapter 7 on psychoeducation.

WHAT ARE PSYCHOACTIVE DRUGS?

Both recreational and medicinal drugs are nonfood chemicals that alter normal biological functions. Some drugs influence neurological processes. Among the functions of neural impulses in the brain are to shape thoughts and behaviors. Neuroscientists believe that psychoactive drugs exert their primary effects by changing the processes by which neural impulses are conducted and transmitted in the central nervous system (Grilly, 2002). For simplicity of language, alcohol is also here classified as a drug because of alcohol's ability to influence baseline brain functions in a manner analogous to other recreational and medicinal drugs. Drugs are introduced into the human body with the intention of creating a specific response (e.g., euphoria, stress relief, or symptom reduction), and all drugs have both desired and unintended (and perhaps undesirable) effects (Doweiko, 2002).

General Characteristics of Psychoactive Drug Use

A drug in and of itself is neither good nor bad because many chemicals administered with clear purposes in carefully selected dosages have known beneficial effects. Problems with substance use can easily arise, however, when unmonitored quantities of a drug are consumed with little attention to duration, frequency, or intention other than to feel subjectively better in the moment (Grilly, 2002).

The user experiences the general impact of psychoactive drugs in terms of alterations in cognition, emotion, and/or behavior, but the specific effects of any drug use incident depend on several interacting variables. The complex interplay of factors determining a drug's effect on the body includes the type and amount of the drug, the duration and circumstances of use, and the characteristics of the user. The body in turn acts in the presence of a drug to metabolize the foreign chemical and eliminate it from the body. Metabolization can vary with the age, sex, medical condition, and race of the individual user. These pharmacological processes of drug action are similar whether the drug is used under a doctor's prescription or under social, recreational, or illicit conditions.

There are numerous kinds of drugs and many schemes for classifying them. Drugs of interest here are those with chemical structures rendering them capable of crossing the blood-brain barrier (BBB). In other words, focus is on the relatively small percentage of drugs with this capacity to act directly on the central nervous system (CNS). The BBB protects the neurons in the CNS with tightly configured brain capillaries wrapped in glial cells. To enter the brain's blood flow, any nutrient or other molecule must pass through several cell membranes in the BBB. Because cell membranes are composed of layers of lipids (fats), only molecules with high lipid solubility or other specific characteristics can cross the BBB (Diaz, 1997). Psychoactive drugs tend to be high in lipid solubility.

Beyond this similarity, drugs that can influence psychological processes come in a wide range of forms. Efforts to classify drugs are complicated by the fact that many drugs have multiple effects, and the same drug can have different effects depending on the dose size and the genetic makeup of the person using the drug (Grilly, 2002). Still a variety of drug categorization schemes have been developed to shape understanding and guide choices regarding psychoactive substances.

Specific Categories of Psychoactive Drugs

Drugs can be classified by their actions on the brain, by the behavior they elicit, or by their typical medical usage (Diaz, 1997). Additional organizational schemes use chemical structure or origin (e.g., natural plant sources or synthetic compounds) of the drug (Lewis, Dana, & Blevins, 2002). Legal classification schemes have also been developed. In the United States, current legal schedules, based on perceived risk of dependence on particular drugs, derive from the 1970 Comprehensive Drug Abuse and Control Act (Bono, 1998; Diaz, 1997) enforced by the Drug Enforcement Administration (DEA).

Finally, drugs can also be classified in terms of their popularity or commonality of use. For example, although alcohol is commonly classified as a sedative drug due to its CNS depressant properties, alcohol is so pervasively abused and (legally) used that it is often treated as its own special category.

In therapy, drug classification schemes are useful for finding out what the client has used and how the drug has affected or could affect the client. Furthermore, the therapist can use knowledge of categorized actions and effects to guide the client's learning and decision making. The categories offered here are largely organized around typical uses of different types of drugs with abuse potential, although within categories each drug has its own unique actions in the brain.

Stimulant Drugs. Stimulants arouse behavioral activity and make the user feel less tired, more alert, and in a better mood. Drugs in this category include cocaine, amphetamines (including methamphetamine), nicotine, caffeine, over-the-counter appetite suppressants, and antihyperactivity drugs. These drugs are sought recreationally for their psychostimulant effects, but are not presently used medically to produce these effects. In a medical context, some stimulants are used to suppress appetite or to treat hyperactivity or narcolepsy (Grilly, 2002).

Sedative and Hypnotic Drugs. Sedative and hypnotic drugs depress activity in the central nervous system. These drugs include alcohol, barbiturates, benzodiazepines, cannabis (marijuana) and other sedative drug compounds. Medically, some of these drugs have been used to reduce anxiety (anxiolytic drugs) and quiet seizure activity (anticonvulsant drugs). Effects sought in recreational use include euphoric relaxation, calmness, and sometimes floating feelings (Lewis, Dana, & Blevins, 2002). At high doses, these drugs typically induce sleep (Grilly, 2002).

Opiate Drugs. Opiates have analgesic (pain-reducing) properties due to their common abilities to act on neural receptors for endogenous opiates (substances naturally produced in the body). Opiate drugs, also called narcotics, include heroin, methadone, morphine, and codeine. These substances produce feelings of sedation and euphoria in addition to analgesia.

Hallucinogens. Also called psychedelics, hallucinogens are drugs taken to distort cognitive and perceptual processes. Currently they have little application in medicine (Grilly, 2002), but are popular in recreational contexts. LSD, PCP, mescaline, ecstasy, and psilocybin are among the best-known drugs in this category. Cannabis, or marijuana, is often classified here as well. However, marijuana is a good example of a drug that is hard to classify because of its mixed effects, which are further differentiated according to dose size. Some (Diaz, 1997) argue that marijuana may constitute its own class of drugs.

Anesthetic Drugs. Anesthetics such as nitrous oxide and ketamine are used medically for surgical procedures to produce loss of sensation and sometimes consciousness (Diaz, 1997). They are typically administered as inhalants or intravenously. The desired effects sought in recreational use of these drugs are dizzy, numbing sensations that may be accompanied by vivid sensory stimulation.

Additional Drugs of Interest. Other psychoactive drugs worth mentioning include those medically prescribed to treat disorders of mood or psychoses. However, these antidepressant and antipsychotic drugs tend to lack reinforcing effects or to have strong, undesirable side effects that greatly limit their abuse potential (McKim, 2003). Still it is important to be aware that medical use of these drugs in combination with recreational drugs can lead to risky drug interactions. Some over-the-counter analgesics can also have toxic interactions when used with alcohol (Doweiko, 2002).

The specific effects of a drug are shaped by several factors. The nature of the substance—including potency, composition, and dose size—will produce certain actions in the user's body and brain. The physical health and current physiological functioning of the user's body will both influence and be affected by the presence of a drug in ways elaborated shortly. The psychological state of the user affects the user's experience of the drug depending on past drug experiences and current mood, expectation, and tasks undertaken during a drug use episode. Finally, the environmental context, including the surrounding place, people, and culture, interacts with the rest of these variables to determine a particular drug experience (Lewis et al., 2002).

HOW DO DRUGS AFFECT THE USER?

Pharmacodynamics

The study of how a drug produces its effects at particular locations in the body is called *pharmacodynamics.* Current theory suggests that most drugs with abuse potential act specifically on the receptor sites of neurons, or nerve cells, in the brain. To clarify these mechanisms of drug effects, recall that neurons communicate messages throughout the brain and body by means of electrochemical conduction and transmission. A neuron, as illustrated in Fig. 4.1, contains a cell body, or soma, from which dendrites and axons extend.

The many dendrites of a single neuron receive numerous messages from several sources, including other neurons, other cells in the body, and even the cell itself. Some messages signal excitation of the neuron, whereas others inhibit neural activity. In the form of many small electrical potentials, this summed information reaches the soma where it is integrated and modulated. If the combined charge of the received signals reaches a threshold that opens ion channels in the cell membrane, the cell's action potential is initiated in the axon at the point where the axon emerges from the soma. Once created, the action potential is propagated down the axon to each of its terminals. In other words, nerve impulses are electrically conducted across a single cell to the axon terminals, where neurotransmitter and enzymes are stored and released when signaled by neuron activation. I later examine what happens at the axon terminals, but first I provide a closer look at the conduction process.

Impact of Drugs on Neural Conduction. Electrical conduction of a neural impulse begins with shifts in the concentrations of positively and negatively charged ions on either side of the cell membrane. Different types of ions (so-

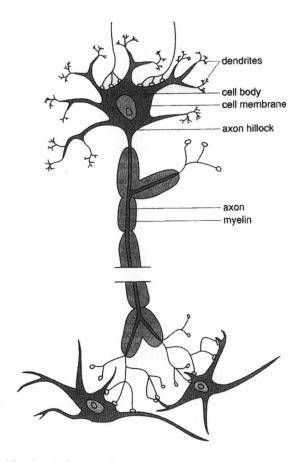

FIG. 4.1. A typical nerve cell. Note that the neuron receives input from synapses from several other nerve cells at its dendrites and cell body, and that it also has synapses on other nerve cells. (From McKim, William A., *Drugs and Behavior: An Introduction to Behavioral Pharmacology,* 5th Edition, copyright 2003. Reprinted by permission of Pearson Education, Inc., Upper Saddle River, NJ.)

dium [Na+], potassium [K+], chloride [Cl–], and negatively charged protein molecules) have different capabilities to pass through the neuron cell membrane, which is believed to cause the differential concentration of ions inside and outside of the cell. In the resting or polarized neuron, negative ions are more densely concentrated within the cell, and positively charged ions are concentrated without. The attraction between ions with opposing charges creates pressure, or voltage potential, on the cell membrane.

A multitude of factors, including the presence of drug molecules in the extracellular fluid, can alter the membrane's voltage potential. When voltage potential shifts to reach or exceed the membrane's threshold potential, ion channels in the cell membrane open to permit a rapid exchange of ions that temporarily reverses the concentrations of ions on either side of the membrane. Commonly referred to as the *firing* of a neuron, this sequence of neural events depolarizes neighboring areas of the cell membrane in sequence until the impulse is propagated all the way to the axon terminals, where the cell's chemical messengers, or neurotransmitters, are stored.

Psychoactive drugs can alter conduction of neural impulses at least three different ways. Drug molecules can influence the permeability of the cell membrane. They can block the ion channels and thus prevent the triggering of an action potential. Also drugs can affect the balance of ion charges across a neuronal membrane. Alcohol is a notable example of a psychoactive substance that directly modifies neural conduction (as well as synaptic transmission; Grilly, 2002). Any of these drug-induced alterations in neural conduction may contribute to the experience and observed effects of psychoactive substances. Emerging evidence indicates that drugs can also induce changes in gene expression within the neuron cell nucleus (Goldstein & Nestler, 1998).

Impact of Drugs on Neural Transmission. Along with their impact on nerve impulse conduction, psychotropic drugs influence neurochemical transmission between neurons. Neurotransmitters, such as dopamine and serotonin, carry messages across the synaptic gap from the axon of the activated neuron to the dendrite of the receiving cell. These messages may either initiate or inhibit activation of adjacent neurons. Communication between neurons is currently understood in terms of endogenous neuroactive chemicals that are released from a neuron, usually from the axon, and then cross the gap between neurons to bind to a receptor on another neuron, typically on the dendrites of the receiving cell. (Intercellular transmission and intracellular stimulation involving neurotransmitters available from nonaxonal sources or binding at nondendritic autoreceptor sites are beyond the scope of this discussion. However, the interested reader can find lucid, detailed descriptions in Grilly, 2002.)

When a neuron's action potential reaches the axon terminal, changes in the axonal membrane occur, which allow neurotransmitter chemicals to be discharged into the synapses (gaps) between neurons. These chemicals passively diffuse through the synapse until they are either degraded by enzymes, taken back into their originating neuron, or bind to the receptors of another neuron. The first two of these neurotransmitter fates result from systemic means of controlling the levels of available neurotransmitters. Enzymes released by the axon terminals help maintain optimal neurotransmitter balance by synthesizing active neurotransmitter molecules, and reuptake pump mechanisms in the axon terminals absorb unused transmitters back into the neuron.

The third outcome of binding to corresponding receptors activates cellular processes in the receiving neuron that stimulate fluctuations in the electrical potential of that neuron. The chemical message delivered by neurotransmitters initiates a flow of ions across the receiving cell membrane, contributing to the potential activity of that cell. Depending on the nature of the messages (excitatory or inhibitory) relayed from multiple receptor sites to the receiving cell soma, the cumulative signals determine whether an action potential is initiated.

Impact of Drugs on the Brain's Pleasure Center.   Psychoactive drugs appear to produce their desired effects (and some undesired ones) by altering the neurotransmission process. The complex mechanisms of neurotransmission are intricately related, with neuroscientists recently finding that the processes are even more complicated than they believed just a few years earlier (Grilly, 2002). Current theory and evidence suggest that drugs with abuse potential act extensively on the neurotransmitter dopamine and on structures in the brain that operate on dopamine (Thombs, 1999). Although several other neurotransmitter chemicals are also believed to influence the actions of drugs in the brain, the discussion to follow focuses primarily on the interaction of drugs with dopamine acting on neural circuits that produce reinforcement. Figure 4.2 depicts the dopamine systems in the human brain.

Research demonstrates that a common effect of drugs with abuse potential is to alter neural impulse transmission in brain pathways associated with the experience of pleasure and reward (Wise, 1998). The mesolimbic dopamine pathway (MDP) is one central reinforcement pathway. Located in the medial forebrain (behind the forehead and frontal cortex), the MDP is comprised of a cluster of cell bodies in the ventral tegmental area (VTA) of the midbrain whose axons pass through the medial forebrain bundle to synapse with neurons in the limbic system structures and the frontal cortex, among other connections. In the MDP, these dopaminergic neurons (operating mostly on dopamine) influence activity in the nucleus accumbens. When stimulated, the nucleus accumbens provides satisfaction or pleasure strong enough that both human and nonhuman subjects will work to obtain this reward (Grilly, 2002; Thombs, 1999). The nucleus accumbens also receives sensory input from the hippocampus and amygdala, parts of the limbic system that regulate learning, memory, and emotion. Based on these combined inputs, the nucleus accumbens provides feedback to the basal ganglia, which play a major role in stimulat-

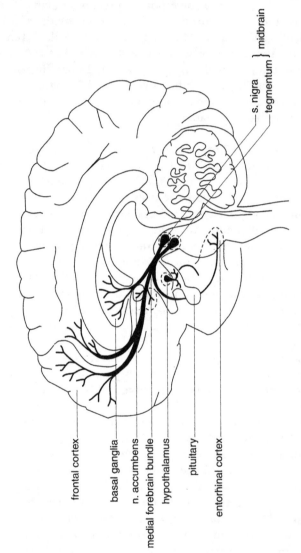

frontal cortex

basal ganglia

n. accumbens

medial forebrain bundle

hypothalamus

pituitary

entorhinal cortex

s. nigra ⎫
tegmentum ⎬ midbrain

FIG. 4.2.   Dopamine systems in the human brain. The mesolimbic system originates in the midbrain in the ventral tegmentum and runs to the nucleus accumbens and forward to the forebrain. The nigrostriatial system originates in the midbrain in the substantia nigra and runs forward to the basal ganglia in the striatum. (From McKim, William A., *Drugs and Behavior: An Introduction to Behavioral Pharmacology*, 5th Edition, copyright 2003. Reprinted by permission of Pearson Education, Inc., Upper Saddle River, NJ.)

ing motor activity. Behavior of the organism is then concentrated on conducting and repeating actions that lead to further stimulation of the MDP reward circuits. Neurobiologists believe that these reinforcement systems serve to maintain behaviors necessary to survival, such as eating, drinking, and sex (McKim, 2003).

The MDP is also a primary locale of drug action. Drugs and alcohol stimulate MDP neural activity either directly or indirectly (Wise, 1998). In general, drug exposure dramatically increases the availability of dopamine in the system, escalating the user's experience of pleasure and strongly reinforcing the likelihood of subsequent drug consumption. Using the brain's reward pathways, drugs interfere with normal MDP transmission and interrupt homeostatic neural mechanisms for maintaining optimal dopamine concentrations. Different types of psychoactive substances accomplish this general effect on the MDP through different processes. Normal neural functions may be enhanced or diminished depending on the chemical properties of the drug and its site of action. The following is a list of some of the specific ways drugs may disrupt neural communication, with examples provided of each. Other neurotransmitters besides dopamine are listed, so the reader should be aware that evidence suggests dopaminergic transmission in the MDP is frequently activated or inhibited by the activity of other transmitters (Wise, 1998).

Psychoactive drugs can:

1. change the amounts of neurotransmitter released (e.g., marijuana, amphetamines [Grilly, 2002], ecstasy, and nicotine [McKim, 2003] all trigger release of excess dopamine; alcohol inhibits glutamates, which in turn increases activity in dopaminergic neurons in the VTA [Grilly, 2002]; benzodiazapines and barbiturates decrease the activity of dopamine, but increase release of GABA, an inhibitory transmitter [Wise, 1998]).

2. alter the rate of metabolic breakdown of transmitters (e.g., amphetamines inhibit the MAO enzyme, slowing the rate of dopamine biotransformation [Grilly, 2002]).

3. bind to receptors to mimic transmitter impact (agonist; e.g., by binding to receptors for endogenous opiates, exogenous opiate drugs activate secondary messengers that normally inhibit dopamine release, thus indirectly enhancing dopamine availability; speculative indications are that LSD mimics serotonin, among other putative effects [Grilly, 2002]; in low doses, nicotine occupies and activates nicotinic cholergenic receptors [McKim, 2003]).

4. bind to receptors to block transmitter impact (antagonist; e.g., in higher doses, nicotine blocks nicotinic cholergenic receptors [McKim,

2003]; PCP and ketamine block glutamate and aspartate [both excitatory] transmitters, which increases dopamine concentration in the nucleus accumbens [Grilly, 2002; McKim, 2003]).

5. change rate of transmitter reuptake (e.g., cocaine, amphetamines, and ecstasy all block dopamine reuptake [Grilly, 2002; McKim, 2003; Thombs, 1999], yielding higher neurotransmitter concentrations available at neuron synapses).

6. cause neurotoxic destruction of nerve tissue (e.g., some animal studies suggest that ecstasy is toxic to serotonergic axons; alcohol appears to be among nutritional and medical factors contributing synergistically to alcoholic brain damage [Grilly, 2002]).

What Do Clients Need to Know About Drug Actions in the Brain?

Even this limited summary hints at the complexity of drug actions in the central nervous system. What of all this does a client who uses drugs or alcohol need to understand? For the therapist whose goal is to teach clients about the risks of exposure to psychoactive substances, the message is that no matter what substance you use, it will change the way your brain operates at least temporarily. These drug-induced changes in specific regions of the brain can trigger strong experiences of pleasure and relief, as users already know. (For alcohol, there is evidence that moderate drinking may also have some health benefits [Grilly, 2002].) However, drug actions in the brain can also cause disruptions in coordination, motivation, mood, learning, and memory, because the parts of the brain that generate pleasure are directly linked by cells in the brain to parts that regulate behavior, thoughts, and feelings. The sense of reward generated by the drug in the brain can temporarily wipe out a person's interest and ability for activities that would otherwise be rewarding, because the substance interferes with the normal balance of brain functions. Sharing this information and exploring its implications with clients are discussed in more detail in chapter 7.

HOW DOES THE USER'S BODY PROCESS THE DRUG?

In addition to knowledge of the action of drugs on the body, the therapist will also benefit from awareness of actions the body takes to rid itself of the foreign chemicals with potential to disrupt the body's equilibrium. There are always risks associated with introducing an exogenous substance into the body, and the body's natural response is to eliminate the drug (Doweiko, 2002). Most chemicals must be structurally modified by physiological processes, known as *drug metabolism*, before they can be excreted from the user's body. These processes, including the absorption, distribution, bio-transformation, and excretion of drug molecules, are also responsible for carrying the drug to its site of action in adequate concentrations to promote the drug's effects.

Pharmacokinetics

The study of processes by which drugs move through the body is called *pharmacokinetics*. The type, degree, and duration of a drug's effects depend on the drug's ability to reach its site of action in sufficient, unchanged strength (Doweiko, 2002). This *bioavailability* of the drug depends on the genetic, medical, physiological, and psychological statuses of the individual, as well as the presence of other drugs (Grilly, 2002).

Absorption. The first step of drug metabolism is *absorption* from the site of entry to the site of the drug's action (Doweiko, 2002). Most recreationally used substances must pass through several layers of cell membranes to get to the central nervous system, where the drugs have their desired effects. The rate of accumulation of the drug at the site of action is influenced by both the nature of the drug molecules and the route of drug administration (Grilly, 2002).

Drugs are carried to the brain through the blood circulatory system. Thus, the faster the drug reaches the bloodstream, the quicker its effects in the central nervous system. Because the cell membranes through which the drug must pass are composed of fatty materials called *lipids*, drugs that are lipid soluble (dissolvable in fat) are more easily absorbed into body tissues. To be transported by plasma in the bloodstream, however, the drug molecule must also have some water solubility. The relative concentrations of a drug in water- and lipid-based media in the body largely determine the different onsets, durations, and intensities of different substances' effects (Grilly, 2002). As examples, alcohol dissolves more easily in water, so it is quickly distributed through the bloodstream, whereas the high lipid solubility of marijuana results in concentrations of the drug in fatty organs of the body (McKim, 2003).

Drug absorption rates of access to the blood are also influenced by the route of drug administration. Drug entrance through the gastrointestinal (GI) tract (the enteral route) is generally safer but slower because the drug molecules have to travel through more layers to reach the circulatory system and ultimately the brain (Grilly, 2002). After entering the body through the mouth, the drug passes first through the stomach, where absorption can be influenced by enzymes in digestive secretions or by contents of the digestive tract, among other factors.

It is thought that drugs administered by mouth are transported from the GI tract into the bloodstream that supplies the liver by means of passive diffusion. This form of transport occurs when chemicals highly concentrated at one site gradually move to regions of lower concentration. The slow action of this method is limiting when quick drug action is desired, as may be the case in either recreational or medical contexts. Another disadvantage occurs when substances irritate the GI tract, causing nausea or vomiting.

Parenteral routes of administration involve introducing the drug directly into the bloodstream by injection. Drugs may be injected under the skin (subcutaneous), into the muscle (intramuscular), or directly into a vein (intravenous). Each of these methods is sometimes used to administer drugs with abuse potential. Intravenous (IV) injection in particular yields very quick, intense effects in the user because the drug administered in this fashion is absorbed right into the circulation of the blood. A drug administered by IV can circulate throughout the entire body in a minute or less (McKim, 2003).

Alkaloid drugs like cocaine, heroin, and morphine that do not absorb well in the acidic environment of the digestive tract are often administered by IV injection (Grilly, 2002). The potential for adverse reactions is high because the body has so little time to adjust to the drug's presence (Doweiko, 2002). Repeated injection, especially with drugs mixed with substances that are not water soluble, can irritate or block blood vessels (McKim, 2003).

Other common methods for administering recreational drugs include sniffing the chemical into the nose (intranasal route) or inhaling the drug as a gas or in the form of particles suspended in smoke. Both the sinuses and especially the lungs are lined with tissues rich with blood capillaries, allowing quick absorption of a drug into the bloodstream (Doweiko, 2002). The lungs in particular provide huge surfaces of extremely thin tissue separating capillaries from inhaled air and any chemicals contained in it. This rapid access allows fast onset and high intensity of drug effects. However, inhaled chemicals can irritate the linings of the lungs and sinuses, contributuing to medical problems like pneumonia, cancer (Grilly, 2002), emphysema, and asthma (McKim, 2003).

Distribution.   As the drug is absorbed, it gets distributed throughout the body. Some of the drug molecules are carried through the bloodstream across the blood-brain barrier (BBB) into the central nervous system, but a portion of the drug is also deposited in other sites in the body, notably the liver and kidneys (Grilly, 2002). To exert their psychoactive effects, most drugs with abuse potential are fairly high in lipid solubility, which also means these drugs accumulate more easily in organs comprised of high proportions of adipose (fat) tissues.

Men and women differ in fat to muscle ratios, so drugs get distributed at different rates and patterns across the sexes. Drug distribution is also affected by the age of the person using the drug, the lipid solubility of the drug, variable blood flow patterns to organs, and the characteristics of tissues in different regions of the body (Doweiko, 2002; Grilly, 2002). Water-soluble chemicals, like alcohol, blend readily into blood plasma and are thus rapidly distributed throughout all body fluids. Drugs lower in water solubility, like marijuana, are transported by chemically binding to fat molecules in the bloodstream, which are capable of easy movement across cell membranes into other body tissues. By this transport system, lipid-soluble drugs get distributed to bodily structures, especially those high in concentration of lipids (Doweiko, 2002), including the liver, heart, brain, and the myelin sheath of neurons.

Some drug molecules can bind to proteins in the body, which delays the body's ability to further metabolize the drug. Protein-bound drugs cannot achieve a biological effect, but can remain stored in the body, often in high concentrations. Over time, protein bonds with drugs held in reservoir are eroded so that newly unbound drug molecules are gradually released back into circulation, giving the drug a longer duration of biological activity (Doweiko, 2002).

Biotransformation. As exogenous chemicals get distributed throughout the body, natural processes are mobilized to get rid of the drug, usually by changing the chemical structure to a form that can be eliminated from the body (Doweiko, 2002). These metabolic activities are called *biotransformation*, whereby the parent compound is altered to produce metabolites that may be more, less, or equally active at drug binding sites. In fact many drugs have multiple active metabolites with different types of actions, so that the subjective effects of the drug depend on the rates of biotransformation of each metabolite (Grilly, 2002).

The high lipid solubility of psychoactive drugs must generally be converted to a more water-soluble metabolite to allow excretion from the body and thus termination of the drug's effects (Grilly, 2002). Much of the work of biotransformation is done in the liver. The liver is thought to have evolved to allow animals to deal with toxins to which their environment exposes them (Guengerich, 1993; cited in Grilly, 2002). Enzymes in the liver create various chemical reactions that alter many types of substances, including drug molecules, producing metabolites (McKim, 2003).

The design of the human circulatory system routes drugs absorbed through the GI tract into the liver before they are distributed elsewhere in the body. This first-pass metabolism process subjects drug molecules to substantial enzymatic action in the liver, breaking down toxins in efforts to protect other organs. This accounts for the slower and often less intense effects of drugs administered orally.

Drugs that do not pass initially through the GI tract or that survive first-pass metabolism intact are biotransformed by enzymatic reactions occurring in virtually every cell of the body. Blood circulation carries drugs to the regions of the body where they can be transformed. Predominant activity occurs in organs involved in excretion of chemicals for which the body has no more use, including the lungs, GI tract, liver, and kidneys (Grilly, 2002).

Most drugs are metabolized at a rate that is proportional to their concentration in the blood plasma. This is the basis of the concept of a drug's half-life, the time span required for the body to inactivate or excrete half of an original dose of the drug. In general terms and in the absence of repeated administrations of the drug, the original dose remains active in the body for the duration of about five half-lives (Doweiko, 2002). A drug's ability to bind with proteins tends to lengthen the drug's half-life and its potential duration of effects. An important exception is alcohol, which is metabolized at a constant rate regardless of the size of dose or concentration in the bloodstream (Grilly, 2002).

Biotransformation is further influenced by previous exposure to chemicals that stimulate or reduce concentrations of enzymes in the liver. Repeated or chronic use of drugs or alcohol activates increases in levels of liver enzymes, making the liver more efficient at metabolizing drugs and alcohol. This in turn means the user will experience a lesser effect with the same dose over time, which is an important factor in the development of drug tolerance (McKim, 2003). Rates of biotransformation further vary with the age, sex, and state of health of the individual.

Elimination. The final stage of drug metabolism is elimination of the drug from the body. The vast majority of drug excretion takes place through the kidneys, which maintain the balance of water and salt in the body. The kidneys filter the circulating blood so that substances needed by the body or insufficiently metabolized for elimination are reabsorbed into the blood circulation. Substances including drug metabolites that are not reabsorbed are excreted in the urine (McKim, 2003). Small amounts of drugs and their metabolites are eliminated through exhalation, perspiration, and lactation, contributing to the characteristic odor of the heavy substance user.

What Do Clients Need to Know About How the Body Metabolizes Drugs?

With this overview in mind, let us again consider how this information is relevant to the client, even clients not that interested in details of pharmacological actions and biological processes. The basic messages the therapist wants to deliver are that drugs must pass through the body in a series of phases to get to the sites of action in the brain where drugs induce their effects. At every phase, from point of entry to site of action, the body is acting on the drug in many ways that both potentiate the drug's effects and rid the body of the drug. The body possesses intricate systems for eliminating foreign substances of no use or of potential harm to the body. Although these homeostatic systems are reasonably efficient at processing reasonable doses of drugs or alcohol, these structures and their functions can be altered and damaged by excessive exposure to drugs.

OUTCOMES OF REPEATED SUBSTANCE USE

Drugs with high abuse potential tend to be those capable of reaching the brain quickly, eliciting intense and rapid reinforcing effects. The swift reward the user experiences is often perceived as more gratifying than rewards associated with alternative nondrug behaviors. Also the costs of substance use typically are delayed to the extent that when an opportunity to use presents itself, those costs become much less salient to the user than the anticipation of more immediate rewards. Reinforcement models of substance use derived from learning theory explain how using drugs is maintained by the strongly reinforcing properties of these substances and the stimuli the user has learned to associate with their use (see McKim, 2003, for a summary of relevant research).

Pharmacological and neurobiological studies of drug effects demonstrate that drugs induce physiological changes in the body and brain that reflect the organism's attempts to restore normal functions under the influence of exogenous chemicals. As the individual continues to use drugs to obtain their rewards, and as the body subsequently modifies both functions and structure to accommodate chemical alterations, the stage is set for the potential development of substance dependence. Of course not all substance users become dependent, so it is important for the therapist to understand how to recognize and distinguish dependence. The therapist can then offer the client psychoeducation (discussed in chap. 7) about addiction and its implications for personal behavior and well-being.

Tolerance

One frequent outcome of repeated substance use is the development of the individual's tolerance to effects of that substance. In general, *tolerance* refers to the reduction in effects of a drug due to prior exposure to that drug. This can mean that the individual requires larger doses of the drug to experience its effects, or that the person cannot obtain previously experienced effects with customary use, or both. Tolerance was once equated with drug dependence, but more recent theory and research indicate that tolerance is neither a necessary nor a sufficient condition of substance dependence. However, tolerance may be among the features that together characterize a dependence diagnosis for a particular individual (American Psychiatric Association, 2000). Also the mechanisms of tolerance subject the substance user to increasing risks of problematic consequences.

This enhanced risk with increasing tolerance stems from several factors. First, users seeking desired effects despite tolerance tend to consume substances more frequently and in higher doses—conditions that are more toxic and potentially lethal. Second, tolerance develops at different rates to the various effects of a single drug (Grilly, 2002). It is thus more accurate to say that tolerance develops not to a particular drug, but to specific effects of that drug (McKim, 2003). Problems can arise when a person becomes tolerant to the desired or euphoric effects of the drug, but not to the toxic effects. The ratio of a drug's effective dose level to its lethal dose level is called its *therapeutic index* (TI). As the TI becomes smaller with increasing tolerance, the effective dose (quantity of drug needed to induce a particular effect) approaches the size of dose that may be lethal to the user (Grilly, 2002). Even if the individual does not die from heavy use, frequent administration of large doses of a substance can cause accumulations of the substance or other alterations of the body that further contribute to health problems. The user may also experience increased or severe side effects when consuming larger doses of a substance in attempts to achieve more euphoric intensity.

Finally, tolerance can contribute to the development of substance dependence (Grilly, 2002). If tolerance leads to such increases in the frequency and quantity of drug use that the user becomes engaged in compulsive use despite punishing consequences, that person will probably meet criteria for a dependence diagnosis.

Pharmacokinetic Tolerance. In general, the greater the amount of a drug the person ingests and the shorter the time between doses, the faster the person will become tolerant to the drug's effects. Tolerance can take several different forms. *Metabolic* (or pharmacokinetic) *tolerance* occurs as the liver increases its rate of chemically breaking down an orally administered drug, thus shortening the duration of the drug's action. The liver responds to heavy concentrations of drug molecules in the blood by producing more enzymes to metabolize the drug more quickly.

Pharmacodynamic Tolerance. Pharmacodynamic tolerance develops when exposure to a drug changes the availability or activity of neurotransmitters in the central nervous system. As seen earlier in this chapter, drugs with abuse potential can change neurotransmission in various ways that all ultimately result in increased levels of dopamine operating in the mesolimbic dopamine pathway while the drug is present. Tolerance associated with pharmacodynamic processes can also take the form of structural changes in neuron receptor systems in response to excessive dopamine availability over long time spans. Exposure to a drug for several hours or more prompts neurons to modify the number and sensitivity of receptors in the cell wall. As neurons adapt to regulate their functions and normalize their firing patterns in the context of drug-modified neurotransmitter activity, cell responses to the drug's presence become reduced, and the person develops tolerance to the drug's effects.

Context-Specific Tolerance. A third form of drug tolerance depends less on physiological mechanisms and more on learned behaviors the user exhibits in association with the drug. Called *behavioral or context-specific tolerance*, these alterations in the user's response to drugs develop through the familiar learning processes of classical and operant conditioning. Through repeated drug use episodes, the user learns to associate contextual cues with the anticipation of drug availability and effects. For example, a refrigerator filled with beer or the pipe used to smoke drugs becomes a conditioned stimulus (CS) to the substance user, signaling that exposure to the substance (the unconditioned stimulus [UCS]) may soon follow. The organism's physiological (unlearned) responses to the substance have already been discussed; from a classical or Pavlovian conditioning perspective, these automatic responses to the drug (UCS) are the unconditioned responses (UCRs). As the user comes to associate the signals (CSs) with the impending drug (UCS) administration, the user begins to respond in preparation (conditioned response [CR]) for the drug.

These conditioned or learned responses occur in reaction to the signal cues even before the drug action is initiated in the user's body. Behaviorally, the individual may engage in seeking and administrating activities (CRs) in response to stimuli such as the refrigerator or the pipe, CSs that would not elicit such a response from the individual without their learned association to the alcohol or drug. Internally, the person may, in the presence of the CS alone, experience craving for the substance or even exhibit physiological compensatory responses in anticipation of the drug (McKim, 2003). Context-specific tolerance thus develops when the substance use experiences reduced effects of the substance because of compensatory responses the user has learned to make in reaction to contextual cues indicating that drug effects are soon to occur.

A classic example of this process is demonstrated in observations of heroin overdose. Tolerance to heroin can be extremely high in frequent users, so that they tolerate doses that would be lethal to a person who has never used heroin. Still heroin users are at high risk for overdose because of fluctuations in their tolerance associated in many cases with taking the drug in unfamiliar circumstances. When using heroin in environments that provide cues and signals that help users regulate their responses to the drug, tolerance requires the user to inject huge doses to achieve desired effects. In atypical contexts, however, where regulatory cues and compensatory signals are not present, a dose the user has easily tolerated in the past can be toxic or even fatal (Siegal, 1982; cited in McKim, 2003).

Context-specific tolerance can also develop according to operant conditioning processes. As many readers will recall, operant or instrumental conditioning occurs when the organism learns to associate a behavior the organism has performed with a particular outcome, influencing the subsequent likelihood of repeating that behavior dependent on the nature of that outcome. *Reinforcers* are identified as those outcomes that increase the odds that the organism will repeat the behavior. Those outcomes that decrease the probability of the behavior are called *punishers*.

Because of their inherent abilities to produce pleasure (positive reinforcement) or reduce discomfort (negative reinforcement), drugs are powerful primary reinforcers. Secondary reinforcers are stimuli that influence the individual's chances of getting access to primary reinforcers, which also include food, water, sex, and so on. In the case of substance use, behaviors that permit the user to maintain control over the detrimental effects of substance use to maintain access to the desirable (primary reinforcing) effects are reinforced in this secondary sense (Grilly, 2002). Thus, the substance user has incentive to learn tolerance to the disruptions drugs initially cause in terms of motor performance, for example. The user who learns to walk, speak, and even drive normally under the repeated influence of drugs is in a better position to continue using the drug without getting into trouble or encountering problems.

This instrumentally conditioned tolerance is also context-specific in that tolerance is exhibited only with respect to specific tasks the individual has performed under the influence that result in reinforcing consequences. McKim (2003) summarized animal and human research that supports this hypothesis (although the reader should be alert to the confusion of negative reinforcement with punishment in his chap. 5).

Reverse Tolerance. Therapists who work with clients who use substances should also be aware of the phenomenon of *reverse tolerance*, or sensitization. Characterized by increased effects of a drug after prior exposure, the enhanced sensitivity to a drug has also been attributed to both pharmacological and learning processes (Grilly, 2002). A good example is the reported tendency for marijuana users to experience euphoria only after repeated episodes of use.

Withdrawal

Another frequent result of prolonged or repeated substance use is the development of withdrawal symptoms, which are physical and psychological disturbances experienced when the effects of a drug cease. Withdrawal can occur when drug administration is discontinued after extensive use or when a specific antagonist drug (one that blocks the effects of another drug) is administered (Grilly, 2002). Withdrawal symptoms can be viewed as manifestations of adaptations the body has made to the drug (McKim, 2003). Different substances produce different specific withdrawal syndromes. Often the symptoms of withdrawal are opposite to the effects of the drug (Doweiko, 2002), as in the cases of fatigue and excessive sleep following a binge with psychomotor stimulants, or anxiety and agitation after abuse of sedative drugs.

The presence of withdrawal symptoms in a substance user alerts the treatment provider to the likelihood of pharmacodynamic tolerance. Recall that this form of tolerance reflects adaptations the neurons have made to restore normal functions disrupted by the drug. When drug use is discontinued, the central nervous system must readjust to regulate activity. Withdrawal symptoms result, to a large extent, from this neuroadaptation process (Doweiko, 2002). Determining the presence of both tolerance and withdrawal is important in specifying a diagnosis of a substance dependence disorder with physiological dependence, to be further considered shortly.

Although withdrawal is included in the criterion set from which a substance dependence diagnosis may be drawn, withdrawal from a drug can occur in the absence of dependence on that drug. For example, according to the *DSM–IV* (American Psychiatric Association, 1994), some patients without opioid dependence or indications of compulsive use exhibit withdrawal reactions to opioid drugs prescribed following surgery. However, because withdrawal discomfort can be relieved by administering more of the drug, the individual's attempts to reduce or avoid withdrawal symptoms can negatively reinforce continued substance use. In time and in combination with other factors to be discussed shortly, the existence of a withdrawal syndrome and drug readministration to avoid it can contribute to the establishment of dependence.

Substance Dependence

In its most general sense, *substance dependence* refers to the compulsory self-administration of drugs despite debilitating consequences, often in response to difficult emotions, physical symptoms, or circumstances that the individual feels otherwise unable to tolerate. The term *chemical dependence* has also been employed in many other ways that vary with the theoretical models embraced by persons expressing their views on problematic substance use. For example, substance dependence may be described differently by professionals embracing disease models versus maladaptive behavior models.

Physiological Dependence. A physical dependence indicates that the user will experience bodily discomfort or feelings of sickness when effects of the drug are withdrawn (Grilly, 2002). To avoid this "abstinence syndrome," the physically dependent person feels compelled to continue substance use despite other adverse consequences.

Psychological Dependence. The user's experience of seemingly irresistible cravings and compulsions to achieve even at high cost the psychic benefits of the drug—be they enhancements in mood, awareness, performance, or relief from stress or affective discomfort—is known as psychological dependence. These two forms of dependence can be hard to differentiate in part because they often appear simultaneously or overlap in the same person (Grilly, 2002). The *DSM–IV* criteria for diagnosing substance dependence specify a distinction between forms of the disorder with (exhibiting tolerance or withdrawal) and without physiological dependence (American Psychiatric Association, 1994, 2000). As noted in the following chapter, a substance dependence diagnosis based on *DSM–IV* criteria rests on evidence that the client displays for a year or more at least three of seven designated problems indicating disordered substance use.

Models of Chemical Dependence. The *DSM* criteria evolved from a disease model of substance dependence disorders. Disease models typically consider substance dependence as an illness resulting from some combination of genetic susceptibility and exposure to psychoactive chemicals (Peele, 1996; cited in Thombs, 1999). Problem behaviors are viewed as symptoms of disease processes. Leshner (1998) considered drug addiction to be a complex brain disease characterized by fundamental, persistent changes in the brain resulting from chronic drug use.

In the 20th century, disease concepts of alcoholism and drug addiction increasingly overshadowed earlier conceptions of excessive substance use as an indication of moral weakness or failure (McKim, 2003; Thombs, 1999). Current legal and social stances toward substance use show that the moral model has hardly disappeared. However, with the emergence of Alcoholics Anonymous (AA) in the late 1930s and the publication of Jellinek's (1960) classic book entitled *The Disease Concept of Addiction*, disease models became widely accepted as the standard basis of treatment. The vast majority of substance abuse treatment centers still utilize the disease model.

Shifting the focus from moral to medical explanations of substance dependence has certainly led to more compassionate care and stimulated important research. The advances in knowledge and technology afforded by such research should be evident from preceding sections of this chapter. Still critiques of the disease model point to several difficulties of the model in accounting for substance dependence phenomena. Proponents of disease conceptions have yet to agree on the nature of the disease (McKim, 2003), with varying emphases on biological, psychological, and spiritual processes. Furthermore, some of the hypotheses generated by the disease model have so far not garnered strong scientific support, in particular the notions that the disease is "progressive" and involves "loss of control" (see Thombs, 1999, for one review of this research).

Thombs (1999) also argued that the greatest weakness of the disease model has been minimization of the importance of psychosocial factors, particularly the crucial role of learning processes contributing to substance dependence. Strict adherence to a disease model can limit the degree to which treatment focuses on learning new skills to counteract chemical dependence, especially for those clients who are not well suited to treatment approaches based on the disease model.

McKim (2003) explained how research based on animal learning models came to demonstrate that neither the assumptions of disease processes nor physical dependence were necessary for the compulsive self-administration of drugs. Maladaptive behavior models of substance dependence postulate that normal learning processes are responsible for establishing addictions. From this perspective, behaviors comprising substance dependence are considered to be conditioned or learned responses. The probability of these behaviors occurring increases each time substance use is reinforced by euphoria, social rewards, and elimination of withdrawal symptoms (McAuliffe & Gordon; cited in Thombs, 1999). Substance dependent persons learn environmental and internal cues to predict when the reinforcement associated with drug effects is available, and the reinforcement these persons actually receive when they use drugs keeps them coming back for more.

In the presence of stimuli the individual has learned to associate with drug use and in the absence of reinforcing effects, strong cravings motivate the individual to seek out and consume more drugs. These cravings are also referred to as *conditioned drive states* (Grilly, 2002). A user's perceived needs and efforts to satisfy these cravings can, over time, teach the user to engage in high rates of drug self-administration. The greater the reinforcement value of the drug to the individual, the faster the individual will respond by administering more drugs (McKim, 2003).

Cognitive factors are also involved in the development of dependence according to some variants of the maladaptive behavior model. Social cognitive models of substance abuse propose that individuals learn to regulate their own drug-related behavior according to internal standards of performance and achievement. The user's self-efficacy and drug outcome expectancies are thought to shape the behaviors a person will attempt (Thombs, 1999). For example, a person with low self-efficacy beliefs for a task—such as passing an exam or breaking up with a romantic partner—and a positive expectancy that using alcohol will enhance competence is more likely than someone with different expectancies to drink while studying or before encountering the partner. Some research evidence suggests that the anticipated outcomes have as much if not more influence on subsequent behavior as the actions of the substance (Kilmer, 2003; Thombs, 1999).

Internal standards and expectations also serve as criteria by which individuals evaluate their own behaviors. In other words, cognitive models hypothesize that individuals internally reward and punish their own performances according to their judgments of their capabilities and limitations. Alcohol and other drug users prone to substance dependence, especially those with low self-efficacy, may compare their behaviors under the influence of substance intoxication versus abstinence and conclude the outcomes are better (e.g., experience of stress is less or ability to verbalize difficult sentiments is increased) when intoxicated.

Efficacy and outcome expectancies can also cognitively reinforce substance dependence from another angle. As rates of drug administration become higher and seemingly more compulsive, individuals may conclude they are incapable of abstaining. Thus, to regulate their behavior, they may withhold self-punishment for using substances in the face of perceived (and possibly real) limitations on ability to resist substance use.

These behavioral and cognitive processes of learning to depend on psychoactive substances have helped address some of the limitations of the disease models by emphasizing normal regulatory learning mechanisms contributing to the development of maladaptive drug consumption (McKim, 2003). However, these approaches have also been criticized for deemphasizing the role of biological and pharmacological factors contributing to substance dependence (Thombs, 1999).

Although different models of substance dependence have offered different definitions, mechanisms, and corresponding evidence, the disease and behavioral perspectives are not necessarily incompatible. To some extent, they describe different but complementary accounts of the incredibly complex phenomenon of addiction. Much of the literature reviewed for this chapter acknowledges the interacting biomedical and psychosocial factors that influence the abuse of drugs and the development of dependence. Leshner (1998) pointed out that successful treatment of chemical dependence requires attention to the "whole person . . . integrating behavioral, pharmacological, and social treatment in ways specific to an individual's needs" (pp. 5–6).

Health Risks and Difficulties

Research indicates that moderate substance use has some conducive effects on personal health, but excessive substance use puts individuals at risk of many physical and mental health problems (Grilly, 2002). Substance abuse by vulnerable individuals can also exacerbate existing medical or psychological problems. Although a comprehensive review of health complications associated with substance abuse is beyond the scope of this chapter, an extensive literature points to potential medical problems affecting the central nervous system, the cardiovascular system, the gastrointestinal system, the reproductive system, and the immune system. Substance abuse during pregnancy can cause fetal distress and birth defects. Substance abuse has been shown to play a significant role in the development of liver disease and cancer and is a factor in many accidental deaths and injuries. Mental health difficulties also frequently co-occur with substance use disorders. Chapter 9 considers how to address health complications of substance abuse in a psychotherapeutic context.

*   *   *

In conclusion, exposure to psychoactive drugs triggers a complex interaction between the user's body and the chemical substance. Drugs can alter both the structures and functions of the brain and body with multiple corresponding effects, some of which are undesirable, but others so desirable that they can reinforce continuing substance use despite great costs. To achieve these effects, the drug must pass through the user's body, which in turn acts on the presence of the drug in attempts to normalize functions of the brain and body. The human body is equipped to regulate itself in response to environmental influences, including exogenous psychoactive substances. However, high degrees of exposure to drugs or alcohol can modify or damage the body's homeostatic mechanisms, contributing to disease and other physical or psychological health problems.

The roles of learning as well as neurological and biological processes are implicated in a comprehensive understanding of chemical addictions. Substance abusers learn extensive networks of cues, signals, incentives, consequences, reinforcements, and punishers that shape the individual's response to the experience of substance intoxication. Changing problematic substance use behaviors is a relearning process, and therapists will be most effective at facilitating such relearning when they consider the multiple interacting processes and outcomes that have maintained a client's substance abuse and that can potentially reinforce behavior change. Therapists can guide clients in articulating a fuller range of awareness of both the desirable and undesirable effects of their substance use, further stimulating clients to explore the implications and their options.

Assessment for Substance Use Disorders

The life stories of substance using clients are so diverse, and the spectra of drugs and alcohols and combinations thereof so broad, that assessment and diagnosis of substance use problems are fascinating but rarely simple, brief, or straightforward processes. The information a client is inclined to provide in an initial meeting often looks quite different from the picture the client is willing and able to reveal after the client gets to know the therapist and to understand the therapy process. Although the importance of incorporating continuing assessment throughout the therapy process can certainly be underscored for any client, careful attention to ongoing assessment of new information about a client who uses psychoactive substances is especially crucial due to the established tendencies of such clients to distort information. The substance abuse therapist thus needs to be skilled at detecting and deciphering relevant details the client offers in early phases of therapy, and he or she must also remain open and attentive to additional data emerging as therapy progresses. It is essential for the therapist to maintain the flexibility of entertaining not only new information that confirms previous diagnostic impressions, but also evidence indicating that the therapist's conceptualization of the client and the corresponding plan of intervention need to be revised.

In this chapter, the time frames of ongoing assessment are described along with criterion sets for determining diagnosis and level of recommended treatment for different manifestations of substance use disorders. Because of the vast number of psychoactive substances with abuse potential and the copious pathways into problematic substance use, it is recommended that therapists and counselors who treat substance use disorders be both well versed in knowledge of widely utilized frameworks and related considerations, and also highly skilled in the application of carefully reasoned and adequately justified clinical judgment.

ASSESSMENT AS AN ONGOING PROCESS

Jarvid presents himself for a mandated substance use assessment following an arrest for trespassing. He claims he has no memory of the incident beyond waking up in an acquaintance's house, but he swears he was not drinking that night, and that he has not done so in the past year of recovery from a former alcohol problem.

Tatlyn confides to her therapist in their third session that she has just confirmed her pregnancy, which Tatlyn has suspected (but never mentioned) for a couple months. Tatlyn admits great worry about the fact that she used drugs (which she is now admitting for the first time) on several occasions before she knew she was pregnant. She is evasive in response to the therapist's question about drug use since finding out for sure.

Ross has been attending therapy sessions for several weeks to address his lack of confidence with women. He claims that in most social and professional situations, he is extroverted and has a wicked wit that makes him popular. However, in dating contexts Ross feels paralyzed by fears of rejection. His history of romantic relationships includes a breakup over two years ago with a woman he had thought he would marry, followed by a long series of brief sexual flings with multiple partners. Ross mentions seven weeks into therapy that he drinks before dates, sometimes starting at noon, to allow himself to be more funny and charming. Probing further, the therapist learns that his fiancée left in part because she got fed up with Ross' drinking habits.

Anna is brought by her mother to meet a therapist for assessment after repeated detentions in middle school for arguing with classmates and teachers. When asked about substance use as part of the routine assessment, Anna replies that she has not yet tried drugs or alcohol, but she figures she will at some point. She explains that she is the youngest of five, and that all her older siblings have experimented with drugs and alcohol, so she sees it as a "God-given inevitability" that she will, too.

Assessment at the Initial Hint of a Possible Substance Use Problem

Each of these clients demonstrates circumstances where further assessment of substance use is needed to determine the presence and nature of current problems and risks. The phases of assessing for substance use disorders begin with screening to determine the need for more thorough assessment. Screening instruments and procedures can be used to identify clients who may be engaging in problematic substance use, experiencing negative consequences of substance use, or be at risk for developing a substance use problem. Standard intake procedures utilized in formal initial assessment of virtually all clients in psychotherapy typically include questions about personal and family history of substance use. This type of screen built into a standard assessment that touches on broad aspects of personal functioning sometimes offers the first hint of a possible substance use issue. With other clients, acknowledgment of substance use may be first mentioned well past the standard intake assessment. In such cases, an alert therapist screens at that point for indications of risk or abuse associated with the client's substance use.

If an initial screen indicates any reason for concern, a more extensive clinical assessment interview can be conducted to explore in more breadth and depth the nature of the client's actual substance use and its implications, as well as the degree to which initial concerns are founded. Written assessment inventories may also be used. If the results of the assessment either confirm or suggest reasons for continuing concern about the client's substance use, ongoing assessment during subsequent therapy sessions of the patterns and consequences of the client's consumption of drugs or alcohol, along with the client's response to therapy, is warranted.

Diagnosis

When thorough substance use assessment indicates the presence of disordered use, the information available about the client's patterns, frequency, intensity, and severity of abuse are incorporated into a diagnosis. The widely used diagnostic criterion sets from the *Diagnostic and Statistical Manual of Mental Disorders, Fourth Edition* (*DSM–IV*; American Psychiatric Association, 1994, 2000) include two general diagnostic categories of substance-related disorders: those induced by exposure to or ingestion of a substance (Intoxication and Withdrawal), and disorders of substance use (Abuse and Dependence). Each of these general categories is further subdivided into disorders associated with the use of particular psychoactive substances, all of which are described in detail later in the chapter. Once the therapist and client agree to undertake a thorough substance use assessment, initial diagnostic impressions are formulated with the therapist's understanding that initial diagnosis may change with new information about the client, including revelations about actual behavior or indications of changes in behavior.

Follow-Up Assessment

Even when the initial screening or assessment does not clearly suggest a substance use problem, the emergence of later information can create circumstances that should prod the attentive therapist into initiating further screening and assessment. Also, with clients diagnosed or treated for substance use disorders, new information about the client's past or present substance-related concerns that comes out after initial assessment may well be different from earlier information. Continuing assessment is then important for understanding the significance of all that information in terms of both client behavior and the therapy relationship. Follow-up assessment of progress achieved in therapy is typically carried out as part of the termination of therapy. In some cases, assessment of changes maintained beyond the end of therapy may also be conducted.

SCREENING

How Drug and Alcohol Screening Is Conducted

Screening for substance use problems consists of asking brief sets of questions used to detect problems or rule out concerns about a person's drug or alcohol use (Doweiko, 2002). The screening questions may be administered in spoken or written form by psychological, medical, or educational professionals, or even by an individual who is worried about personal use. Computerized screening is possible, and biological testing of urine, blood, or breath is also broadly utilized. Emerging technology further permits laboratory testing of saliva, sweat, or hair to detect the presence of illicit drugs (Verebey, Buchan, & Turner, 1998).

A screening may be conducted at the first hint of a problem, such as the passing mention during intake of heavy drinking a few nights per week. The need for screening may arise later in therapy, too. Consider Ross, the client described earlier lacking confidence with women. Ross mentions during Session 7 that his unusually irritable mood that day is due to a bad hangover, which the client promptly dismisses as "no big deal." Even if the therapist has never witnessed Ross in such a foul mood before and has not previously considered substance abuse as one of this client's problems, her current memory of Ross' comment at intake that he "parties a lot" causes her to reflect on the mixed messages in what the client has told her about his substance use so far. Imagine that Ross told this therapist at intake that his alcohol consumption was no different from any normal person and that he had no troubles associated with drinking. Although the therapist may have taken this information at face value at intake, now the therapist cannot help noticing that today's hangover, despite Ross' attempts to downplay it, has certainly compromised his state of mind. Not a problem? Perhaps not, but the responsible therapist should ask some additional questions to provide a finer screen besides the client's assurances and attempts to change the subject.

The CAGE. Screening instruments ask a few questions that have been widely observed to discriminate persons who exhibit substance use problems from those who do not. Used to screen for alcohol problems, the mnemonic device CAGE prompts treatment providers to inquire about a client's typical substance use and its aftereffects. The CAGE instrument (Ewing, 1984) presents four questions and an acronym for screener recall: Have you ever felt you ought to *CUT DOWN* on your drinking? Have people *ANNOYED* you by being critical of your drinking? Have you ever felt bad or *GUILTY* about your drinking? Have you ever had a drink (*EYE-OPENER*) first thing in the morning to steady your nerves or to get rid of a hangover? An affirmative response to any one question triggers further assessment.

The MAST. The Michigan Alcoholism Screening Test (MAST; Selzer, 1971) is another instrument widely used to screen for alcohol problems; it is particularly useful for detecting dependence, but not less severe problems (Doweiko, 2002). To identify possible disorders associated with substance use in addition to or instead of alcohol, Brown, Leonard, Saunders, and Papasoulioutis (1997) recommended asking two simple questions: In the last year, have you ever drunk or used drugs more than you meant to? Have you ever felt you wanted or needed to cut down on your drinking and drug use? Doweiko (2002) cited these authors' findings that 45% of persons answering "yes" to one item and 75% of those answering "yes" to both items were diagnosed with substance use disorders.

How a Therapist Responds to a Positive Screening Result

A positive result, indicating a possible problem, leads the screener to recommend more extensive assessment. Often the screener is an educational, social services, or medical professional who refers the client to a specialist for further substance use assessment. The screener and assessor may also be the same person, if qualified. If the screener is a mental health professional and the screening suggests a reason for continuing concern, the professional should either conduct a thorough substance use assessment or refer the client to an appropriate assessor.

It is important not just to list, but also to discuss the options with the client, including exploring the client's reactions to the recommendation for further assessment. A good screener can offer a rationale for more extensive assessment that is relevant to the client's circumstances and appeals to the client's motivations. For example, with a resistant or skittish client, the screener might say,

> Your answers to my questions suggest this is worth further attention. We haven't talked about this enough yet for me to say you do or don't have an alcohol [or drug] problem, but I'd like to propose that we look at this in more detail. I suggest we spend some time together assessing your experiences with alcohol [and/or drugs] so we can decide together whether or not there is reason to be concerned. Would you be willing to take me up on that recommendation?

Methods of assessing substance abuse are discussed shortly in this chapter, but if the screener decides to refer the client, some follow-up is advisable to enhance the chances that the client will make contact with the referred assessor. Referral without follow through to facilitate contact may result in an ambivalent or reluctant client's loss of momentum or failure to receive services. If the client has been referred elsewhere for substance use assessment and possible treatment, but the screener is continuing to work with the client on other issues, follow-up to the screening includes requesting a report of the assessment as well as considering with the client, and possibly the other treatment provider, how to coordinate the components of the client's counseling and therapy.

How a Therapist Responds to a Negative Screening Result

When the client's responses to screening questions are negative, as in the case of Anna (the middle-school student with older siblings who use substances), the screener in an ongoing relationship with the client still has responsibilities to educate the client about risk where relevant. While the therapist communicates trust in the data provided by the client, the therapist also keeps listening for any further indicators of substance abuse risk or problems.

Passing through a screen indicates that the client has answered "no" to all questions used to detect substance abuse problems. A client who "passes through" the screen may well have no problems associated with alcohol or drug use. However, in some cases, clients will "pass" because they have not been entirely accurate in providing answers.

Options When Negative Results Are Ambiguous.   If the screener suspects that substance abuse is occurring despite the client's negative reply to screening questions, the screener has at least two viable options. First, the screener can tell the client that, on the basis of the honor system, the screener will take the client's answers at face value, but that the screener also acknowledges some evidence that contradicts the client's responses. Screeners are advised to share specifically both what they have heard their clients say and any contradictory evidence, and to inform clients that all this information will also be documented. Of course this means the therapist should carefully record the content of the discussion as well as the client's responses to the screening questions. The therapist should also continue listening for and commenting on any additional indicators of problems that might arise. This is not to imply that the screener should take the stance of waiting to catch the client in a mistake or a lie (and the therapist will need to be prepared to discuss the chosen professional stance with a skeptical or accusing client), but rather to encourage therapists to keep open both the possibilities of the client's subjective truth and alternative interpretations.

Second, the screener with lingering doubts about the client's honesty (with self or the screener) may ask the client to submit to biological testing. Obviously such testing provides an even finer screen for substance use, although actual detectability depends on the type of drug, the size of the dose, the frequency and recency of use, the route of drug administration, individual differences in metabolism, the time of sample collection, and the sensitivity of the specific test (Verebey, Buchan, & Turner, 1998). Furthermore, a laboratory detection of substance use is not automatically equivalent to a determination of chemical abuse. Still the client's reaction to the request for a urine, breath, or blood test reveals another useful piece of information to the screener. Clients who willingly or even grudgingly comply because they have "nothing to hide" are less likely to elicit ongoing concerns about deceptive self-report during screening, compared with clients who refuse to be tested. Although refusing clients offer various reasons (e.g., citing their rights to privacy, freedom from coercion, medical conditions, menstrual periods, etc.), refusal of a breathalyzer, urinalysis, or blood test to screen for substance use is viewed by many professionals as equivalent to an admission of recent use.

The screener should be further aware that "treatment-savvy" clients develop and share means of achieving negative biological test results—for example, by ingesting concoctions designed to "cleanse" the client's system of drug residues before the test, or by substituting someone else's bodily fluids to avoid a "dirty drop." Thus, if the screener chooses to request that the client be "dropped" or tested using laboratory analysis of drops of the client's urine or blood, or an alternative approach, the screener will find the results most useful if the tests are conducted as soon after the screening interview as possible and if the screener remembers that both false positives and false negatives can occur with biological testing (Doweiko, 2002).

Motivational Factors. The screener who plans to refer the refusing client or a suspected false negative client for additional assessment and possible treatment is wise to attend to motivational and relationship factors at this point. An attitude of "I know you're lying and I'm going to prove it" or "I'll give you enough rope to hang yourself" is not likely to facilitate client participation. Even a reluctant client is more willing to proceed with a therapist who communicates the message,

> If you say you haven't been using drugs, I believe you because I take people at their word. But that also means I will be honest with you and tell you that some other things I've picked up about you don't fit with what you're telling me. Let me tell you my observations and concerns, and then I want to hear what you think about them.

The Importance of Documenting Screening Results

Positive or ambiguously negative screening results, then, can be used as the basis for recommending that the client participate in a more detailed substance use assessment interview. Screeners should adequately document the type of screen and results along with any salient information about the client's behavior, appearance, or responses to the screening process. Any recommendations or referrals discussed with the client should also be recorded. Any client screened may be provided with psychoeducational or motivational resources about using substances safely if at all, identifying substance use problems in self or others, or engaging in therapy for substance use concerns.

IN-DEPTH ASSESSMENT OF CLIENT SUBSTANCE USE

At the point where a concern is raised, in-depth assessment of a client's drug or alcohol use is conducted with two related purposes. First, the assessor collects information to determine whether the client's substance use and related behaviors meet the diagnostic criteria for abusive, dependent, or otherwise disordered consumption. In general terms, diagnosis involves critical analysis to determine the nature and cause of a disorder through examination of the patient history and relevant clinical data. The *DSM–IV* (American Psychiatric Association, 1994, 2000) criteria are among the most widely utilized frameworks for diagnosing substance use disorders, and are thus presented next as guidelines for assessment. The criteria for substance use disorders were not changed in the 2000 Text Revision of the *DSM–IV*.

If in fact the assessment supports the conclusion that the client is at risk of developing or already exhibiting a substance use disorder, the second purpose of assessment is to determine the appropriate level and format of recommended treatment, setting the stage for the development of a treatment plan (to be covered in chap. 6). The American Society of Addiction Medicine (ASAM) has published and revised placement criteria (Mee-Lee, 2001b; Mee-Lee, Shulman, Fishman, Gastfriend, & Griffith, 2001) to help determine the level of care that best serves clients with particular severities of substance use disorders. The ASAM placement criteria are presented after the *DSM–IV* diagnostic criteria, and together these two frameworks are used to shape the subsequent discussion of substance use assessment.

With these purposes of diagnosis and placement in mind, the assessor is encouraged to also build rapport with the client in efforts to engage the client in the assessment interview. The assessor who can connect on an affective level with the client and share the client's story is better able to motivate the client to consider the treatment recommendations the assessor makes toward the end of the assessment interview.

DSM–IV Diagnostic Categories of Substance Use Disorder

The fourth edition of the *Diagnostic and Statistical Manual of Mental Disorders* (*DSM–IV*, American Psychiatric Association, 1994, 2000) classifies disorders directly related to psychoactive substances into four general categories: Intoxication, Withdrawal, Abuse, and Dependence. Substance Abuse and Dependence are both considered disorders of substance use behavior, whereas Intoxication and Withdrawal are among the syndromes that can be induced by exposure to or ingestion of substances including illicit drugs, alcohol, medications, or toxins. To a certain extent, each of the four general categories of substance-related disorders can be manifest by users of various different substances, which allows for conceptualization and documentation of the common factors among substance-related disorders.

In addition to these four general diagnostic categories, the *DSM–IV* offers further specification of characteristics that indicate disordered use or induced syndromes connected with each class of substances. The *DSM–IV* identifies eleven classes of abused substances and associated disorders. These classes consist of alcohol, amphetamines, caffeine, cannabis (marijuana), cocaine, hallucinogen, inhalant, nicotine, opioid, phencyclidine (PCP), and sedative/hypnotic/anxiolytic drugs. Additional categories include polysubstance dependence and other or unknown substance-related disorders (covering steroids, nitrous oxide, and self-administration of prescription drugs, among others).

Substance-Induced Disorders. Exposure to a psychoactive substance can occur through deliberate ingestion or accidental or intentional poisoning. *Disordered Substance Intoxication* refers in the context of assessment to a syndrome of reversible psychological or behavioral changes caused by exposure to a drug (including alcohol) that influences the person's central nervous system functions. Furthermore, to meet the criteria for a diagnosis of disorder, these changes induced by intoxication will be maladaptive in that they contribute to the individual's distress or impairment within the person's social and environmental circumstances. Every category of chemical substances listed in the *DSM–IV* is capable of producing an intoxication syndrome, and each type of substance has specific sets of characteristic symptoms of intoxication following recent ingestion of or exposure to that substance. Substance use assessors should be familiar with and have easy access to criterion sets for diagnosing Substance Intoxication.

As a substance is gradually eliminated from the body of a substance user, particularly after a period of abstinence from or reduction of prior heavy use, the user may experience symptoms of withdrawal. *Substance Withdrawal Disorders* are diagnosed when the substance user experiences the withdrawal symptoms typical of the type of drugs ingested as interfering with normal functions. An individual exhibiting Substance Withdrawal reports significant distress or impairment in fulfilling important roles or activities because of the withdrawal symptoms. (Other Substance-Induced Disorders associated with cognitive, mood, anxiety, psychosis, sleep, or sexual function problems are briefly listed in the *DSM–IV* chapter on Substance-Related Disorders, but further described in detail in chapters of the manual that cover the types of disorders induced by exposure to a chemical substance. For example, Substance-Induced Delirium and Persisting Amnestic Disorder are both included in the *DSM* chapter on cognitive disorders, and Substance-Induced Anxiety Disorder is covered in the chapter on Anxiety Disorders.)

The presence of intoxication or withdrawal at the time of assessment alerts the assessor to the possible need for medical attention and appropriate referral, to be discussed shortly. The very behavior of showing up to a professional consultation under the influence of substances calls into question the individual's judgment regarding appropriate times to use substances. Information indicating patterns of repeated intoxications or withdrawal problems serves as the basis for further assessment for substance use disorders.

Substance Use Disorders.   Among the general disorders of intentional use, Substance Dependence can be considered a more severe subset of Substance Abuse. Both are defined as "a maladaptive pattern of substance use leading to clinically significant impairment or distress . . . occurring in a 12-month period" (American Psychiatric Association, 1994, pp. 181–182). The first criterion for Substance Abuse requires only one recurrent behavioral manifestation of impairment or distress, whereas a diagnosis of Dependence rests on the client's meeting at least three out of seven possible criteria. The second criterion for Substance Abuse Disorder states that the client's "symptoms have never met the criteria for Substance Dependence for this class of substances" (p. 183). In conducting an assessment of a client's use of a particular substance, it is most practical to start by looking for the presence of Dependence, and, if Dependence can be ruled out, to next determine whether the client also meets the first criterion for Substance Abuse. This procedure is more efficient because every Substance Dependent client will meet the first criterion for Abuse, but not all clients who abuse substances will meet the more restrictive criteria for Dependence. If the more severe problem cannot be ruled out, there is then no need to assess for Abuse. If Dependence can be ruled out, the client meets the second criterion for the diagnosis of Abuse, but must still be assessed with respect to the first criterion.

To be diagnosed as *Substance Dependent,* a client will, over the course of at least one year, exhibit any three of the following seven criteria: tolerance, withdrawal, ingestion of larger amounts or over longer time periods than intended, wishes or failed efforts to control substance use, excessive time spent in substance-related activities, neglect of previously important activities because of substance use, or continued use despite known problems associated with substance use. The first two criteria of tolerance and withdrawal specify Substance Dependence with *Physiological Dependence.* *Tolerance* is defined as either the need for greater amounts of the substance to become intoxicated or "high," or the experience of reduced effects with continuing use of the same amount of a substance. Withdrawal occurs when the concentrations of a substance decline in the blood or tissues of the heavy user, resulting in physiological or psychological symptoms of discomfort that often prompt the person to resume substance use to eliminate or avoid the withdrawal symptoms. Withdrawal takes on different characteristic symptoms depending on the specific substance(s) being abused. (The reader may recall that factors contributing to the development of tolerance and withdrawal were detailed in chap. 4.)

The assessor asks clients general questions about their experiences of tolerance and withdrawal, which for some clients may require providing definitions in language the clients can understand. Revisiting the earlier example of the pregnant client: Tatlyn questions what the therapist means by *tolerance.* The therapist replies, "Did you ever need to use more and more of the drug to get the same feeling of high, or ever find that you couldn't get the kind of highs you used to with the same amount of the drug?" In addition, the assessor should directly ask whether the client has experienced the symptoms of withdrawal and tolerance associated with the criterion sets linked to the substances the client has been using. For example, the withdrawal symptoms for alcohol and other sedative drugs include hyperactivity, agitation, and anxiety, whereas withdrawal from stimulant drugs like cocaine or amphetamines encompasses dysphoric mood, fatigue, and either retardation or agitation of psychomotor functions. This, of course, means that the substance use assessor should become familiar with the substance-specific criteria as well as the general criterion sets, and he or she should have access to appropriate reference material (such as an available copy of the *DSM–IV*) to prompt thorough assessment.

A client can meet the criteria for a Dependence disorder without exhibiting either tolerance or withdrawal, and in such cases the disorder is specified as *Without Physiological Dependence.* A diagnosis of Dependence without evidence of physiological dependence still reflects a client's tendency to persist in self-administering a drug of choice despite significant problems connected with that compulsive use. These individuals may organize their life activities around obtaining and using their preferred substance(s) and recovering from the effects. They may try to regulate or control their consumption, perhaps having tried to limit the amount they ingest or quit using altogether, but have been largely unsuccessful in those efforts. Like Ross, who kept drinking heavily after the love of his life threatened to leave if he did not control his drinking, clients may sacrifice relationships, give up formerly gratifying activities, or abandon important responsibilities to continue using. Even when faced with knowledge of severe adverse health, vocational, social, or psychological consequences of substance use, like the pregnant Tatlyn is, the substance dependent person keeps on taking the drug of choice.

The *DSM–IV* includes additional course specifiers to reflect changes in substance dependent behavior over time. Often during therapy the client diagnosed as Substance Dependent engages in a period of abstaining from or greatly reducing consumption of a drug or alcohol. Sometimes the client even enters therapy already abstinent, but still working on coping with the impact of prior substance dependent behavior. Jarvid, the client in the opening example, was arrested for trespassing when someone he just met reported Jarvid passed out in the man's home, allegedly uninvited. Jarvid was referred for substance use assessment based on these circumstances as well as his documented history of Alcohol Dependence, although he insisted that he had not had a drink or used recreational drugs in over a year. In such cases, where the client has not exhibited the criteria for Dependence for some time (at least one month according to the *DSM–IV*), the remission specifiers can be applied to clarify the diagnosis.

Early Remission refers to the period from one to twelve months after the client no longer engages in behaviors characteristic of Substance Dependence. Early remission is distinguished from *Sustained Remission*, occurring for more than twelve months, because the first year of remission is frequently a time period when the temptations and cravings to resume substance use are strongest, and the risk of relapse is high. Remission can also be qualified as *Full Remission*, indicating the client has been free from symptoms of Substance Abuse or Dependence for the specified time frame (early or sustained), or as *Partial Remission* (early or sustained), indicating presence of at least one symptom of Substance Abuse or Dependence.

For clients who do not currently exhibit a full set of Substance Dependence symptoms, but are presently undergoing medical or other intensive intervention, the specifiers of *On Agonist Therapy* or *In a Controlled Environment* are applied instead of remission course specifiers. The former specifier refers to a substance dependent person who is taking medication prescribed to reduce cravings for the abused substance by substituting a safer alternative, such as methadone or buprenorphine for an opiate dependent person or antabuse or naltraxone for an alcoholic. The latter specifier is applied when the client is in a closely supervised, substance-free environment, such as a jail, hospital, or therapeutic community.

The Distinction Between Remission and Recovery.   Some controversy exists over whether a client who has met the criteria for Substance Dependence at any point over a lifetime should thereafter be considered Substance Dependent even after a long period (several years) of Sustained Remission. Does a Substance Dependent person ever relinquish the diagnosis? If so, under what conditions? Is total abstinence necessary for recovery? Additional debate about the need for total abstinence assuming the chronic nature of addictions has generated high levels of tension between addictions researchers and treatment providers (Thombs, 1999).

The majority of treatment programs for chemical dependence promote abstinence as a goal, although some research findings indicate that controlled drinking may be a viable strategy for some clients (Harris & Miller, 1990; Miller & Hester, 1980; Sobell, Wilkinson, & Sobell, 1990). Many substance abuse experts are skeptical at best about the therapeutic potential of attempts to resume moderate social drinking (Buelow & Buelow, 1998; Doweiko, 2002). The *DSM–IV* (American Psychiatric Association, 1994) specifies that the distinction between Full Sustained Remission and complete recovery depends on the length of the disorder, the duration of the remission, and the need for continued evaluation. Buelow and Buelow

(1998) offered the following conditions under which they believe that clients should be encouraged to maintain total abstinence from mood-altering substances:

1. Repeated failure to cut down the amount or limit the frequency of drinking or use of other legal drugs
2. Use of illegal drugs
3. Physical problems that alcohol or other drugs can exacerbate in any way
4. Pregnancy or risk of pregnancy
5. Prior dependence on, or addiction to, any drug
6. Concurrent use of medications known to be affected by alcohol or other drugs
7. Prior decision to abstain

Thombs (1999) noted the need for more comparative research to address this controversy.

The Distinction Between Abuse and Dependence. To qualify for a *DSM–IV* diagnosis of Substance Abuse, the client will not presently meet nor ever have met the criteria for a Substance Dependence diagnosis for that category of substances. In addition, the client will exhibit at least one form of recurrent impairment, distress, or problem characterized by any of the following patterns: failure to fulfill work, school, or household obligations due to substance use; repeated substance use in hazardous situations (such as driving a car or rock climbing); legal problems associated with possession or consumption of substances of abuse; or continuing substance use despite persistent, substance-related interpersonal or social difficulties. Although only one of these factors needs to be evident, the problem must have occurred more than once (to be considered recurrent) within a twelve-month period. Thus, the assessor should carefully question the client about frequency and timing of incidents and should document responses thoroughly to support a diagnosis of Substance Abuse.

Use of these diagnostic categories and criteria is discussed at length later in the chapter. First, an additional framework is presented for choosing an appropriate level of treatment in light of assessed client characteristics.

ASAM Patient Placement Criteria

In addition to the *DSM* diagnostic criteria for substance-related disorders, the assessment process to be offered in this chapter is modeled in part from the recently revised placement criteria (Mee-Lee et al., 2001) developed by the American Society of Addiction Medicine (ASAM). ASAM's guidelines for recommending level of care incorporate six dimensions of the assessed severity of a person's disordered use of substances. Using these dimensions, clients or patients are assessed in terms of:

1. Acute Intoxication/Withdrawal Potential
2. Biomedical Conditions and Complications
3. Emotional, Behavioral, or Cognitive Conditions or Complications
4. Treatment Acceptance/Resistance/Readiness to Change
5. Potential for Relapse, Continued Use, or Continuing Problems
6. Recovery Environment

The ASAM guidelines help decide, based on the assessed levels of severity and functioning along each of these six dimensions, which level of care is the most appropriate for the client's needs. Levels of care range from:

0.5   Early Intervention
I.   Outpatient Treatment
II.   Intensive Outpatient Treatment/Partial Hospitalization
III. Residential/Inpatient Treatment
IV.   Medically Managed Intensive Inpatient Treatment

The ASAM framework permits the assessor to develop a "multidimensional risk profile (the acuity, urgency, and priority of clinical risk of each assessment dimension) [which] integrates all of the biopsychosocial data [about the client] into a more succinct summary" (Mee-Lee, 2001b, p. 2). This summary can be used to match the client with treatment modalities that best fit the assessed priorities. This is facilitated using detailed tables, which cross dimensions of client substance use with levels of treatment and which describe the characteristics of clients who fit each cell. The ASAM dimensions are useful for assessing the severity of a substance use problem whatever the specific diagnosis. Furthermore, the ASAM guidelines can help a practitioner determine whether adequate care can be provided through that practitioner or whether referral is warranted to another source of treatment that meets the identified needs.

Each section of the assessment format proposed next is thus linked to one or more of the ASAM dimensions for assessing severity of substance-related problems. The potential for withdrawal or the presence of biomedical conditions (Dimensions 1 and 2) can indicate a higher risk for immediate medical problems and a higher relapse rate (American Psychiatric Association, 1994). Thus, when severity is rated high on ASAM Dimensions 1 or 2, referring the client for a medical consultation is often of paramount importance (Mee-Lee, 2001b). Ongoing or later psychological intervention can in many cases serve as a useful adjunct to medical attention, especially when problems are also determined on ASAM Dimensions 3 to 6, as is often the case.

In the absence of current concerns regarding intoxication, withdrawal, or medical complications, psychologically oriented treatment to address the emotional, behavioral, or cognitive complications of the client's substance use (Dimension 3) is typically a pressing need for clients who exhibit a substance use disorder. The assessor, then, should thoroughly investigate the client's subjective experiences of moods, thought processes, and risky behaviors. The anticipated degree of client cooperation with treatment is estimated in terms of the client's readiness for change (Dimension 4), encompassing both the client's awareness of the need for some change and the client's commitment to changing behavior. The assessor also takes into account the apparent likelihood that the client will be able to abstain from or control future substance use, or that the client will resume or continue problematic consumption (Dimension 5). Using Dimension 6, the assessor further investigates the extent to which the client's living environment poses barriers to or provides supports for the client's efforts to stabilize or change.

Proposed Template for In-Depth Substance Use Assessment Interview

The template provided next can be used with clients who are new to the therapist or with clients the therapist knows well, but for whom substance use concerns have only recently emerged in session. The template organizes a structure the therapist can use to conduct a thorough substance use assessment, but it is by no means the only format available for this task (see e.g., Donovan & Marlatt, in press; Lewis, Dana, & Blevins, 2002; McLellan, Luborsky, Woody, & O'Brien, 1980; McLellan et al., 1992; Ott & Tarter, 1998). Readers are encouraged to use this template flexibly, in accordance with their own experiences and with their places of employment or training. The important point is for assessors to be aware of the broad range of considerations to be addressed in piecing together a picture of the client's substance use issues. Confidentiality provisions and limitations should be addressed with the client prior to starting the assessment, and these are discussed in detail later in this chapter.

Introduction of the Assessment Process. For clients who have never taken part in a substance use assessment before, especially those clients who have attended reluctantly at best, the assessor should make an effort to establish rapport and explain the process about to unfold. Even clients who have been through a prior assessment are more readily engaged in the immediate process if the assessor gives an idea of what will happen in the present session. Neutral terminology at the beginning can facilitate the interview. For example, with clients specifically requesting a substance use assessment, the assessor might say:

> We're meeting today to assess your experience with alcohol and drugs. That means I'm going to ask you a set of standard questions I ask every client whenever we agree to do a substance use assessment. This way I can try to get a broad picture of your own use of drugs or alcohol and any related consequences.

The deliberate reference to "use" rather than "abuse" and "consequences" rather than "problems" is intended to avoid making presumptions about the client's reasons for coming and also to prevent triggering resistance in clients who do not consider their substance use either abusive or problematic. Any questions the client might have can be invited and answered up front.

With clients in therapy who did not present with substance abuse issues or request substance use assessment, the therapist may take a different approach to introduce the in-depth assessment process. First, this includes explaining the reasons, including corresponding observations, for recommending the joint undertaking of assessment of the client's substance use and related experience. For example:

> You've made three or four references now to "getting high," and to me that is sounding like a big enough part of your life that it would be worth talking about more, if you're willing. I'm interested because I think finding out more about that part of your life would help us decide together if your drug use is related to any of the other concerns we have been talking about.

The therapist using this introduction will also be ready to hear and respond to the client's reactions to this proposal.

Next, the assessor often describes the assessment process to the client in enough detail so the client knows what to expect. For clients who are agreeable to the assessment, this may be less crucial than with a reluctant client, but it still helps prepare the client and structure the discussion when the therapist describes what will happen. When the client is unconvinced of the need for substance use assessment, the therapist's description can emphasize taking a nonjudgmental stance to gather information that will be used to determine whether a focus on substance use issues is relevant to plans for continuing therapy. For example, the assessor might say:

> I'd like to take at least part of our session this week or next to ask you a series of questions about substance use that may or may not be related to your own history, but will give us a broader picture of your own actual experience, past and present. By learning more about any role substance use may have played in your life and where you stand on the topic, I'm in a better position to either be convinced we don't need to talk more about your substance use, or to think about other options open to us.

Finally, the therapist invites the client's questions or other reactions to the assessment proposal, giving them full weight of consideration through discussion as needed. The therapist asks for the client's agreement to proceed according to a negotiated schedule. If the client is willing and there is time left in the immediate session, the therapist may launch right into the substance use assessment. If this topic arises toward the end of a session or if the client wants time to think about the prospect, an agreement can be formulated to resume the discussion at the beginning of the subsequent session.

With clients who dismiss the need for further assessment of their substance use even after the therapist has made the request and offered a rationale, the therapist can honor the client's refusal and still hold open the possibility that the discussion may resurface at another time.

Client History of Substance Use.   Once the client asks for or agrees to an assessment, a logical next step is to inquire about the client's history of involvement with alcohol and other drugs. The diverse backgrounds of clients who use drugs or alcohol necessitate detailed history of each individual client's substance use.

The assessment history begins with asking the client's reasons for seeking the assessment (Buelow & Buelow, 1998). The therapist should record the answer in the client's own words (see Table 5.1, Section a, for a possible format); if paraphrasing is needed, the therapist is recommended to read the written reason back to the client and negotiate the wording until the client agrees with the reason(s) included in the record. With clients presenting specifically for substance use assessment and with whom the therapist is meeting for the first or second time, much important content is typically revealed by how the client answers this question. For example, a client's report that his wife threatened divorce indicates the need for attention to relationship issues, a client frightened by frequent blackouts and tremors probably needs referral for medical consultation, and the client who says she was ordered by a judge to get assessed following a DUI in-

TABLE 5.1
Template for Assessing Client Substance Use History

a. Client's Reason for Seeking Assessment _____

b. Substance Use History

Category of Drug	First use?	Pattern of use over time?	Frequency of use in past month?	Date/Amount of most recent use?
Alcohol				
Marijuana				
CNS Stimulants or "Uppers"				
Cocaine, Ritalin, Methamphetamine				
Anxiolytics/Sedatives/Hypnotics or "Downers"				
Barbiturates: Secobarbital/Quaaludes				
Benzodiazepines: Valium, Xanax, Rohypnol				
Opiates or "Painkillers"				
Heroin/Morphine/Methadone/Oxycodone				
Hallucinogens				
LSD/PCP/Ecstasy				
Inhalants/aerosols				
Steroids				
Cigarettes				

Have you ever used any of these
drugs in combination?

cident alerts the therapist that consents for releasing information to third parties will be necessary. In addition, the client's reasons for seeking assessment often provide some initial information about the client's attitudes toward personal substance use, toward motivations for changing current habits, and toward engaging in therapy to promote such change. Whether the client's attitude is compliant, sheepish, defeatist, defiant, dismissive, hostile, or some other variant, the assessor can maximize the client's cooperation by empathizing with the client's perspective and reasons. The therapist's communication of acceptance, understanding, or tolerance of the new client's fears or frustrations must of course be couched in a firm frame of therapeutic boundaries. In most basic terms, the therapist's implicit message is, "I hear what you're telling me and here's what I have to offer."

When the assessment is conducted in the context of substance abuse concerns raised during the course of therapy with a continuing client, the reasons for the assessment have most likely already been discussed during collaborative decisions to incorporate this in-depth assessment into the treatment strategy. Still asking the client to elaborate on his or her understanding of the reason for assessment at the start provides opportunities for the therapist to hear how the client is approaching the activity and also to clear up any possible confusion.

Once reasons for the assessment are established, the therapist informs the client that a detailed list of commonly used and abused substances will be covered. Table 5.1, Section b, provides a template for requesting and recording information about the client's personal substance use history. (The tables have all been compressed here in the interest of space, but a roomier version along with the entire assessment interview questionnaire developed and explained here is compiled in Appendix A.) The therapist may start assessing substance use history by saying something like,

> I'm going to go through a list of drugs and other substances that are widely used and abused, and I want to find out if and when you have personally tried any of them. I'll start with alcohol, because as you probably know, that's one of the most common recreational substances.

For each category of substances, the assessor then asks if the client has ever used it. If the answer is affirmative, the rest of the questions across the top of the grid in Table 5.1 are relevant as well. The assessor, interested in the frequency, intensity, and severity of any substance use by the client, can ask the following questions for each drug category the client admits using:

> At what age or approximate date did the client first try that drug? How has the client's use increased or decreased over time? When was the period of heaviest use, and what was it like? How much and how often has the client used over the past month? And what was the date and amount of most recent use?

Obviously asking each of these questions for each category of substances can be time-consuming, especially with clients who have lengthy histories or who have used multiple drugs. However, such extensive histories help pinpoint the nature of the client's issues and the most appropriate treatment options. Assessment may take more than one session.

The assessor who shows interest in the client's full story also helps establish rapport. In circumstances where time is limited, the assessor can express this interest without necessarily hearing the whole story at once. For example, if the client continues at length or brings up important information toward the end of the session, the assessor can let the client know, "What you're telling me sounds very important, and we will definitely come back to it because I want to hear more about it." (Or, if referral is in order: ". . . and I strongly encourage you to bring it up with the therapist you will be working with. . . .") "But to make sure we cover what we need to get to today, let me first ask you about. . . ." In these instances, the assessor should make note of the topic to ensure that further assessment and discussion are conducted when time permits.

The history assessment starts with alcohol both because it is a legal drug and one consumed by people in virtually every segment of society. Clients are sometimes put at ease by first discussing their experience, if any, with this "safe" substance. The type of alcohol a client drinks (wine coolers, beer, mixed drinks, straight liquor, etc.) should be determined. For each subsequent category, the assessor also inquires about and records information about the form in which the client has used the drug. For cannabis, as an example, the assessor should determine whether the user has ingested the marijuana by means of joints, pipes, bongs, blunts, brownies, hash, chew, or some other form. By the time the assessment reaches the category of central nervous system (CNS) stimulants or "uppers," the assessor using the template in Table 5.1, Section b, will note that a few examples of that category (e.g., cocaine, Ritalin, methamphetamine) are included to generate further questioning if the client is unfamiliar with the general category. The categories of sedative ("downer"), opiate (painkiller or analgesic), and hallucinogenic drugs also include examples that can be offered to prompt clients who may not be aware how the drugs they have consumed are classified or how those drugs operate on the brain. For example, a client who took a "roofie" (Rohypnol) pill given to her at a party, in search of a fun "high" at the time, may not know that the so-called "date rape" drug depresses the CNS and creates a sedative effect on the body.

This history-taking phase of assessment also provides opportunities, then, for the therapist to begin educating the client about the nature and biological impact of the drugs the client has ingested, inhaled, injected, or been curious about using. Many therapists discover that the education goes both ways: Clients experienced with substance use and effects can help therapists better understand the impetus for and effects of taking drugs in addition to extending a therapist's list of drugs to be assessed for along with their "street names."

Walking through the client's drug history will also yield encounters with signals of issues the therapist will wish to record and pursue if ongoing therapy is recommended. Some clients are quite willing to tell their stories to an attentive, caring therapist, and some end up sharing personal details they had not planned on discussing. Clients' descriptions of their initiations into drinking or drug use or of the forces encouraging their continuing use can uncover links to co-morbid symptoms or interpersonal, educational, or occupational concerns. The effective assessor will take careful note of such hints or details and encourage the client to use ongoing therapy as an opportunity to explore these issues more deeply. Even at this early stage, the therapist can offer recognition of a difficulty and hope of finding a better way to deal with it.

Once the substance use history is completed, the assessor often already has some diagnostic impressions. At the least, the assessor can narrow the focus from generalized substance-related disorders to consideration of disorder(s) associated with a particular class of substances. Distinguishing among diagnostic sets depends on not only the drug that has been used, but also on the conditions under which the drug was used and the consequences of use. Thus, the rest of the assessment template offered here explores the physical, psychological, interpersonal, educational, vocational, financial, and legal factors linked to the client's drug or alcohol use.

Physical Symptoms of Substance Abuse.   The importance of first addressing or ruling out any need for medical attention has already been mentioned. Thus, the next section of the assessment template corresponds to ASAM Dimension 1 (Acute Intoxication/Withdrawal Potential) and helps determine whether the client meets the *DSM–IV* Substance Dependence criteria for tolerance or withdrawal. Because each drug has its own particular effects on the brain and the body, the criteria that identify intoxication or withdrawal for cocaine, for example, are different from those indicating marijuana intoxication or alcohol withdrawal. Table 5.2 includes lists of numerous physical consequences and psychological symptoms associated with problematic substance use. The table further incorporates all the indicators of withdrawal summarized in the *DSM–IV* for each class of substances with which withdrawal symptoms have been demonstrated. Compulsive use of alcohol, opioids, sedatives, hypnotics, or anxiolytics (anti-anxiety drugs) each produces significant and measurable withdrawal symptoms, whereas stimulants like cocaine or phencyclidine (PCP) elicit less obvious but still evident signs of withdrawal, and hallucinogens show no evidence of a withdrawal syndrome (American Psychiatric Association, 1994). Withdrawal potential is also determined in part based on the client's replies to the earlier history questions about most recent use and amounts of use in the past month.

Working with a format like the template in Table 5.2, Section c, the assessor first tells the client,

> I am going to read through a list of physical consequences that some people experience when they are using drugs or alcohol or coming down from an episode or a "high," and I want you to let me know if you've ever experienced any of these consequences in the past or present associated with your own use.

The assessor should certainly ask about all the criteria associated with the substances the client has reported using, but it is also useful to inquire about symptoms associated with the dependence on other drugs in case the client's self-report has underestimated actual use. The assessor can use the "past" and "present" columns to record a "Y" for the client's response of

TABLE 5.2
Assessing Physical and Psychological Consequences of Substance Use

c. Physical Consequences	(past/present)	d. Psychological Symptoms	(past/present/AOD cause?)	
Headaches	/	Concentration difficulties[e]	/	/
Nausea[a,f,g]	/	Memory loss/lapses	/	/
Nosebleeds	/	Disorganized thinking	/	/
Tolerance[a,b,c,d,e,f,g]	/	Hallucinations[a,d,g]	/	/
Sweating[a,f,g]	/	Bad dreams[b,c]	/	/
Increased appetite[b,c,e]	/	Flashbacks[d]	/	/
Fatigue[b,c]	/	Irritability[e]	/	/
Vomiting[a,f,g]	/	Anxiety[a,e,g]	/	/
Using to avoid withdrawal symptoms	/	Restlessness[e]	/	/
Rapid pulse rate[a,g]	/	Low mood[b,c,e,f]	/	/
Decreased heart rate[e]	/	Depression	/	/
Chronic cough	/	Mood swings	/	/
Hand tremors[a,g]	/	Sedation	/	/
Insomnia[e,f,g]/hypersomnia[a,b,c]	/	Suicidal thoughts	/	/
Hangovers	/	Suicidal gestures	/	/
Blackouts	/	Anger[e]	/	/
Passing out	/	Paranoia[b,c,d]	/	/
Psychomotor agitation[a,b,c,g]	/	Homicidal thoughts	/	/
Psychomotor retardation[b,c]	/	Violent behaviors	/	/
Seizures[a,g]	/	Inability to care for self	/	/
Muscle aches[f]	/	Other _____	/	/
Lacrimation/rhinorrhea[f]	/			
Diarrhea[f]	/			
Yawning[f]	/			
Fever[f]	/			

Note. Superscripts indicate the category of substance with which each symptom is associated in the *DSM–IV*: [a]alcohol, [b]amphetamine, [c]cocaine, [d]hallucinogens, [e]nicotine, [f]opioids, [g]sedative/hypnotic/anxiolytics.

"yes" and "N" for "no." At times the therapist will need to prompt the client to clarify or add information about whether the experience was in the past, present, or both. Sometimes the therapist will need to reword the criteria in language that makes sense to the client. For example, the therapist may need to explain that *tolerance* means "using more and more often or in larger and larger amounts to try to get the same high," or that *lacrimation* refers to watery eyes and *rhinorrhea* to a runny nose. Taking notes on any details the client shares about experience of symptoms is also important for future treatment planning. Such comprehensive assessment reduces the chances that significant or serious problems will go undetected.

Psychological Consequences of Substance Abuse. Like many other assessment protocols, the template offered here includes a list of psychological as well as physical symptoms of withdrawal, also compiled from the criterion sets for each substance associated with Dependence in the *DSM–IV*. This section of the assessment template in the right-hand column (d) of Table 5.2 corresponds to the assessment of ASAM Dimension 3 (Emotional, Behavioral, or Cognitive Conditions). The assessor informs the client, "Now I have another list of symptoms, but the set we just discussed were more physical and this next set is more psychological; about thoughts, feelings, and behaviors." Again, the assessor asks clients whether they have ever experienced these consequences, either in the past or the present, and records any relevant detail clients provide. Using the present template, affirmative responses are followed with the therapist's question about whether the clients perceive that symptom as caused by alcohol or other drug (AOD) use, and "yes" and "no" responses are documented in the columns provided in the template.

The assessor can begin formulating a diagnosis by checking the extent to which the symptoms, both physical and psychological, reported by the client overlap with those indicating a disorder of use for the client's drug(s) of choice. The review of consequences can also be utilized as a chance to educate the client about risks associated with continuing substance use. The therapist's inquiries about psychological distress or dysfunction often yield information that will guide ongoing assessment and treatment planning. A detailed substance use assessment frequently takes sufficient time to preclude a complete diagnostic assessment of possible co-morbid disorders or other concerns of clinical significance, at least in the same session. However, the assessor's broad scope—touching on questions about depression, anxiety, irritability, memory, concentration, and the like—will help focus attention on setting treatment goals and objectives, including plans for further assessment in subsequent sessions if needed. Psychological inventories—such as instruments assessing for depression, anxiety, and other psychological complications—can also be useful in this context. Ott and Tarter (1998) reviewed instruments with well-established psychometric properties and utility for assessing substance use disorders.

Client's Risk of Endangering Self or Others. For some clients with substance-related disorders, the anger, depression, or anxiety they experience due to consequences or losses associated with their substance abuse lead to defeatist thoughts and/or destructive behaviors. The items embedded in Table 5.2, Section d, to assess for psychological conditions and complications include estimation of the client's level of risk for danger to self or others. Violent behavior sometimes occurs in concert with drug or alcohol abuse, probably in parts attributable to both the mind-altering, disinhibiting properties of psychoactive substances as well as to the illegal status accorded to most drugs of abuse and to the use of alcohol under specified conditions (e.g., underage drinking, driving while intoxicated, etc.). As with any client, the admission of suicidal or homicidal ideation requires the therapist to immediately and sensitively determine whether the client has a plan of action and, if so, also has the means and intent to carry out that plan. Thorough assessment of suicidality or homocidality cannot be postponed. If the therapist considers the risk to be high or a threat to be significant, the therapist is obligated to take appropriate action, advisably in consultation with a colleague or supervisor. If, on further questioning, the client actively denies intent, means, or plan to harm self or others, the therapist can still express empathy for the suicidal or homicidal thoughts the client is reporting and the feelings underlying them.

It is also worth asking whether the client's thoughts or impulses toward hurting self or others tend to increase, decrease, or stay the same when the client is using psychoactive substances. The therapist can offer the client opportunities to learn to better cope with violent thoughts and potentially dangerous behaviors as part of the therapy and recovery processes. Confidentiality considerations in risk assessment implanted in a substance use assessment are further discussed later in this chapter. As with other aspects of the assessment, thorough documentation of risk assessment discussions is good and recommended practice.

Client Intoxication at the Time of Assessment. On occasion, substance use assessors and therapists will encounter clients who are under the influence of a drug or alcohol at the time of the interview. To detect and appropriately respond to intoxicated clients, the therapist should be familiar with the different criterion sets indicating states of intoxication with each category of substances. Buelow and Buelow (1998) provided a comprehensive list of indicators of intoxication with various substances. If the client's behavior, appearance, or odor suggests intoxication at the time of the interview, the assessor should directly inquire whether the client has used substances that day. The assessor can explain that a thorough assessment is difficult, if not impossible, while the client's thought processes are compromised. (The assessor needs to be prepared to discuss this position with a client who counters that his or her faculties are not affected or are even enhanced by substance use.) If the client denies use, the assessor may request a biological screening test. If the client admits to use, the therapist can ask that a follow-up session be scheduled at a time when the client is clean and sober (Doweiko, 2002).

If the client is too intoxicated to participate in an assessment interview, the therapist can suggest not only rescheduling assessment for a time when the client is clean and sober, but also may decide to refer the client for medical intervention or detoxification. Based on the client's behavior, appearance, and answers to questions about physical and psychological symptoms, the therapist will need to make a judgment about whether immediate medical attention is needed. If so, the therapist can arrange for the client to contact someone the client knows to transport the client to a detox center. If that option is not available, the therapist may call a crisis center or the police to assist with transportation. Buelow and Buelow (1998) underscored the wisdom of never offering a ride to a client unless the treatment provider is trained and employed for such services. The assessor should be aware of state laws and employer policies regarding professional responsibilities when a client appears intoxicated.

Unless the client is obviously incapacitated, however, it is advisable for the therapist to spend some time talking to the client who has made the effort to come. By engaging the client who has already shown up in the assessor's office, the therapist can began to establish a base of information about the client, emphasize the importance of coming to future sessions sober, and educate the client about available professional services. The block of time spent in the interview also allows the client to "sober up" or "come down" before leaving the assessor's office. It is recommended that the assessor not only schedule a second appointment for the client, but also to ask for the client's commitment to abstaining from drug or alcohol use for 24 hours prior to the next and any future appointments. This stipulation can be combined with the request that the client cancel the session if the client becomes intoxicated the day of a session. The expectation of sobriety during sessions should be reiterated and discussed at the next contact with the client.

Concurrent Medical Concerns and Treatment History.   As demonstrated earlier, the client's potential for acute intoxication and/or withdrawal (ASAM Dimension 1) can be determined from the types of questions posed in Table 5.2 plus the recent use questions in Table 5.1. Assessment of psychological complications of substance use (ASAM Dimension 3) begins with items like those in Table 5.2, Section d. ASAM Dimension 2, Biomedical conditions and complications, can be assessed using formats like Sections e and f of Table 5.3. The client's past and current medical problems, medications, and instances of outpatient interventions or inpatient hospitalizations are all important for assessing the degree to which health issues and treatment history are likely to complicate any current substance use and treatment.

A good example is the case of Tatlyn's pregnancy, outlined at the beginning of the chapter, involving multiple instances of substance use in the two months following conception. Any medical conditions that may be relevant to the conceptualization and treatment of the substance-related disorder should be noted on Axis III (General Medical Conditions) of a *DSM–IV* diagnostic summary. This promotes thorough evaluation of the client's situation and improves communication with other providers of care to the client

TABLE 5.3
Assessing Medical Concerns and Treatment History

e. Medical Concerns	f. Treatment History
Past	*Outpatient therapy* (incidence/outcomes)
Problem(s)?	For substance use?
	For mental health concerns?
Medications?	Other?
(prescription or OTC)	Were providers aware of your AOD use?
Current	*Inpatient treatment/hospitalization* (incidence/ outcomes)
Problem(s)?	For substance use?
	For mental health concerns?
Medications?	Other?
(prescription or OTC)	Were providers aware of your AOD use?
(for women) Are you Pregnant?	(If Pregnant) Are you receiving prenatal care?

(American Psychiatric Association, 1994). Assessors should facilitate appropriate referrals when the client's health concerns or medical symptoms are outside the assessor's own area of expertise.

Note in Section f of Table 5.3 that past treatment episodes may include interventions for substance abuse, mental health, or other medical concerns. It is useful to assess the client's relationships with or impressions of doctors or treatment providers with whom the client has worked. For example, did the client inform any health care providers of alcohol or other drug use? Does the client have an established medical provider? To what extent has the client been satisfied with services received? To what extent and on what criteria does the client consider those treatment episodes to have been successful? Such exploration of the outcomes as well as the incidence of past treatment helps gauge not only the need to refer the client for medical consultation if biomedical concerns appear to be exacerbating substance use problems (or vice versa); it also helps locate starting places for planning a client's treatment.

A substance abusing client who reports no past treatment interventions will require different treatment plans than one who reports successful past interventions, but is now experiencing depression or impulse control problems when faced with consequences of past alcohol or drug abuse. Still other motivational treatment strategies are needed when the client reports any history of unsatisfactory interventions for either substance abuse or mental health issues, or when the client reveals current use of prescription drugs suspected by the therapist to have potentially dangerous interactions with recreational substances the client is also using. Formulating treatment plans is the focus of chapter 6, but the point here is the importance of thorough assessment of medical and psychological history in driving subsequent decisions about treatment strategies.

In addition to biomedical concerns, the assessment of the client's symptoms and treatment history is also intended to elaborate on psychological difficulties the client may be facing. The checklist of psychological symptoms in Section d of Table 5.2 has already been discussed for assessing severity on ASAM Dimension 3, but Section f of Table 5.3 and Section g of Table 5.4 also cover information relevant to psychological functioning.

TABLE 5.4
Assessing Contextual Factors Linked to a Client's Substance Use

---

g. Environmental Factors

Residential situation
  Anyone else living with you?
  Anyone else in your residence an alcohol or other drug (AOD) user?
  Is your living situation safe?

Social support system
  Whom do you count on for support?
  Anyone in your social network an AOD user?
  Has your AOD use interfered with any of your relationships with people?

Family and developmental history
  Messages received growing up about AOD use?
  Anyone in your family an AOD user?
  Has your AOD use affected your family? How so?
  Any mental health concerns in your family?
  Significant events during childhood?

Educational/vocational factors
  Relevant history (if student, indicate status: full-time/part-time)
  Has your AOD use interfered with any of your school/work obligations or goals?

Financial factors
  How much would you estimate you spend on alcohol and/or drugs per week?
  Has your AOD use contributed to any financial problems?

Transportation factors
  How did you get here today?
  Do you have a valid driver's license?
  Do you have access to a car or other vehicle?
  Have you ever driven under the influence of alcohol or drugs?

If so, how many times in the past year?

Legal concerns
  Ever been arrested?
  Number of times/reasons?
  Charges/disposition?

Clients' responses to Section f on treatment history, especially regarding any past mental health therapies, can augment information clients have already provided on psychological symptoms or may uncover information clients have not yet revealed, or suggest hypotheses for the assessor to pursue. Examples include clients who admit few if any psychological symptoms in the past or present, but acknowledge fairly extensive treatment histories, or clients who say that past treatment was successful yet report current psychological distress or dysfunction.

Environmental Factors Associated With Substance Use.   Section g of the assessment template, in Table 5.4, on the environmental milieu in which the client's substance use is occurring, provides a context in which the assessor can test or further develop hypotheses and diagnostic impressions. After introducing the topic of environmental issues, the assessor specifically questions the client about her or his residential situation, social supports, family and developmental history, educational and/or vocational status, financial factors, transportation issues, and legal concerns. Assessment of each of these areas helps target the situations and factors (a) that the client subjectively considers problematic, (b) around which the symptoms occur most intensely, and (c) which can become a focus of treatment planning and intervention. In other words, any client who indicates environmental difficulties—for example, beliefs that one's residence is unsafe, or limited social supports, or family members with substance use diagnoses or problem behaviors—could understandably be reporting or demonstrating emotional, cognitive, or behavioral problems during the assessment. A client with a history of educational failures, financial difficulties, job losses, or legal troubles is also likely to be assessed as more severe on ASAM Dimension 3.

Client Motivations for Treatment and for Behavior Change.   Assessment of the client's readiness to change (ASAM Dimension 4) is saved for the end of the interview using the present template (see Table 5.5) because logic and experience indicate that it is most effective to gather as much standard information as possible before asking clients loaded questions like whether

TABLE 5.5
Assessing a Client's Treatment Readiness

h. Motivation for Treatment
Do you think you have a drug or alcohol problem?
Do you plan to stop or reduce your AOD use?
If yes, how confident are you that you will be able to do so?
Do you think you need treatment?
Has anyone urged or required you to get an assessment or treatment? Who?
Do you have any questions about AOD assessment and/or treatment?

they believe they have substance use problems or whether they think they need help addressing problematic substance use. Two related reasons are that questions about the client's motivation for change carry the potential to trigger client resistance, which can limit further information gathering, but also, more important, that the interview process provides opportunity to develop rapport and establish a basis of trust with the client. The demonstration of genuine interest and positive regard while gathering relevant information helps the assessor elicit less defensive responses from the client once the time has come to assess readiness to change. Therefore, assessment of relapse potential (ASAM Dimension 5) and recovery environment (ASAM Dimension 6) is discussed as part of this assessment protocol prior to ASAM Dimension 4.

Client Relapse Potential.   Despite many good intentions, once the client has presented for an assessment or is committed to therapy, relapse into old habits or former problems remains a thorny barrier for many substance abusers. Chapter 8 addresses in detail the problem of relapse and means of intervention that help clients prevent and cope with relapse. For now, assessment, both initially and ongoing, can be used to estimate how the potential for relapse is likely to be manifest for a particular client. For some clients, relapse is defined in terms of continuing substance use with its associated problems. For many others, even current abstinence from substance use does not erase the difficulties caused by their prior use, and the continuation of associated problems often begs for therapeutic intervention. In the present edition of their Placement Criteria, ASAM has revised the title of Dimension 5 (Potential for Relapse, Continued Use, or Continuing Problems) from its original title of Relapse/Continued Use Potential to reflect an expanded conception of the term *relapse* (Mee-Lee, 2001b).

In the assessment template developed here, relapse potential is assessed in terms of substance use history (Table 5.1, Section b), presence of tolerance and withdrawal symptoms (Table 5.2, Sections c and d), treatment history (Table 5.3, Section f), and plans and confidence regarding future reduction of substance abuse (Table 5.5, Section h). Higher relapse potential is indicated by longer histories and greater frequencies and intensities of use, by greater recency of use, by lesser amounts or lesser success of past treatment interventions, and by lower motivations and intentions to reduce substance use.

The Client's Recovery Environment.   The client's recovery environment (ASAM Dimension 6) is a crucial factor in terms of the forces that support or inhibit any efforts the client makes to change problematic behaviors. Environmental assessment using a format like that presented in Table 5.4, Section g, allows the therapist to identify any aspects of the client's situation that may threaten the client's safety, well-being, sobriety, or efforts toward change, and to make treatment recommendations accordingly. In addition, the assessor can determine strengths inherent in the client's environment that can be utilized to promote recovery. Discussion of both bolstering and limiting factors in the client's environment also helps establish rapport and hope, as well as further setting the stage for treatment planning.

For example, consider a cocaine dependent client who has reported reasonable social supports and no residential or legal problems, but is facing extreme debt due to his expensive drug habit, complicated by the threat of job loss. The assessor can segue into treatment recommendations by saying something like,

> It seems that improving your situation would involve addressing not only your cocaine use, but also the financial problems it's caused, and maybe also the problems at work. Luckily you feel you can count on some family and friends to support you, but I can also offer the option of working in therapy on how to cope with the complications in your life. In fact, the next time you come in could be used to flesh out a plan for using your time in therapy to deal with the things you see as problems.

More on Assessing Treatment Readiness and Offering Recommendations.   By the time assessors reach this point in the assessment, they have learned a great deal about their clients and are in the position of offering some suggestions about how therapy could be useful to the client. However, the potential utility of therapy depends, to a large extent, on the client's willingness to partake. This movement in session from assessment of the client's situation to presentation of treatment recommendations nicely parallels the estimation of the client's motivation for change (ASAM Dimension 4), assessed in the present template by items in Section h of Table 5.5.

To increase chances that the client will choose to take advantage of the therapy option, the assessor needs to assess the client's readiness to change and be prepared to fashion recommendations that correspond to the client's level of motivation. Few people are willing to change a behavior they do not consider problematic, so the first question the assessor asks regarding readiness to change is whether the client perceives a personal problem with the use of drugs or alcohol. Asking the client about intentions to modify substance use behavior as well as about confidence in one's ability to actually change behavior is also part of assessing readiness to change. Using open-ended questions with neutral wording is important. Miller and Rollnick (2002) recommended assessing the client's perceptions of the importance of making a change and of confidence in one's ability to do so.

Some people who perceive a substance use problem and indicate readiness to make a change believe they can do it themselves, whereas others are convinced they need external help. Some other people who do not consider their drug or alcohol consumption to be a problem may still agree that their efforts to deal with other issues in their lives could benefit from therapy. The client may see no connection between those other difficulties and the client's substance use even though the assessor suspects a link. Still other clients will inform the assessor in no uncertain terms that they see no need for or have no interest in therapy. In each case, it is important to ascertain whether the client believes behavior change is desirable or needed, and whether clients see themselves as seeking therapy voluntarily or pressured into it by some third party. The assessor may at times concur that further intervention is unnecessary for certain clients. Yet when the assessor decides to recommend therapy, the client is more likely to be receptive when the assessor has carefully and accurately determined the client's level of motivation for change. Motivational interviewing strategies (Miller & Rollnick, 2002) are useful in this context.

The questions posed in Section h of Table 5.5 help assess motivations for seeking help and for change during the initial contact with a client, and shape the form in which the assessor will present therapy recommendations to the client. The assessment of motivation for change continues to be a relevant concern beyond the beginning of treatment as the therapist plans and evaluates the course of treatment to fit the client's expectations and efforts as the work proceeds. The art of piecing the assessment findings into the client's treatment plan is sketched out in chapter 6 with the elaboration of the stage model of change (Prochaska & Norcross, 1994). This influential, transtheoretical model is worth introducing in this assessment chapter, too, because unless the assessor responds appropriately to the client's level of readiness for change as assessed on ASAM Dimension 4, the client may not return to allow any therapist a chance to plan further treatment.

The Transtheoretical Model of Change

Prochaska and Norcross (1994) summarized the literature on behavior change as a process that occurs as a person moves through a series of italicized stages from *Precontemplation,* in which the person is unable or unwilling to see a need for change, to *Contemplation* of the possibility of change, *Preparation* to take *Action,* followed by further steps for *Maintenance* of the change. The assessment template presented in this chapter can be used as a rough assessment of the client's stage. The assessor can then offer recommendations the assessor believes the client is likely to accept given the stage of change at which the client currently operates.

A client who denies a drug or alcohol problem or the need for change, especially in the face of contradictory evidence, is probably in the Precontemplation stage, and the assessor will need to present recommendations with this in mind. The assessor might say,

> I hear you saying you don't see a problem, and I respect your viewpoint. I also heard you say some other things that don't quite match up with that perspective, and here's what they are. [Assessor names any evidence suggesting a problem without yet labeling it as a problem.] So I'm not saying there is or is not a problem, but I am saying there's a lot going on here and it seems worth coming in for one or two more sessions to talk about this some more and decide what to do about the situation. Even if we end up deciding together that there is no problem with your alcohol (or drug) use, it still sounds like (this person or that situation) is a hassle for you, and we could use our time together to figure out what you can do to make it better. Would you be willing to talk to me or to someone about this for a couple more sessions?

This "foot-in-the-door" approach validates the client's opinion, but also offers an alternative for the client to consider as well as a limited time frame for additional contact that encourages the client to keep thinking about the alternatives without making an indefinite commitment to an unknown process.

The client in the Contemplation stage of change at the time of initial assessment is identified by affirmative answers to questions about an alcohol or drug problem and the need for change, but negative replies to questions about intentions and confidence to actually make the change occur. To this client, the assessor could say something like,

> What I'm hearing is there's one part of you that wants to change your habits and solve this problem, but there's another side to you that isn't convinced you can or even want to. I recognize and accept the aspect of you that doesn't want to change, but I also encourage you to give fair consideration to the aspect that wants to improve your situation, because I believe you can. Therapy could help you sort that out. How would you feel about coming talk to me, or to someone else if you prefer, for a few weeks to weigh your options and then you will have a fuller set of information to help you decide if you want to take further action at this point?

Again the assessor attempts to obtain a short-term commitment from the client that will permit decision making about next steps. For clients at this stage, the decision is about whether to move toward action on an identified problem rather than about whether a problem even exists.

The Preparation stage is identified in the client who reports intentions to change, but has not yet taken active steps and may lack confidence in doing so. In such cases, the assessor's recommendations could take a form similar to the following:

> It sounds like you're motivated to make a positive change in your behavior, and I'm glad to hear it! I also know it can be a hard thing to do at times, and I give you a lot of credit for coming this far already. Even when you feel ready and you're starting to plan your strategy, it's still important to have some support and a sounding board as you prepare to take those steps. Therapy can help with that. If you decide to come in for a few sessions, you and I (or your therapist) can put together a plan of action and track your progress over time.

Here the assessor offers therapy as a potential context in which the client can work on deciding how to take action.

Some clients during initial assessment report already taking direct Action toward the process of change. They will readily admit some problem associated with drug or alcohol use, and when asked if they plan to stop or reduce use, they will say they have already begun to do so. Clients just starting the Action stage are sometimes discouraged that change is even more difficult and progress more slow than they had hoped, and signs of actual change may still be minimal at best. Fears of relapse into old habits or problems are common among clients who present at this stage of the change process. With such clients, the assessor can recommend,

> Therapy can provide a secure place where you can keep actively working on the changes you're already starting to make. Yes, I can see that it's frustrating when change is slow and not yet obvious, and the pulls back to old familiar tendencies are strong. But you decided to make this change and you're already doing some of the things you need to do, and I'm confident that if you stick with this you will see the payoff in the long run. You can do it! How about coming in once a week to support your efforts, check up on your progress, and tighten up plans as you get clearer on what works for you?

The last stage in the transtheoretical stages of change model is Maintenance. A client in this stage presenting for assessment has not only made efforts to change, but has experienced some success and is working on keeping the momentum going and holding onto the improvements already accomplished. One example would be a client who kicked a long-standing drug habit during a period of incarceration, has not used for a few years, and is fairly confident that he will not return to drug use, but is still mandated to obtain an assessment and possible therapy by terms of his parole, and he reports to his assessor that he still struggles with managing the anger he used to blot out by using drugs. Or another who is not sure how to handle contacts with old friends who still use drugs and occasionally offer her the opportunity to do so, too. For a client at the Maintenance stage, the assessor can validate and reinforce progress achieved by the client, and can offer therapy as a means of keeping on track with goals the client has set and is continuing to refine for oneself during the long course of remission from a substance use disorder.

For each client, then, the assessor carefully conceptualizes the client's readiness for change and willingness to engage in therapy. Accurate conceptualization depends on the assessor's attention to the client's present reaction to the assessment process, including discussion of immediate and longer term needs. With clients who abuse substances, the assessor's determination and recommendations should account for some special factors that are likely to arise in assessment.

CONSIDERATIONS FOR ASSESSMENT GIVEN CHARACTERISTICS OF SUBSTANCE USE DISORDERS

Possibility of Distorted Information

Some clients are not honest with themselves about their behavior, whereas others intentionally downplay their substance use to avoid expected sanctions. Because many forms of substance use are illegal, because abuse of psychoactive substances is widely stigmatized, and because many substance abusers are ambivalent at best about giving up an inherently pleasurable habit, many clients minimize their actual use or consequences when talking to an assessor. Especially if the client is meeting the assessor for the first time at the assessment interview, or if the client feels coerced by a third party to be assessed, the client may not trust the assessor to use the information in a manner that is favorable to the client. Clients often suspect that the assessor may report them, shame them, or try to make them quit using drugs or alcohol. Many will test the therapist by feeding false information to see how the therapist handles it, or even by confronting the therapist with questions like, "Why should I tell you anything? You won't believe me anyway" or "How do you know I'm not lying to you?"

Many substance abuse professionals take the stance of assuming information given by substance abusing clients is not entirely accurate (e.g., Doweiko, 2002). It is also crucial for the assessor to strike a balance between validating the client and entertaining reasonable doubt. Validation in this context does not entail blind or absolute acceptance of the client's word as truth. Rather, it means letting the client know that the assessor takes what the client says seriously and respectfully, and remains open to the possibility that the client's information is true even as competing and possibly contradictory information is being simultaneously considered. The assessor who tells the client overtly or otherwise, with no benefit of doubt, that the assessor believes the client is trying to deceive the assessor runs the risk of alienating the client. Even if that client returns for therapy to satisfy some third-party obligation, real progress in therapy will be difficult if the client does not think the therapist believes or respects the client. Likewise, if clients believe they have successfully duped a gullible therapist, those clients will probably view the therapist as incompetent.

Thus, the recommended, balanced message for the therapist to give is:

> I trust you to be straight with me, and I also take into account any other information that's coming to me along the way. So I believe what you tell me unless I have substantial reason to do otherwise. And then we can talk about that.

This approach tells the client that the therapist will listen carefully and try to fairly evaluate the situation, rather than jump to a snap judgment. Thus, the therapist can encourage the client to return for future sessions. This approach also buys the therapist time both to demonstrate expertise and trustworthiness to the client and in that context to glean more information to help verify or refute the therapist's hypotheses about what is actually going on with the client.

The problem of client deception or distortion in assessment interviews points to the next two considerations in substance use assessment—the utility of multiple data sources and the necessity of data privacy considerations.

The Utility of Multiple Data Sources

The assessor sometimes has access to sources of information about the client in addition to the client's self-report. These may include discussions with family members or friends who accompany the client to the assessment site, documents such as referrals or releases brought to session by the client or requested by the therapist, or consultations with involved parties such as social service or law enforcement personnel. Any such information should be collected with the client's knowledge and consent. This is because a therapist is obliged to avoid revealing that an individual is a substance abuse client to anyone else unless certain conditions are met, as elaborated shortly.

Incorporating data from outside sources into the assessment can help verify a client's position, or it can provide alternative interpretations of the client's situation that help the therapist establish a base of evidence with which to confront the client if needed. Either way, using sources of information external to the client where available allows therapists to expand their conceptualizations of intervention needs and options. Attention to multiple data sources can also help identify potential barriers and resources potentially influencing the client's progress toward meaningful change.

The Necessity of Data Privacy Considerations

The protection of confidentiality and provision of clear advice to clients on its limits are paramount in any therapy, but professionals working with substance use disorders should be aware that records on drug and alcohol treatment are held to an even higher standard of confidentiality than other mental health and medical records (Lopez, 1999). Title 42, Part 2 of the Code of Federal Regulations governing Confidentiality of Alcohol and Drug Abuse Patient Records specifies that, to permit clients with substance use problems to address their drug or alcohol concerns in counseling or therapy without fear of legal recrimination or public disclosure, federally funded treatment programs and their practitioners are prohibited from disclosing that any individual is, ever has been, or has plans to become a client for substance abuse treatment except under specified exceptions. Generally, this means that a provider of assessment, therapy, or other relevant services is obligated to withhold knowledge of contact between a client and the treatment provider from any third party unless one of the following conditions applies (Lopez, 1999).

Informed Consent by Client. First, disclosure is permitted when the client has explicitly by signature waived the right to privacy through written, informed consent, in which case the release should specify precisely what information is to be disclosed, to whom, by whom, and for what purpose. Clients should be informed that they may revoke their consent at any time, by oral or written form, and a date of expiration of the release is to be included. This allows the therapist to assure the client that no information will be revealed to family members who contact the therapist with questions about the client without the client's permission, and no authorities will be contacted if the client admits to illegal substance use unless the client wants or requests a report to be made, say to a probation or parole officer or to a judge. Confidentiality of the information disclosed remains protected by federal law, and the person making the disclosure is required to include a written notice warning the recipient against redisclosure of the information disclosed (Lopez, 1999). In cases where the client is mandated to seek therapy by court order or as a condition of probation, the client is often required by the person(s) issuing the mandate to consent to communication between the therapist and designated third parties about the client's treatment, or to be considered in violation of the mandate, a practice that raises some ethical questions about the actual nature of consent.

Confidentiality Rights of Minors. None of the United States of America explicitly requires parental consent or notification for a minor to obtain substance abuse treatment, and 44 states plus the District of Columbia have passed legislation specifically authorizing minors to consent to confidential counseling, therapy, and medical care for substance abuse (Boonstra & Nash, 2000). Such regulations reflect established opinion that minors engaged in behaviors that put them at risk of physical or mental heath complications may resist seeking care if their parents must be involved. The six states without relevant laws or policies found at the time Boonstra and Nash (2000) published their report include Alaska, Arkansas, New Mexico, South Carolina, Utah, and Wyoming.

The questions of whether a minor has the right to keep their treatment records confidential from their parents or to authorize access to their records without parental knowledge are less clear. Recent changes in privacy rules have "sever[ed] the existing link between minors' right to consent to health care and their ability to keep their medical records private" (Dailard, 2003, p. 7). Current federal regulations cited by Dailard (2003) permit minors to control their records only when states have legislated authorization for them to do so, and most states are currently mute on the subject. Under these circumstances, it is up to the provider of care to determine whether to disclose information a minor client reveals about substance use to the client's parent(s).

Disclosure to Authorized Treatment Providers. Disclosure of client-identifying information is allowed when the recipient of the disclosure is either part of the organizational unit providing substance use services or employed by a qualified service organization having a written agreement with the treatment program to refrain from re-disclosure and abide by Federal confidentiality regulations (Lopez, 1999). In either case, the information to be disclosed must be necessary to the provision of services to the client. For qualifying service organizations, the services provided should be those not available internally to the treatment program (such as laboratory analyses, accounting, legal, medical, or other professional services). All parties receiving confidential client information under such conditions are bound by confidentiality regulations to refrain from further disclosure unless allowed exceptions are in effect.

Additional Conditions Permitting Limited Disclosure. Other sets of conditions allowing disclosure to certain persons are when a crime has been committed on program premises or against program staff, in cases of medical emergency (including suicide threat, drug overdose, or immediate threat of the client's behavior to the health of another individual), or when child abuse or neglect is suspected. Such situations permit disclosure only to relevant authorities or medical personnel, and not to other third parties including family members. In the event of reporting child abuse, the discloser of a suspicion against a particular client must continue to protect the client's drug or alcohol treatment records from further disclosure unless the client consents to or the court orders their review in child abuse proceedings against the client.

A court can order a treatment provider to disclose confidential substance abuse treatment records in court, but only when certain conditions specified in the regulations are met. A subpoena or search warrant alone is not enough to justify identifying an individual as a substance abuse client. The provider and client must be given notice of and time to respond to the application for a court order, except for the party to a crime the information sought will be used to investigate or prosecute. A court must determine that the need for disclosure in the public interest is greater than any potential harm that may accrue to the client. Even when such "good cause" for the disclosure has been established, the information to be disclosed and the persons to receive it must remain limited to that required by the stated purpose of the court order. Disclosure of confidential communication can be ordered by a court only when the information

> is necessary to protect against a threat to life or of serious bodily injury, is necessary to investigate or prosecute an extremely serious crime [the list of which does not contain the sale or possession of illegal drugs], or is connected with a proceeding in which the patient has already presented evidence concerning the confidential communication. In all other situations, not even a court can order disclosure of a confidential communication. (Lopez, 1999, p. 6)

Disclosure of client-identifying information may also be permitted for purposes of research, program audits, or evaluations. Those who receive confidential information for any of these purposes must have established qualifications as well as plans for protection and use of the information, including obligations to avoid unauthorized redisclosure. Research uses require independent approval by a committee for the protection of human subjects.

Informing Clients About Confidentiality Protections and Limitations. The confidentiality regulations summarized earlier emphasize the sensitivity of substance abuse treatment participation and the need to protect the rights of those who seek help for drug and alcohol concerns. Assessors and treatment providers are advised to let clients know up front about the provisions and limitations of confidentiality, and to find out early in the first interview whether the client plans to request disclosure of information about the assessment to any third party.

If the client says yes, the assessor should complete and explain a consent form authorizing the release of information, and discuss with the client the purpose of the disclosure, the nature of information to be disclosed, and any questions the client has about the terms and procedures of disclosure. If the client says no or expresses uncertainty, the assessor can still inform the client that if situations arise where the client or some third party requests a disclosure, the request and next steps will be discussed with the client to the extent required by law before any disclosure will be made. Some clients are not sure or even aware at the time of assessment that third-party disclosure could be requested or required, so a straightforward discussion of confidentiality issues is important with all clients for legal, ethical, and therapeutic reasons.

Client Occupational and Interpersonal Problems

Aside from frank mental health disorders, substance abusing clients frequently present with problems in their social and vocational transactions. Excessive substance use can diminish a person's development of, implementation of, or motivation for effective interpersonal or occupational skills. Whether the client reports using substances to cope with skills deficits or admits that substance use is contributing to an interpersonal or occupational problem, the assessor will better conceptualize and engage the client by acknowledging problems mentioned in addition to the substance use.

The assessor needs to ask questions to tease out how, if at all, the client perceives substance use to be related to problems at work, school, home, or with friends. If the therapist learns that the client is trying to blunt feelings about or avoid dealing with socioenvironmental difficulties by using drugs or alcohol, the client can be offered help finding more effective coping strategies. If the assessment indicates that the client's job or relationships are in jeopardy because of the client's refusal to admit or inability to reduce substance abuse, the assessor can suggest future use of therapy as a venue to work through the vocational or relationship issues by, among other approaches, looking at the extent to which the client's substance use is in fact contributing to the problem.

The essential point is that goals of assessment—establishing an initial diagnosis and recommending treatment—should not be conducted as if substance abuse is isolated from the client's other personal or occupational concerns. When using the *DSM–IV* format for diagnosis, such concerns can be recorded on Axis IV (Psychosocial and environmental problems). A recommendation for substance abuse therapy can certainly encompass plans to address interpersonal tensions or vocational problems in concert with substance use behavior. Even when the client does not acknowledge a substance use problem, the astute assessor who has just collected information about a client's substantial history of substance use can recommend that the client think about using therapy to tackle other concerns the client has identified. The assessor can focus efforts on engaging the client through appeals to problems the client has named, trusting that if the past or present substance abuse is relevant, it will emerge in subsequent therapy sessions. In other words, offering therapy to address concerns other than substance abuse to a client who has used substances with high frequency and intensity is still a form of substance use therapy.

THERAPIST BARRIERS

Appropriate assessment, diagnosis, and treatment recommendations for clients who abuse psychoactive substances depend on a therapist who is sensitive to the client's perspective and receptivity, tolerant of ambiguity and possible resistance, open to both alternative interpretations of the data at hand and to the impact of future information, and skilled at complementing various clients' interpersonal styles. Therapists who conduct substance abuse assessments need to be aware of their own values, strengths, and limitations. Making use of supervision, consultation, and introspection, therapists learn to detect and address their own barriers to effective assessment.

A therapist who has difficulties interacting with defiant, combative, or noncompliant personalities can explore the feelings and reactions that such people elicit in the therapist and can learn to implement more productive responses to resistant client behaviors. Those with the tendency to jump to conclusions about a client's dishonesty or lack of motivation to change can practice communicating to clients, supervisors, colleagues, and self that, although the therapist is formulating a knowledgeable opinion, the therapist is also amenable to the possibility that new information or changing circumstances can call for a revision of that opinion. Therapists who feel overwhelmed by the complexities of working with clients who exhibit substance use disorders can consider how to empower themselves to take steps to sufficiently serve those clients who do present with substance use concerns, whether that means learning more about how to conduct competent services or how to provide suitable referrals.

As therapists face up to barriers such as these, they frequently find they have capacities for dealing with hard situations and complex transactions beyond what they realized they possessed. They also encounter lessons in using self-care to prevent burnout. Learning to assess for substance abuse teaches therapists much about themselves in addition to putting them in positions to make meaningful differences in the lives of their clients.

*   *   *

In summary, assessing clients for drug and alcohol problems involves initial screening based on hints of a possible concern, and then further assessment for persons who do not filter through the screen. Assessment involves collecting detailed personal history and environmental information to detect and properly diagnose a disorder where one is evident. If warranted, the assessor formulates recommendations about the appropriate type and level of treatment to be offered and tries to motivate the client to consider and hopefully accept the treatment recommendations. Continuing assessment over a course of therapy is also relevant to planning intervention and evaluating client response and progress. The utilities of the frameworks provided by the *DSM–IV* diagnostic criterion sets, by the ASAM Patient Placement Criteria, and by the transtheoretical model of change have all been demonstrated and further incorporated in this chapter into a template to guide therapists through the assessment interview. A continuous version of the assessment template is provided in Appendix A.

Thorough assessment and accurate diagnosis drive the development of a treatment plan customized to the client's particular interests and needs. In the next chapter, the link is drawn from assessed history, current symptoms, and environmental context to specific goals, objectives, and strategies to be pursued in therapy.

Chapter **6**

Planning Treatment Across the Course of Therapy for Substance Use Disorders

A therapist's work with a client to establish meaningful goals and a strategy to reach them begins as soon as assessment results in a diagnosis and the client accepts the corresponding treatment recommendation. Treatment planning continues as long as the client keeps returning for therapy sessions. Ideally, a treatment plan emerges from negotiations between the client and therapist to decide what problems are to be addressed in therapy, what goals are reasonable and worthwhile, what pathways and techniques are available, and what steps the client is willing and able to take toward those goals. Periodic review is built into the plan because treatment plans often change as new details come to light or as the client's situation and the therapeutic relationship evolve.

A plan for therapy gives both the therapist and client a sense of direction for their work together. A well-articulated plan also potentially enhances treatment efficacy by providing a clear means for tracking progress toward established goals. The therapist has several purposes in developing a treatment plan for a client with a substance use disorder. First and foremost, the therapist wants to motivate and empower clients to make beneficial changes in their substance use behaviors. To that end, the therapist structures the task at hand by helping the client identify a range of available options, and by encouraging the client to make informed choices from among those alternatives. In addition to increasing the client's knowledge, the therapist also plans treatment to boost the client's sense of self-efficacy, so that clients will have some confidence in their abilities to make good choices and implement plans of action. Treatment plans that are negotiated directly with clients invite the client to share both initiative and responsibility for determining the course of therapy, including both end goals and the steps to take in striving to reach those goals. In summary, a workable treatment plan is responsive to the client's stated interests, provides flexible structure, reinforces client choice, supports decision making, and promotes responsibility for outcomes of client behaviors.

COMPONENTS OF A TREATMENT PLAN

Therapists accomplish these purposes by organizing plans into meaningful components. The first component is the rationale provided to the client for generating a plan; this includes the therapist's thoughtful response to the client's reaction to the planning proposal. Once the client agrees to collaborate on a plan, the second component specifies the problem(s) to be addressed in therapy. Third, planning involves clarification of goals to be attempted, with the desired general result to be either resolution of the problem or at least reduction of its detrimental impact. The fourth component, setting objectives, consists of breaking the distance between the problem and the goal down into identifiable, meaningful, and achievable steps. These steps toward the goal help make the process of changing behavior more understandable and manageable for both the client and therapist. Fifth, planning specifies methods to be used for working on each objective or tasks to be undertaken in attempts to move toward goals. Finally, the therapist and client may wish to agree on time frames for attempting specific tasks, reviewing the plan to assess progress, and achieving objectives and goals.

The present chapter is structured around these six components of a treatment plan. The rationale for involving the client as much as possible in formal planning of a course of substance abuse therapy is followed by a presentation of some common problems focal to many cases of substance use disorders. These include low motivation and low self-efficacy for changing problematic behaviors. General goals for addressing these focal problems are elaborated in the context of relevant theoretical and empirical literature. These goals include (a) increasing the client's motivation and self-efficacy for change; (b) enhancing clients' understanding of their thoughts, feelings, and behaviors associated with substance use and related problems; and (c) engaging clients in action planned to promote change. Within the sections covering each general goal, feasible objectives, methods, and time frames are outlined, with a particular focus on pertinent objectives for each goal. Methods and time frames are considered in greater depth in chapters 7 (Psychoeducation), 8 (Relapse Prevention Strategies), 9 (Interventions to Address Problems Linked to Client's Substance Abuse), and 10 (Terminating Therapy).

OFFERING CLIENTS A RATIONALE FOR GENERATING
A SUBSTANCE ABUSE TREATMENT PLAN

Substance abusing clients often lack structure in significant parts of their lives. Because their time is highly organized around alcohol- or drug-related activities, or because their substance use blunts their capacity for executive functioning (or both), they may have trouble setting realistic goals, developing workable plans, or maintaining motivated effort in realms of life outside of substance use and the activities necessary to keep using. The *DSM–IV* criteria for Substance Abuse disorders capture the potential for life disruption through repeated risks or troubles encountered under the influence of psychoactive substances. The criteria for Substance Dependence further allude to the chaotic nature of a substance use disorder in specifying that the substance dependent individual tries to quit using but cannot, neglects important life roles in favor of continued substance use, or keeps on drinking or drugging even in the face of seriously negative consequences. Individuals whose days have been organized around drugs or complicated by alcohol have much to gain from the structured activity of planning treatment with a therapist.

Treatment Planning as a Collaborative Intervention

Skilled therapists can use the initial treatment planning discussion to explore with clients how they are presently dealing with life and how that compares with what they ultimately want from life. By thus identifying problems and goals, the therapist can help clients choose how they can use their time together in therapy sessions to promote progress toward those goals. Motivational interviewing strategies (Miller & Rollnick, 2002) are often useful in this context and are discussed later in this chapter. Once the client agrees to a negotiated plan, the therapist will refocus on the planning process when needed to clarify problems through further assessment. Therapists can also undertake review of the treatment plan to help specify client options and choose and implement actions. Additionally, review of a treatment plan also encompasses evaluation of the outcomes of those actions and revision of the plan as the work progresses. Sample treatment plans are provided to illustrate these points.

Engaging a client in collaborative treatment planning is an intervention that contributes to progress in therapy. Hopefully it is already clear that I wish to focus on the active process of planning treatment as well as the obtained product of a document to be filed in the client's record. Often a written plan is a desirable—and in some settings, a required—commodity. It can serve as a contract of sorts to guide subsequent transactions in the therapy relationship. Yet the premise of this chapter is that without incorporating the client's perspective and activating the client's initiative, the document will be worth little more than the paper on which it is written. Telling an alcoholic client that he needs to stop drinking will not help until the client agrees to quit. Insisting that a woman who has stated a goal of reducing habitual marijuana use should stop hanging around with her friends who still use pot will not keep her from smoking until the client decides she can and wants to implement steps to keep her from smoking. The most useful plan for a client is a living, working document that reflects the client's perceptions, motivations, and input as well as the therapist's definitions, suggestions, and expertise. A productive plan mobilizes the therapist to assess the client's motivation for treatment and address any resistance. Effective planning elicits client input, encourages client choice wherever possible, provides structure and an underlying rationale for treatment, and helps select formats and goals that meet clients where they live.

Inviting the Client's Participation. The therapist commences treatment planning by explaining to the client the purpose of developing a plan. The therapist tells the client,

> I suggest we start by coming up with a written treatment plan. I like to do that with new clients for at least two important reasons. First, a plan that we both can read, discuss, and sign helps make sure we agree on how we're going to use our time in these sessions; and second, it gives us a way to track progress over time. A treatment plan is like a road map to give us some direction, but it's also not engraved in stone. We can take it out and look at it now and then, and if we want to, we can pick a new route or even redraw the map.

Most clients, when asked their reaction to such a proposal, will consent to a discussion of planning either because they have problems in mind to address or because they are willing to give their new therapist, who seems to be offering a reasonable starting point, the benefit of the doubt. The therapist's opening educates them about what to expect next and also piques curiosity about what the therapist will do. Notice that therapists do not say that they "have to" come up with a plan, nor does the therapist tell the client that the purpose of writing a plan is to satisfy agency requirements or any other third party. The client will be more motivated to engage in the planning process with the therapist when the plan is presented as the therapist's own initiative in the client's interest and with the client's active participation, rather than as an externally imposed obligation.

It is not imperative that the plan be written together in session. In some settings and with some clients, it is acceptable to talk about the plan for therapy and negotiate an agreement without putting it on paper in the client's presence or requiring the client's signature. However, it is highly recommended that the therapist develop some plan, ideally in collaboration with the client, to guide the therapy process. Also the therapist is advised to keep a record of any plans discussed with the client. Careful documentation of plans as a component of progress notes is essential to therapist memory, credibility, and accountability. The ongoing process of treatment planning involves clearly and consistently communicating to the client what the therapist proposes to do and why. The process also incorporates the client's reactions and ideas. Although it is important to maintain a written summary, not every aspect of a plan can be put into writing. At many points during a session, a therapist is planning what to say next, with aims to offer choices to the client wherever therapeutically viable so that the client will be empowered by the act of choosing in the interest of therapeutic change. This emphasis on collaborative choice underlies the present recommendation for a written plan developed and signed together in session.

Identifying a Focus.   Once the client has agreed to engage in planning, therapists then ask whether the client has concerns or problems on which the plan can focus. If the client mentions more than one, the therapist notes each one and asks the client to prioritize them. Starting with the client's definition of the problem, even if the client sees the problem outside the domain of substance use, enlists the client's involvement in planning. After listening to the client's description of each concern, the therapist writes the problem down in the client's own words or paraphrases it as closely as possible. (To establish rapport, the therapist is encouraged to listen carefully and empathically before writing.) Then therapists can read back to their clients what they wrote, asking whether the written statement captures the client's concern and revising the wording if needed according to the client's suggestions. When a client is vague, verbose, or uncertain in describing a problem, it is important for the therapist to negotiate and help refine the wording of the problem statement into one the client will endorse.

Some clients who use drugs or alcohol say they do not have any problems, or at least none they are interested in discussing with a therapist. The therapist then asks the client's reason for coming to therapy, being careful not to imply that the therapist agrees the client has no good reason to be present. In response, clients referred for substance abuse therapy often reveal or reiterate external pressures placed on them to attend. The therapist can reframe this encumbrance as the client's problem to be addressed. For example:

> So your main problem right now is that your spouse is threatening divorce if you don't come to therapy, even though you don't see your drinking as a problem, and you'd like to get him (or her) to lay off of you. So is figuring out what to do about that problem something we could work on in here?

To elicit participation from a client who feels coerced into therapy, the therapist's message is, "Well, as long as you have to be here, is there anything you and I could talk about or sort through that would be worth your time?"

Specifying Goals and Objectives.   Once the therapist has a firm conception of the client's definition of a problem and a sense of the client's motivation to work on it, the therapist aims to articulate relevant goals and corresponding objectives, which can be explained as steps toward a goal. Beginning with the client's conception of the problem and the work to be done means that the therapist attempts to pace the course of therapy to move only as far and as fast as the client is willing to go, testing that boundary by pushing gently against it and adjusting the approach according to the client's reaction.

At the outset of planning treatment, the client may report many troubles, a small number, or none at all. The therapist refines the focus by helping the client select a workable number of issues to target. For clients with clear ideas about personal goals and priorities, this part is not difficult. However, clients with diffuse or multitudinous problem statements can be reminded that setting and clarifying priorities makes more efficient use of the time available in sessions. The therapist can acknowledge the legitimacy of all the client's expressed concerns and still encourage sharpening the focus of the treatment plan. When clients deny any problem or cannot think of a specific one, the therapist can create momentum by reflecting one complaint the client has mentioned already even if the client did not label it as a focus for therapy. A viable treatment plan requires only one goal that both (or all) parties agree to work on, although it certainly may consist of more goals depending on the client's current understanding. The therapist who responds, "You're telling me the main thing you want out of coming here is to get out of trouble by satisfying the judge's order that you get therapy. I'd say that's something we can work on together," will often obtain the client's willingness to continue the conversation. That one goal can become the basis for an initial treatment plan to satisfy all aspects of the court order by considering what steps the client would need to take to do so. A sample plan written to reflect such a discussion between a court-mandated client and his new therapist is presented in Table 6.1.

Planning Treatment in the Face of Client Resistance

Certain clients object even to the process of planning treatment. They may indicate that they "just want to talk" or that they "don't really like things so structured," or even that discussing a plan "feels like going through the mo-

TABLE 6.1
Initial Treatment Plan for Cody, Client Diagnosed
With Alcohol Abuse and Assessed in the
Precontemplation Stage of Readiness for Change

I. *Problem:* Cody has been ordered by Judge Carson to complete 25 hours of alcohol treatment subsequent to Cody's arrest for driving under the influence of alcohol. At the time of the DUI arrest, Cody's blood alcohol content (BAC) was measured at 0.11, although the client disputes both the accuracy of this measure and the claim that he is a problem drinker.

  A. *Goal:* Satisfy the judge's order so that current legal troubles can be resolved.

    1. *Objective:* Clarify all tasks that will need to be completed to fulfill the obligations of the judge's order.

      a. *Method:* Bring copy of court order document to next session with the therapist.

      b. *Method:* Discuss options and priorities in next session.

    2. *Objective:* Generate a schedule and plan of action for completing required tasks by the court's deadline.

  B. *Goal:* Avoid similar troubles in the future.

    1. *Objective:* Identify any lessons learned from present situation.

      a. *Method:* Review the circumstances leading up to, during, and after the DUI incident.

      b. *Method:* Discuss steps client can take to prevent similar circumstances from recurring.

tions" to fulfill someone else's expectations. If such a client repeatedly resists the therapist's attempt to establish a formal plan, the therapist may, rather than losing the client, agree to proceed by minimizing immediate overt discussion of the plan. Instead the therapist can reiterate reasons for suggesting a plan and request to revisit the topic later if either party sees the need arise. By at least temporarily deferring to the client's wish to decline planning, the therapist can listen attentively to whatever the client talks about instead and can tease out information relevant to the therapist's own conceptualization and planning. The therapist can use this information outside of session to formulate a tentative plan that can be offered to the client in a subsequent session.

In this manner, the therapist is still involved in planning, with emphasis on how to engage the client in collaboration with the planning process. Initially reluctant clients frequently buy into a plan that the therapist developed outside of session and offered in a subsequent session because the therapist accepted their initial stance, took time outside of session to work on the client's case, and wrote up a plan that not only reflects the client's behavior and words, but also takes up only a small fraction of a session to go over unless the client has questions or clarifications.

Revising the Treatment Plan as Needed

Thus, in addition to the client's starting point, the therapist simultaneously entertains ideas about problem definitions and resolution strategies based on what the client has said and done in sessions. The therapist is devising plans as the therapist gets to know the client. In negotiating a plan with the client, the therapist continually estimates how far the client's ideas are from the therapist's own, and how ready and willing the client seems to be to hear alternative perspectives the therapist has to offer. The therapist continually decides how and when to introduce the therapist's private thoughts into the joint planning process. The therapist's decisions will rest on an assessment of how far the client has come, how far the client is willing to go, and what resources the client has available to support taking the next step between those two points. The therapist can enhance opportunities for collaboration by telling the client up front that together they can review the treatment plan periodically to decide whether to stick to the game plan or go back to the drawing board.

To facilitate collaboration in planning with clients, the therapist needs skills for balancing structure with flexibility. Planning treatment for substance abuse can involve negotiation with clients who are unfocused, skeptical, or resentful about treatment, or who may be trying to test or deceive the therapist. The therapist tries to give the client a framework to clarify expectations and guide progress, but also to remain open to modifying that framework as suggested by the client's interests, needs, and attitudes.

Table 6.2 gives an example of a revised treatment plan developed by a therapist with her client, Barry, who was at the time of intake reluctant to commit to intensive outpatient therapy even though he met criteria for long-term Alcohol Dependence. The initial treatment plan had thus been negotiated to specify that Barry would try weekly outpatient therapy for six weeks; if at the end of that time period he had not made sufficient progress toward his abstinence goals, he and the therapist would reconsider the recommendation for intensive outpatient therapy.

After four weeks, Barry told his therapist that he appreciated her efforts, but he could already tell that therapy once a week was not enough to keep him from stopping at his regular liquor store on the way home from work. Although he had reduced his weekly average number of binge nights, he still found himself sneaking into his garage about three times per week to drink one or more of the fifths of vodka he had hidden there. He said he was now ready to try intensive outpatient treatment. His therapist validated Barry's honesty, efforts, and reduction of drinking, and suggested they revise his treatment plan, as summarized in Table 6.2.

TABLE 6.2
Revised Treatment Plan for Barry, Client Diagnosed With Alcohol
Dependence and Assessed in the Preparation Stage of Readiness for Change

I. *Problem:* Despite genuine efforts in outpatient therapy and reduction of drinking episodes from five to three days per week, Barry continues to drink excessively to the point of blacking out on a regular basis. Barry is coming to believe that he won't meet his goal of abstinence from alcohol without more intensive treatment.

   A. *Goal:* Increase Barry's hopes for and beliefs in the possibility of meeting his abstinence goal.

      1. *Objective:* Develop and expand ways for Barry to acknowledge and reinforce the progress he is making.

         a. *Method:* Address in ongoing individual outpatient therapy.

         b. *Method:* Enroll in intensive outpatient (IOP) therapy group starting next Monday.

      2. *Objective:* Further assess the typical thoughts, feelings, events, or other triggers that precede alcohol binge episodes.

         a. *Method:* Explore difficulties involved in driving past the liquor store on the way home from work.

         b. *Method:* Discuss feelings of letting wife and son down.

         c. *Method:* Address memories of mother's drinking during Barry's childhood.

      3. *Objective:* Identify possible alternative responses client believes he could make to the above triggers without resorting to alcohol use.

         a. *Method:* Map and take a different route home, and decide on strategies for passing liquor stores without stopping.

         b. *Method:* Eliminate the stash of bottles in the garage.

         c. *Method:* Consider the possibility of self-forgiveness for past mistakes and resulting problems that Barry associates with his alcohol use.

         d. *Method:* Review in individual therapy what client learns from other IOP participants.

         e. *Method:* Expand client's support systems and leisure options.

II. *Problem:* Barry continues to worry about the future of his marriage given his wife's increasing complaints about his lack of success, as she perceives it, in quitting drinking.

   A. *Goal:* Barry hopes not only to save, but to improve, his marriage.

      1. *Objective:* Continue working on stopping alcohol use.

         a. *Method:* Continue weekly individual outpatient therapy.

         b. *Method:* Begin intensive outpatient therapy group.

      2. *Objective:* Work with wife to address problems they both link to having each grown up in families with an alcoholic parent.

         a. *Method:* Talk to wife about the possibility of future couples therapy after Barry completes IOP.

         b. *Method:* In individual therapy session, role play possible approaches to this discussion with wife, including anticipated outcomes and plausible responses.

Addressing Therapists' Issues With Treatment Planning

Therapists are advised to be aware too of their own issues with imposing structure. When a therapist is either overstructured or understructured, difficulties may ensue in attempts to conduct substance abuse treatment.

Therapists who have a hard time asserting a format, offering suggestions, or interrupting a tangential or verbose client may be at a loss with clients who are uncertain about what to expect from treatment or unconvinced that they have a problem. Yet therapists who dictate treatment expectations, goals, and objectives without allowing for client input or feedback risk alienating the client and will probably elicit resistant behavior. Over the course of a career, supervision and consultation with respected professionals can help a therapist expand the capacity for flexible structure, especially by providing means to work through issues surrounding appropriate structure.

ADDRESSING FOCAL PROBLEMS OF LOW SELF-EFFICACY AND LOW MOTIVATION

Client initiative can be mobilized through the choice of problems to be addressed in therapy. A problem therapists routinely encounter in planning substance abuse treatment is clients who do not take responsibility for active roles in changing their circumstances. Therapists cannot bring about beneficial change without clients' involvement. The corresponding issues from a client perspective are that clients either lack interest in changing or perceive themselves unable to change their problematic substance use. In other words, low motivation and low self-efficacy are common focal problems for clients with substance use disorders. Therapists try, using treatment planning as one important tool, to motivate clients to take initiative for change by offering clients options, encouraging them to make choices, and supporting their efforts toward implementing their choices. The options a therapist presents at a given point in a course of therapy can be differentially selected based on the client's sense of self-efficacy and the client's degree of readiness to change. Miller and Rollnick (2002) recommended attention to both the client's sense of the importance of making a change and the client's confidence in personal ability to make that change. Both are viewed as aspects of a person's intrinsic motivation.

Goal 1: Increase Client's Self-Efficacy to Make a Beneficial Change

Research on cognitive models of therapy demonstrates that treatments are effective to the extent that they enhance clients' expectations of efficacy in dealing with personal problems (Thombs, 1999). Efficacy expectations are defined by Bandura (1997) as beliefs that one is capable of sustaining a course of action intended to achieve a particular outcome. Outcome expectations are reflected in the individual's level of confidence that the anticipated outcome will actually occur. Together efficacy and outcome expectations comprise self-efficacy. Clients who do not genuinely believe either that things can change or that they are capable of bringing about change are not likely to take either initiative or responsibility for changing problematic behavior.

Chemical addictions by definition put clients in positions where they find themselves seemingly unable to stop using their drug of choice even after persistent wishes or multiple attempts to quit. Or they give up activities that were once important to them to continue drinking or using even in the face of damages probably caused by their substance use. Those clients who abuse substances without fitting the full criteria for Substance Dependence still encounter repeated difficulties associated with their excessive substance use. It is understandable then that clients exhibiting substance use disorders often display low expectations of efficacy to change undesirable behaviors or circumstances. An essential component of planning treatment is motivating clients to believe that change is possible and that they are capable of making change occur. Only when clients have realistic hope and expectations of efficacy will they make choices in favor of positive change and take initiative and responsibility for promoting change. When the goal is increasing self-efficacy, therapists can assist in identifying objectives with the potential to augment the client's efficacy and outcome expectations.

Research shows that when persons experience enhanced personal competence, their abilities to function improve, whereas when perceptions of competence are diminished, the risk of relapse into problematic behaviors dramatically increases (Thombs, 1999). A treatment plan designed to enhance a client's perceptions of self-efficacy has the potential to improve the client's functioning by promoting the client's ability to regulate one's own behavior in healthier ways. Social cognitive theory (Bandura, 1977) specifies four means by which efficacy expectations can be altered, and these can be directly incorporated into treatment plans as objectives for moving toward the goal of improved self-efficacy. The sources of information, from strongest to weakest, that influence efficacy expectations are (a) performance accomplishments, (b) emotional arousal, (c) vicarious experiences, and (d) verbal persuasion. The subsequent discussion looks specifically at the relevance of these four general categories of information to a therapist's efforts to alter a client's self-efficacy for personal change in the context of substance abuse treatment.

Objective 1a: Choosing Tasks With Strong Chances of Client Success. A client's performance accomplishments provide powerful information about the likelihood of success in reaching identified goals and objectives. Substance abusers who have encountered repeated troubles, often despite goals of avoiding them, tend to doubt the possibility of change. In some cases, this lack of conviction gets rationalized into a lack of desire for things to be different. Such clients argue and may genuinely believe that they prefer using drugs and invite the consequences over the alternatives. The therapist who shows curiosity and interest in the client's perspective and explores that client's sense of performance accomplishments in more depth will often run into the client's ambivalence. Many clients report some version of the sentiment that they would like to be able to continue using their drug of choice and enjoy its pleasurable effects, but simultaneously wish to forego the uncomfortable or debilitating effects.

A treatment plan can incorporate performance accomplishment objectives by specifically looking at what the client can do to reduce or eliminate difficulties the client has previously been unable to manipulate satisfactorily. In some cases, this involves temporarily suspending judgment about whether giving up substance use altogether will be a necessary condition for successful problem reduction. For example, when the client asserts lack of willingness or ability to abstain from alcohol use, he may still agree to performance objectives including harm reduction strategies, such as monitoring number of drinks, sticking to a limit of drinks per sitting, avoiding drinking on an empty stomach, avoiding drinking when in a bad mood, refraining from driving under the influence, and so on. In any case, the therapist's job is to shape the treatment plan by setting up methods and time frames that are likely to meet the objective of giving the client the experience of successfully accomplishing a meaningful task. This, of course, is best accomplished through the method of discussing with the client what constitutes an outcome worthy of the client's effort, and what type of effort the client is willing and able to exert. Additional methods relevant to this objective include expanding the client's awareness of alternative tasks for approaching the problem at hand, encouraging the client to make deliberate choices from among available options, guiding client efforts to perform the chosen task, helping the client evaluate the outcomes of task performance, and revising the plan as needed to accomplish the objective.

An example of negotiating performance objectives occurs with Jason, who says a month before his college graduation that he is thinking about giving up his daily cannabis habit when he starts his new job right afterward. However, when he has tried abstaining, he repeatedly capitulated to his urges to smoke. Jason is afraid if he waits to quit until the job actually begins that he still will be tempted to use, but he also wants to enjoy graduation festivities with the additional enhancement of marijuana. He calls himself a "pothead," admitting that it has been weeks, maybe months, since he has skipped a day of smoking. His therapist recommends that Jason commit to abstaining until final exams are over to see what it is like for him to do so and to clear his head for upcoming exams. Jason is obviously reluctant to agree, saying he could if he wanted to, but he is not ready yet. The therapist suggests that Jason try refraining from any use for the coming week, and then reporting back in the next session how it went and what he wants to do from that point. The client says he would be willing to forego marijuana use on the weekdays, but is not willing to commit to that objective for the weekend because of big plans on which he elaborates. The therapist agrees to this weekday abstinence plan, but expresses concern for Jason's well-being over the weekend and raises considerations for Jason to take responsibility for his behavior, both now and in the longer term. The therapist reiterates the plan to talk more next week about Jason's experience of abstinence on weekdays and his thoughts about next steps in light of his overall goals, and the client agrees.

Another example is Rhonda, who reports a number of physical symptoms she associates with her substance use, but who says she has not had a complete physical in years. When her therapist recommends that Rhonda make an appointment with a medical doctor, the client says it is not worth it because she knows from past experience that she will just spend money to be examined and told that nothing is wrong. In this case, the therapist might suggest objectives such as exploring Rhonda's doubts and fears about a medical consultation, weighing her alternatives, preparing and even rehearsing what she wants to ask the doctor if she does decide to go, or looking up her symptoms on the Internet or at the library. The therapist should certainly find out as well if other objectives occur to Rhonda. From the list of options they generate together, the client can indicate the ones she is willing to try, and the therapist can further explore the client's reasons.

Encouraging the client to make deliberate choices about the course of action in therapy and guiding action along an achievable course both increase the client's chances of accomplishing successes that will motivate additional action and further commitment to the therapy process. Treatment plans can evolve as clients partake of the powerful information about their efficacy offered by their successful performance of treatment objectives. The therapist tries to steer the client toward objectives that are likely to provide the client with the experience early in therapy of successfully mastering a relatively simple task, and then moving toward attempt and mastery of more complex tasks. The types of tasks that can be offered are gauged according to the client's stage of change, as elaborated in later sections of this chapter.

Objective 1b: Learning to Manage Affect Associated With Treatment Efforts. Emotional arousal in response to a task or goal is a second form of information that affects a person's self-efficacy, to the extent that a task elicits anxiety about the possibility of failure or confidence about the anticipation of success. Strong anxiety can easily dampen confidence and resolve, leading the anxious individual to question his or her ability or deny responsibility for attempting the task at hand. Thus, the therapist can plan treatment to promote client self-efficacy by building in objectives centered on alternative means of managing intense negative emotions aroused by the client's problems and efforts at resolving them. Clients who have been dealing with their anger, sadness, frustration, or anxiety by masking feelings behind substance-induced affect can benefit from a therapist's suggestions about other effective strategies for coping with difficult emotions. Chapter 9 addresses interventions to help clients manage difficult affect tied up with the problems that bring them to therapy. The present section focuses specifically on addressing fear or anxiety raised in attempts to master treatment objectives.

Clients who agree to objectives of managing emotional arousal that interferes with effective performance typically need the task broken down into manageable steps. To help plan treatment methods for emotion management objectives, the therapist can draw on the classic approach–avoidance conflict paradigm posed by Dollard and Miller (1950). Already mentioned is the tendency for substance abusers to feel ambivalent about changing their patterns of consumption because their substance use yields both pleasurable and uncomfortable results. This represents a prototypical approach–avoidance conflict, where the user is both drawn to and repelled by the prospects of reducing or eliminating substance use. Dollard and Miller (1950) empirically validated their hypotheses that the tendency to approach a goal would be stronger when the individual is farther from the goal, but avoidance activity increases rapidly and eventually overtakes the approach tendency as the individual gets closer to the goal.

The substance abuse client sitting in the therapist's office with primed awareness of the undesirable aspects of substance use that landed the client there is at that point more motivated to approach the goals of therapy than the client will be during the time between sessions when opportunities arise to act counter to goals and objectives. When the chance to drink, take drugs, or engage in problematic behavior presents itself, the client's motivation to avoid treatment goals escalates. Frequently the client gets anxious about the conflicting pulls. The client may be more tempted to avoid thinking about either the goals or the related conflict by giving into the urge to use the substance, which promises relief from conflicting feelings, however temporary.

A client who worries about handling friends who pressure him to drink with them can benefit from consideration in therapy of what he can do in those moments to stick to his goals and deal with the corresponding feelings. Another client who is thinking about trying a support group, but struggling with her pervasive shyness, can also profit from specifying therapy objectives for managing her fears of inefficacy.

The therapist who can help the client recognize the dynamics of emotional arousal in response to approaching goals and objectives in therapy will be in a position to teach the client new ways of managing negative affect states as they are aroused. The relative distance of the therapy interaction from situations in which the client has the realistic option to relapse can be used to identify and practice strategies for managing intense anxiety, anger, or sadness. Methods for working toward emotion management objectives include identifying the circumstances the client believes will trigger difficult emotions, generating ideas about how to respond to intense feelings without resorting to substance use or other problematic habits, practicing new responses both in and out of therapy sessions, and rewarding valid attempts and successful outcomes of applying new responses. Establishing clear objectives gives the client hope that progress is possible. As a client learns to better manage the emotions aroused by responding to circumstances that conflict with treatment objectives, the client is likely to increase efficacy expectations for continuing progress.

Objective 1c: Learning From Vicarious Experiences. Vicarious experiences of success and failure can influence self-efficacy by allowing an individual to observe the behavior of other persons and learn from others' successes and failures. Clients can learn to fine-tune their abilities to regulate their own behavior by imitating what they have seen work for others and by avoiding strategies they have observed leading to another's failure to achieve a similar objective. A treatment plan can set up opportunities for vicarious learning through considering participation in group therapy or a self-help group.

Not all clients are ready for group encounters, so therapists need to screen based on both group selection criteria and client expressions of willingness to try a group. It is not unusual for clients to express at least some reluctance to engage in a more public form of therapy or self-help. Yet for clients who are willing to at least experiment, the therapist can emphasize the value of comparing experiences with others who are blazing their own paths to the goal of improving their own circumstances. For those clients currently refusing even to attend one group session to evaluate its potential, the therapist can suggest further discussion at a later point in time of the benefits and limitations of group therapy. If the client agrees to write this time frame into the treatment plan, both parties will be prompted to reconsider the possibility of a group intervention at the next treatment plan review (or at some other date agreed on at the time the method is specified).

In addition to group therapy or support groups, vicarious learning can be promoted by asking clients to name anyone they know who has successfully confronted a problem related to drugs or alcohol. The treatment plan can then include the method of having the client talk to the identified per-

son(s) about their successes and failures. The client can then be encouraged to report back to the therapist or to journal in private about what the
client learned from these conversations. Therapists may also at times share
their own observations of struggles and successes among their other clients
as long as, of course, no identifying information is revealed.

A therapist should be prepared to respond to a client's request for vicarious experience through the therapist's self-disclosure of thoughts, feelings,
or behaviors associated with drugs or alcohol. Some therapists are comfortable and highly effective using their personal histories or values in a selective manner to motivate clients, whereas other therapists are reluctant to
self-disclose or do so inappropriately. Careful self-disclosure can be useful
in substance abuse therapy under the following conditions: (a) the therapist explores with the client the reason for the request, (b) the therapist has
a therapeutic rationale and intent for the disclosure, (c) the therapist feels
reasonably comfortable making the disclosure, (d) the therapist maintains
a focus on the relevance to the client, and (e) the therapist assesses and responds to the client's reaction to the disclosure.

Being caught off guard by client questions about the therapist's personal
use, opinions, or values with respect to drugs and alcohol can damage the
therapist's credibility. Even if a therapist declines to disclose personal history, the planning process is best served if the therapist can offer a convincing rationale. For example, the therapist could respond to client probes by
explaining the "Catch-22" implied in the question (M. Combs, personal
communication, November 1996):

> I must admit that I'm torn about answering your question. On one hand, if I
> were to tell you I have never had my own substance use problems, you could
> tell me I don't know enough to help you. But if I tell you I have, you could tell
> me I have my own problems, so how am I in the position help you? So either
> way, I'm not sure how it will be useful to talk about me. I'd rather focus on you
> to see if we can find any way to work together on your own concern.

This response will obviously not work for every therapist or every client, but
the point is that therapists are advised to think through not only how they
feel about personal disclosure of drug and alcohol history, but how and under what circumstances they would communicate those thoughts and feelings to a client. Therapists who are prepared to answer clients' questions in
a genuine, straightforward manner will not only earn their respect, but can
model effective communication and elicit valuable new material about vicarious and interpersonal learning regarding the broad range of substance
use issues.

Planning ways for the client to vicariously experience the outcomes, but
especially the successes, of other people who have also struggled with chem-

ical dependency or substance abuse can contribute to the client's increased self-efficacy for change. Not only does interpersonal sharing teach the client new perspectives and coping strategies, it also decreases a client's isolation and potentially enhances social support.

Objective 1d: Persuading Clients That They Should and Can Change. Verbal persuasion is the final source of information that Bandura (1977) specified for shaping efficacy expectations, but by itself trying to convince clients that they are capable of change is rarely sufficient. Regular, sincere expressions of faith in clients' abilities and potential can reinforce their efforts to change, but persuasion alone will be weak in promoting change until the clients decide to make the effort.

Recognizing the limits of verbal persuasion alerts the therapist to use it judiciously in planning a client's course of therapy. Self-efficacy theory suggests that individuals are most likely to attempt designated tasks when they believe the desired outcomes are attainable and they are reasonably sure of their abilities to attain those results. A therapist's verbal persuasion is most motivating when clients are already considering a task they have some confidence to achieve, but have not yet accomplished. Through exploration of what clients are willing to try, the therapist can selectively coax clients to endorse objectives with strong chances of yielding performance accomplishments, vicarious experiences of success, and manageable levels of emotional arousal. Although verbal persuasion without attention to other facets of a client's efficacy expectations usually misses its mark, a therapist can usefully harness persuasive efforts to the therapist's assessment of where the client is willing to focus energy and attention. The specific objectives and methods that the therapist persuades the client to accept and implement as part of the treatment plan can usefully be matched to the client's level of readiness for change.

TAILORING THE TREATMENT PLAN TO THE CLIENT'S STAGE OF READINESS FOR CHANGE

Planning treatment according to a client's assessed readiness for change ties back into the transtheoretical model of personal change (Prochaska & Norcross, 1994). The stages of change associated with the model were already described in chapter 5 in the context of making treatment recommendations that a client will accept following a substance use assessment. The client's stage of change is also crucial for the task of treatment planning because therapists who try to persuade clients to engage in activity that is inconsistent with the client's current level of readiness usually elicit client resistance in some form. For example, asking clients in the contemplation stage to take the action of abstaining from drug use before the clients have committed to taking this step and prepared themselves for the task has lower chances of keeping clients' emotional arousal at manageable levels and of giving clients experiences of successful task performance. Another example of mismatched methods would be to require the client to attend thirty Alcoholics Anonymous (AA) meetings in thirty days if the client is still in the precontemplation stage, not yet acknowledging any problem with alcohol. Clients who resist therapists' recommendations such as these are sending a message that their therapists may have initially misjudged clients' readiness to change. In such instances, therapists are recommended to alter their approaches accordingly.

To set goals and objectives that clients are willing to attempt, the therapist considers what steps are feasible given the client's circumstances to nudge clients from their current locations on the path toward change to the next logical point. Continuing from the examples given in the preceding paragraph, the therapist in the first example could try prodding a contemplative client toward preparation to take action by suggesting that the client engage in further discussion with the therapist about the perceived advantages and disadvantages of future abstinence. The client could also be asked to keep a log of current drug consumption and related thoughts and feelings, or to try abstaining or reducing consumption as an experiment for a finite period of time (perhaps a week or a month, to be negotiated with the client) with the understanding that further discussions and decisions will be made after the designated time span has ended. These methods keep the client engaged in contemplation and urge movement toward eventual action when the client is ready without foregoing the preparation stage. In the second example, the therapist could recommend that the precontemplative client attend just one AA meeting with an open mind, to see what it is like, and report back. Again the method is responsive to the client's conception of the absence of a problem, but still invites the client to gather new information that will be useful in making decisions about next steps in facing whatever circumstances brought this person without a self-perceived alcohol problem to substance abuse therapy.

These strategies are consistent with the motivational interviewing approach developed by Miller and Rollnick (1991, 2002). Motivational interviewing prepares people to change by inviting the interviewee to collaborate in the process of evoking the person's own motivation for change, and by respecting the individual's autonomy and responsibility for choices about personal change. The principles that guide motivational interviewing strategies are to express empathy, develop discrepancy, avoid argumentation, roll with resistance, and support self-efficacy. Motivational interviewing is particularly useful in the context of treatment planning. Using methods based on these principles, motivational interviewing helps establish interpersonal conditions within the therapy relationship that communicate the therapist's interest in working with the client's perspective, rather than imposing the therapist's viewpoints, thus promoting trust and hope. This approach also prompts the client to expand and explore his or her own perspective to consider both good and bad points about substance use, as well as both advantages and disadvantages of change. With this elaborated picture, clients can then be encouraged to reflect on implications of discrepancies in their own viewpoints, and to develop treatment plans that are both realistic and meaningful in light of this mutual reflection with the therapist.

In discussion of their transtheoretical model, Prochaska and Norcross (1994) pointed out that most theories of psychotherapy emphasize either insight (e.g., analytic and cognitive models) or action (e.g., behavioral therapies) goals. Their transtheoretical model presumes that change requires both. The merger of models into cognitive-behavioral approaches has similar implications. Prochaska and Norcross further listed five categories of activities people employ to change themselves, noting that different types of activities are more useful at different stages of change to stimulate transition to the next stage. Activities or methods to elevate awareness include consciousness-raising, emotional catharsis, and choosing from among available options. Action-oriented activities include modifying the stimuli that control learned responses, and controlling the contingencies that result from behavioral responses. Prochaska and Norcross further subdivided each of these categories into activities that occur at the level of subjective experience and those operating at the environmental level, again illustrating how different theories of psychotherapy emphasize different types of activities leading to preferred goals. Although the authors note the general applicability of these stages and processes to change occurring under circumstances both outside and inside of therapy relationships, the goals, objectives, and methods embedded in the transtheoretical model can be directly utilized by therapists in negotiating treatment plans with clients.

Applying this model to planning treatment for substance abusers, the choice of goals and corresponding objectives, methods, and time frames rests on determination of what the client needs to facilitate movement from a current stage of change to the next logical stage. Transitions through the first three stages of change (Precontemplation to Contemplation to Preparation) are marked by increasing awareness of a problem and insight into the dynamics that sustain or resolve the problem. For change to occur, the individual makes further transitions from these insight-oriented stages to the action-oriented stages, called Action and Maintenance. In chapter 5, the client's stage at the time of assessment was accounted for in terms of offering treatment recommendations in a manner that the client can accept.

Once this first objective is met, of getting the client to agree to try therapy, planning treatment activities that suit the client's stage of change (and relatedly provide experiences of success that will motivate further action) gives tools to keep the client invested in the therapy process. The therapist does not make change occur for clients, but helps clients realize the potential to change themselves. The transtheoretical model offers two general goals, insight and action, on which therapists and clients frequently negotiate in planning efforts aimed at changing problematic substance use.

Goal 2: Increase Insight Into the Thoughts, Feelings, and Behaviors Associated With Clients' Substance Use, Related Problems, and Potential Solutions

Objective 2a: Determining Whether There Is a Problem to Be Addressed. The client in the precontemplation stage is not yet interested in making a change. Clients who report symptoms consistent with a diagnosis of a substance use disorder, but deny that their drinking or drug use is a problem, are in this stage. So are clients who distort or minimize their actual substance use behavior, although this is obviously harder for the therapist to identify. To move to the contemplation stage, these clients would need to raise their awareness of any undesirable results of their substance use. Prochaska and Norcross (1994) recommended a few types of activities at this stage to move the precontemplative client toward contemplation. The first is consciousness-raising, including both feedback about the individual's behaviors and education about more general consequences of substance abuse. (Psychoeducational interventions are addressed more fully in chap. 7.) These activities are intended to present a fuller range of information to clients so they will be in a more knowledgeable position to decide whether they have a problem and whether they wish to change. They prompt clients to address the discrepancy between their own stated beliefs that their substance use is not problematic with the beliefs or suspicions of others who got the precontemplators to show up for therapy.

Another way to conceptualize this is for the therapist to propose further assessment as an initial treatment objective. The therapist can explain to the client that it makes little sense to decide on actions before they have a clearer, shared understanding of the situation and the problem, if in fact there is one. The objective may be phrased in terms of continuing their shared assessment of the client's complex situation, whether that entails further exploration of the role drugs or alcohol have played in the client's life, or of the relationship between the client's substance use and the interpersonal, occupational, financial, or legal problems that pushed the client to seek therapy. The neutral wording implies that the designated assessment will take place before conclusions are drawn, and that therapists will withhold opinions until they have firmer bases on which to make interpretations. This stance can be explicitly stated to clients who express doubt about the value of more assessment and therapy. The therapist can further propose that this extended assessment will be followed by a review and possible revision of the treatment plan. Both the client and therapist are likely to learn valuable new information from taking the time to discuss the client's history in greater detail. Among other lessons, the client learns that the therapist is not going to push an agenda or rush to judgment without comprehensive understanding of the uniqueness of the client's circumstances. The therapist will probably glean a clearer picture of the nature of the client's substance use and its relationship to other problems in the client's life.

As treatment progresses, the dyad can consider their joint evaluations of the extended assessment outcomes in formulating additional objectives and updating the treatment plan. Consciousness-raising interventions are probably more effective when the therapist honors the client's choices about how to use the information brought to the client's awareness. If the therapist communicates that the therapist knows the right conclusion and is just waiting for the client to see it, feedback and education will not overcome the client's resistance. When the therapist does offer feedback through interpretations or confrontations, precontemplators may hear alternative perspectives with less resistance if the therapist clarifies that this is the therapist's opinion, that clients are entitled to their own opinions, and that the therapist is interested in hearing what feedback the client has to offer.

Therapists can suggest plans to explore clients' feelings about their substance use histories. According to Prochaska and Norcross (1994), catharsis of pent-up or denied emotions can also help move clients into contemplation. Catharsis relieves internal pressure and releases energy, formerly used to ward off emotion, now available for other purposes. Sometimes the expression of deep emotion about causes, consequences, or related aspects of substance use can also help raise the client's consciousness of the negative impact of problematic behavior on the client's life. For example, a precontemplator who hinted at a traumatic initiation into marijuana use was invited to tell the story of how he started smoking pot in the first place. The client revealed that at age twelve, he was pinned down by two older brothers and their friends, and a "joint" was forced into his mouth until he inhaled several times. The client said he had never talked about that incident since it happened and recalled the fear, anger, and disgust he felt at the time. These recollections, along with other current considerations, stimulated this client to begin contemplating the possibility of quitting smoking.

By collaboratively planning therapy so that precontemplators gain increased awareness of the complexities of their situations and the feelings associated with them, such clients may make transitions into the contemplation stage of change. When clients come to acknowledge a problem that is worth addressing further in therapy, the next step is to consider options about how to address the issue.

Objective 2b: Identifying and Deciding Among Options for Responding to Problems That Have Been Targeted for Attention. Clients in the contemplation stage have acknowledged a need to change and are typically preoccupied with considerations of what to do about it. Clients who are contemplating change can spend long periods of time evaluating themselves, their environments, and their options. This necessary stage is a natural outcome of prior efforts to expand individuals' awareness of information and alternative perspectives. A first method to move clients through this stage is to generate options for how to construe the problem and how to promote change. Once potential goals or actions are clear, a second method is to weigh the pros and cons of each option. For clients to move into the preparation stage, they need to choose from among these options and commit to taking action in the foreseeable future.

The sample treatment plan in Table 6.3 revisits the case of Jason, the self-proclaimed pothead with the new job starting soon. Jason's written treatment plan summarizes a fifteen-minute discussion with his therapist in the session following his initial intake assessment, and illustrates the utilization of objectives and methods discussed in this section to facilitate transition from contemplation to preparation for action toward behavior change.

The individualized treatment plan needs to account for the reality that the transition from contemplation to preparation can be a very hard one. Many contemplators have difficulty making choices about how to confront an acknowledged problem. In such cases, the therapist can direct the focus using additional consciousness-raising and catharsis to explore with the client the barriers blocking the client from choosing a course of action. Asking clients what they believe is interfering with their decisions to take action to address identified problems will often yield insights into additional specific objectives clients need to address before they can let themselves decide to change.

Clients who express concern that family members or friends will reject or ridicule them if they no longer "party" together can plan with their therapists how to handle interpersonal tensions with particular individuals. They can also be advised to talk about their plans and feelings regarding possible change with those persons the clients are most worried about, and possibly report back to the therapist how those conversations went. (Many will find that others are more accepting and understanding than anticipated!) For clients who voice doubts that they are capable of enforcing their own decisions to change, therapists can suggest methods to boost the client's self-

TABLE 6.3

Initial Treatment Plan for Jason, Client Diagnosed With Cannabis Abuse
and Assessed in the Contemplation Stage of Readiness for Change,
Working Toward Preparation for Action

I. *Problem:* Jason has decided he will not continue to smoke marijuana once he starts his
    new job in a month, but he is unclear about the most desirable and effective strategy
    for quitting. He has been smoking daily for several months and wants to continue
    through his graduation, but he suspects it might then be hard to stop abruptly right af-
    terward when his new job begins.

    A. *Goal:* Choose and implement a workable strategy allowing Jason to refrain from
        marijuana use that might compromise his success on his new job.

        1. *Objective:* Identify and weigh all reasonable options ranging from stopping mari-
            juana use immediately to continuing current use until graduation.
            a. *Method:* List and discuss options with therapist this week and next.
            b. *Method:* Think about reactions to each option, adding to the list if other
                ideas arise, between now and next session.
            c. *Method:* In next session, discuss the pros and cons of each option, along with
                thoughts and feelings in reaction to this assessment.

        2. *Objective:* Based on assessment of pros and cons, make a choice and develop a
            plan for implementing the chosen strategy.
            a. *Method:* Decide on specific steps Jason will take to put the strategy into ac-
                tion.
            b. *Method:* Discuss anticipated barriers to taking these steps, plus how to deal
                with them.
            c. *Method:* Plan incentives and rewards for completing each step.

        3. *Objective:* Take some time off from marijuana use this week as an experiment to
            determine how easy or hard it will be when Jason is ready to stop smoking for
            the sake of his job.
            a. *Method:* Jason agrees to abstain from smoking marijuana Sunday through
                Thursday of the coming week.
            b. *Method:* Jason will report back in next week's therapy session about what this
                experiment of abstinence was like and what he learned regarding next steps.

efficacy and self-esteem. Plans can include agreements to discuss best- and
worst-case hypothetical outcomes of making a decision. During the planning process, therapists can empathize with and validate the client's feelings about being stuck as well as the client's hope for change.

Therapist expressions of empathy are crucial for creating therapeutic
conditions in which treatment plans can be made and implemented. Clients stuck in the contemplation stage face not just one decision to alter
problematic substance use; they confront daily, hourly, and even moment-
by-moment chances to change their minds. The client who decides to quit
smoking, drinking, or using so much (or at all) is repeatedly bombarded
with both internal and external messages to go ahead and indulge one
more time and start enforcing the decision "tomorrow." Beer ads, social
events, drug-oriented music, an available "stash," the promises of quick euphoria and distance from troubles are among the signals of opportunity to

continue chasing the familiar highs. Clients who have time and time again postponed decisions to change can come to doubt whether they can or want to enforce their own commitments, which may actually serve as a justification for simply giving into an immediate urge to use rather than suffering the agony of resisting the inevitable. They may tell their therapists that they cannot make decisions about how to address their problems because either they do not want to change or they do not see the point in trying in light of multiple experiences of vowing to control their substance use and then not doing so. Therapists who empathically encourage ruminations on the possibilities and difficulties of changing behavior will help clients to vent frustrations and other negative affect. This activity furthermore gives a client and therapist time to anticipate exactly what situations may goad the client into using excessively despite decisions to abstain from or limit substance use.

It is in those moments, when clients are telling themselves that "just one more time won't hurt, so why not?" or "If I don't just go ahead and do it, I'll be immobilized by my preoccupation with wanting to do it anyway," that clients most need tools to counter their impulses to postpone decisions to take control. Unless therapists can empathize with the strong conflicts contemplators feel as they move to prepare for change, and can empathize in a manner that clients can hear and believe, clients have few reasons to trust in therapists' expertise. Thus, in negotiating treatment plans, it is essential for therapists to offer or endorse methods that fully address clients' obstacles to change as well as their motivations to change.

Methods that can be discussed with contemplators and written directly into treatment plans include (a) identifying optional responses to specified problems, (b) weighing those options, (c) addressing any barriers to making decisions, and (d) choosing a viable strategy for responding to the problem. By breaking the process of contemplating a decision into meaningful steps, the therapist validates the contemplator's dilemma and offers guidance toward the objective of taking responsibility for choosing a course of action. In this manner, the therapist meets the contemplator at the point where the client is willing to focus and proceeds at a pace that the client is able to progress.

Objective 2c: Preparing to Undertake a Course of Action. When the client has reached the point of deciding on a change strategy and making initial gestures toward implementing that strategy, the client has reached Prochaska and Norcross' (1994) preparation stage of change. Individuals with substance use disorders may present themselves for therapy at this stage, especially if they are having trouble enforcing changes in behavior that they have committed to make, or they may be clients continuing therapy efforts that started with a different therapist during an earlier stage of change. Regardless, clients in the preparation stage have made important decisions about how they wish to tackle problematic substance abuse and have established some groundwork on which to base their planned actions. However, they have yet to manifest significant change in substance-related behaviors or consequences. They may be encouraged by early indications of success in moving this far toward change, but they can be just as quickly discouraged by even small signs of regress. To effectively individualize treatment plans for clients in the preparation stage, therapists need to employ methods that reinforce even small steps toward treatment objectives and also address obstacles to the implementation of the chosen strategy.

Clients who are strongly committed to a decision and capable of undertaking relevant action move quickly through the preparation stage. More often substance abuse clients struggle with uncertainty about the strength of their convictions or the extent of their abilities to follow through with the options they have selected for responding to problems. The inherent reinforcing qualities and easy availability of psychoactive substances to habitual users conflict with increasing awareness of the problematic consequences of habitual substance use, creating ambivalence even in clients who are preparing to change their habits. They sometimes vacillate from preparation back to contemplation as they encounter unanticipated complexities or setbacks. The process of treatment planning can help clients maintain progress by spelling out realistic expectations of the course of change and by providing tools for combating barriers to continuing progress.

When planning treatment with a client in the preparation stage, the therapist can help break down a more abstract strategy on which the client has decided into concrete tasks. Often agreeing on time frames in which a task is to be carried out assists clients in enforcing decisions. Therapists can offer time in session to anticipate possible outcomes of specific tasks and to plan how the client might respond to these different outcomes. A therapist can also build into the treatment plan time for discussing the actual outcomes of a client's attempts at implementing tasks that are part of the larger strategy, with the stated objectives of rewarding the client's successes and learning from mistakes.

A good example of this process came about with Paul, who was preparing to abstain from alcohol use on an upcoming business trip by inviting a good friend, Karen, to travel with him. He told his therapist he knew he would drink if he went alone, and because Karen does not drink, he felt confident he could avoid drinking when he was with her. However, on further questioning, Paul admitted that Karen was not aware of Paul's plan to quit drinking, nor his reason for asking her to accompany him. The therapist thus proposed spending some time in the present session, because the trip was coming up soon, talking about what might happen if Paul did or did not let Karen know what was going on with him. Paul agreed to this plan, acknowledging that the temptation to drink could still be high and might make him cranky even with Karen alongside.

When the therapist pointed out that Karen might be confused or upset by Paul's irritability if she did not know what was causing it, Paul decided he should tell her about his intentions. The therapist asked if he was worried that Karen might not want to go if she was aware of his plan, but Paul expressed certainty that she would be interested in helping him. He just did not know how and when to bring it up with Karen. So the therapist worked with Paul to generate a plan for where and when he would raise this topic, and the rest of the session was spent role playing what Paul wanted to say to Karen and how he could respond to her possible reactions.

During the preparation stage, clients lay foundations of commitment, effort, and responsibility from which more substantial actions will be launched. From the understanding of the problem cultivated in working through the precontemplation stage, and from the expanded awareness of possible responses contemplated in the second stage of change, the client decides on a response and establishes the cognitive, affective, behavioral, and interpersonal conditions under which change can occur. This preparation in terms of how the client chooses to think, feel, act, and relate can be facilitated by carefully negotiating treatment tasks at this stage to match the intentions the client has come to endorse. Prochaska and Norcross (1994) indicated that individuals in this stage need to set priorities and can experience self-liberation through the conscious creation of new alternatives.

Progress through these first three stages of change parallels clients' acquisition of insights into the nature of personal problems and the process of changing them. As clients expand their insights into the desirability and feasibility of change, the goal of taking explicit action to reduce problematic substance use emerges in prominence.

Goal 3: Engage Clients in Action to Promote Change

By the time individuals are ready to focus on the goals of action and maintenance, they have already exerted significant efforts toward prioritizing and planning. An action plan specifies criteria of change, often in terms of behaviors that demonstrate a difference from prior habits. Some examples include a client with a diagnosed alcohol dependence who successfully refrains from drinking for an entire week and resolves to continue abstinence. A cocaine binger overcomes former reluctance to try residential treatment, after numerous failed attempts to quit drugs through outpatient treatment, and checks himself into an inpatient treatment facility. A client who has been planning to stop smoking marijuana turns down an invitation from a friend to attend a party where the client knows people will be smoking, and instead attends a group therapy session for the first time.

To help clients put insight into action, therapists can propose altering the stimuli or consequences that shape client behaviors. When the goal is to change patterns of substance use, clients need to exert some control over the stimuli to which they are exposed, often by avoiding contact with certain people or situations that elicit temptation to abuse substances and replacing those stimuli with new stimuli associated with healthier and still rewarding behaviors. Treatment plans at this stage of change also acknowledge that many stimuli that activate urges to drink or use drugs are not under the individual's control. In designing action objectives to deal with uncontrollable stimuli, the therapy dyad aims to practice new responses to "trigger" situations. Emphasis is placed on the outcomes of the client's behavior, with attention to promoting reinforcements to increase the likelihood of continuing new learned responses. Also the punishing consequences of continuing old habits may be analyzed and, to the degree possible, accentuated to help clients resist resumption of behaviors they are trying to change. For example, the client in the action stage of change may endorse the objective of reminding himself whenever he feels the old, familiar impulse to get high about the worst-case scenarios he encountered during his days of heavy drug use.

Prochaska and Norcross (1994) demonstrated that methods derived in particular from behavioral and cognitive approaches fit the action and maintenance stages of change. The two general objectives and corresponding treatment methods offered next borrow extensively from their formulation of therapy at the action stages of client change. The objectives vary in terms of focus on classically versus operantly conditioned behaviors, and the methods are distinguished in terms of the extent to which the individual has direct control over the stimuli or outcomes influencing individual learning and behavior.

Objective 3a: Severing The Connection Between Particular Stimuli and Learned Responses.   From a classical conditioning paradigm, this objective concentrates on extinguishing a learned behavior tied to the substance use disorder. Of course this objective can also be worded in a treatment plan in terms much more familiar to the client than psychological jargon. The therapist informs the client that the purpose is to change behavior by cutting the link between a signal (that substances are available and desirable) and a response (abusing a substance) that the individual has learned to make to that signal. The therapist further explains that this is accomplished by learning new responses that shrink the power of the signal and reducing one's exposure to potent signals. For example, the stated plan could be to help a client find alternative, healthier means of reacting to boredom, anger, sadness, or frustration without resorting to drug or alcohol use. In another case, the plan might be to avoid exposure to people, events, or other cues that the client associates with drug use. In both examples, the action involves substituting a new behavior for a former one. In the first method, a new behavior is learned to respond to the same old difficult emotions. In the second case, the plan is to make changes in the client's environment so that the stimuli that trigger substance use are less available. Prochaska and Norcross (1994) distinguished these two methods of altering classically conditioned responses by pointing out that the first, counterconditioning, focuses on changing the individual's experience, which the second, stimulus control, emphasizes change of the person's environment.

Counterconditioning is an especially useful method when a stimulus that elicits substance use cannot be strictly controlled. This is a crucial concern for substance abusers who have become accustomed to reaching for their substance of choice when family members get on their nerves, when they feel blocked from completing required tasks, or when the end of the work week arrives because these types of events cannot be entirely eliminated. On occasion, spouses, parents, and offspring will continue to annoy the individual, work will still need to be done, and paychecks keep arriving. The client who wants to stop using drugs or alcohol in response to such stimuli needs not only to be aware of alternative responses besides using substances; the client must actually employ those new responses. The client's action plan is to implement new responses to signals that formerly elicited abuse of drugs or alcohol.

A treatment plan for a client in the action stage helps countercondition the client by stating the new responses the client agrees to emit in response to unavoidable stimuli previously linked to substance use. The plan should also include criteria that will indicate when the client has successfully completed the action, along with stated intentions to examine the client's thoughts, feelings, and experiences of the new behavior. When the plan gives the client clear ideas about what to expect both from the therapist and the process of trying something new, the client may be more motivated to follow through with the action.

In situations where the client has some degree of control over level of exposure to a stimulus that cues substance abuse, treatment methods for promoting new behavior involve minimizing the client's exposure. The therapist typically cannot control the stimulus for the client, but rather teaches the client means of stimulus control. Meeting this objective goes beyond listing situations or people the client will wish to avoid (although this is an important first step). The therapist will further inquire about what it will be like for the client to stay away from triggering stimuli, how the client expects to minimize exposure, and how the client feels about doing so. Methods to build into a plan include identifying particular events that will confront the client with stimuli the client wishes to avoid, articulating specific steps the client can take to minimize exposure, providing behavioral rehearsal of those steps during therapy sessions, giving homework to implement those steps in a relevant context outside of session, and reviewing outcomes of actions aimed at stimulus control in subsequent therapy sessions.

To illustrate, Juanita has successfully stopped smoking cigarettes for one week and two days. She knows it will be hard to deal with urges to smoke when she is studying for upcoming exams. Her favorite place to study used to be a campus coffeehouse, but she tells her therapist that the smoky atmosphere there could add to the temptation to light up a cigarette. The therapist suggests taking some time to decide on other places to study, and on how Juanita can resist inclinations or invitations to go to the coffee house. The treatment plan Juanita and her therapist generated together can be viewed in Table 6.4.

Another example of planning stimulus control involves Angie, who stopped smoking pot as soon as she discovered she was unexpectedly pregnant. She has decided to keep the baby, but the new stresses of her changing circumstances make her want to indulge a familiar habit of listening to music to help her relax. The problem is that in the past she typically

TABLE 6.4
Maintenance Treatment Plan for Juanita, Client Diagnosed With
Nicotine Dependence and Assessed in Transition From Action
to Maintenance Stages of Change

I. *Problem:* Juanita wants to maintain her initial success at quitting smoking for nine days, but she is worried that she might relapse if exposed to certain cues and triggers.
   A. *Goal:* Abstain from all use of cigarettes and learn to handle potential relapse triggers.
      1. *Objective:* Stay away as much as possible from places where she knows people will be smoking or cigarettes will be available.
         a. *Method:* List in session the places and situations Juanita plans to avoid.
         b. *Method:* Specify alternatives Juanita can use, including other things she can do and other places she can go.
         c. *Method:* Practice in session how to talk with friends and family about her decisions to avoid trigger situations.
      2. *Objective:* Develop ways to resist urges to smoke when unavoidably exposed to environmental tobacco smoke or other cigarette cues.
         a. *Method:* Identify the kinds of situations that are likely to be hard to entirely avoid and also likely to tempt Juanita to smoke.
         b. *Method:* List possible responses Juanita could make to such events without smoking.
         c. *Method:* Explore Juanita's thought and feelings about these nonsmoking options.
         d. *Method:* Decide how Juanita can reward herself when she successfully deals with any of the identified triggers without smoking.

---

smoked pot while listening to favorite music. Angie tells her therapist that a recent attempt to play these songs was anything but relaxing because she found herself preoccupied with cravings to get high. The therapist recommended discussion of other strategies Angie could use to control this stimulus and manage her stress, perhaps by choosing other music or other activities. Angie accepted the rationale for this plan, but indicated sadness at the prospect of giving up music she loved along with her drug use. Her therapist explained that their plan could include future consideration of reintroducing the music once the new habit of abstaining from smoking was more firmly established. In other words, controlling the stimulus until its connection to the learned response has been extinguished may eventually lead to the possibility of increasing exposure to the neutered stimulus; in this case, Angie's beloved music.

When the learned behaviors of substance use are entrenched to the point where individuals see the behaviors as parts of their identities, extinguishing the behaviors is rarely quick or easy. Even when the individual has reached the action stage of change, unrealistic expectations and fears about the pace of success are likely. The therapist can use the ongoing process of planning treatment to prepare the client to anticipate ups and downs, to rely on the support of the therapist in learning from both successes and failures, and to maintain faith and hope in eventual progress and increasing efficacy. The therapist can assure the client that, although the nature of change can be frustrating at times, the steps the client is taking are worthwhile and the therapist commends the client's efforts.

Objective 3b: Changing the Rewards and Punishments That Follow Behavior. From an operant conditioning perspective, substance abuse recurs because of the strongly reinforcing properties of the behavior (detailed in chap. 4). Therapy in the action stage of change can utilize operant learning principles by planning methods to modify the patterns of reinforcement for the client's behaviors. According to Prochaska and Norcross (1994), to the extent that the consequences of behavior are under control of either member of the therapy dyad, the method of contingency management involves identifying and applying meaningful rewards for behaviors that are incompatible with substance abuse. If healthier, incompatible behaviors, such as abstinence, result in desirable outcomes, especially over time, the "action" client is more likely to repeat the newly learned response as an alternative to continuing substance use.

As behavioral therapists have often noted, the nature of reinforcement is tricky because the potency of a reward varies across individuals and because the factors reinforcing an individual's behavior are not always obvious (Cahoon & Cosby, 1972). Functional analysis is prescribed in behavioral therapies to tease out the reinforcement mechanisms particular to individual clients. With those who abuse psychoactive substances, analysis of reinforcement patterns in the service of contingency management should not underestimate the strength of rewards the client derives from using the substance. The pleasure and relief that come with the impact of the chemical on brain functions are frequently bolstered by social reinforcers.

What this means in planning substance abuse treatment is that efforts to modify the contingencies of behavior, starting with a functional analysis of reinforcement patterns, will work better if the therapist acknowledges the benefits as well as the costs the client has incurred from substance use (Sobell, Sobell, & Sheahan, 1976; Tucker, Donavan, & Marlatt, 1999). In addition, clients are more likely to collaborate in planning with the therapist who validates the sense of loss (i.e., negative punishment by withdrawal of a reinforcer) and fears of not ever finding an equally gratifying reinforcer. Consistent with motivational interviewing principles (Miller & Rollnick, 2002), the therapist needs to balance this empathy with consciousness-raising about the detrimental consequences of continuing use, thus developing discrepancy.

Empathy and discrepancy are important in planning treatment in the action stages of change for two reasons. First, the client's heightened awareness of such strong, mixed motivations for and against changing behavior helps to anticipate the difficulties associated with taking action that achieves the criterion goal. When clients (and therapists) understand that the desired consequences of action are not always immediate and that competing pulls contribute to a gradual and often erratic process of change, they are better equipped to navigate the journey.

Second, the therapist's stance of empathy with discrepancy communicates the therapist's appreciation of the salience of reinforcers competing with the client's attempts to change. The therapist's comprehension of the client's competing motivations helps the therapist "roll with resistance." A client who senses that the therapist shares the difficulty of the client's struggle to maintain action tends to feel supported rather than criticized. Under these conditions, the client will feel safer in carrying out the action plan, more confident that even small steps are worthwhile, and even immediate failures can be learning opportunities to modify the plan and promote eventual success. Such experiences also contribute to increases in the client's self-efficacy for change.

The research literature on treatments of substance use disorders contains several studies of contingency management methods where the rewards for client behavior consistent with therapy goals were under the therapist's control (e.g., Budney, Higgins, Radonovich, & Novey, 2000; Carroll, Sinha, Nich, Babuscio, & Rounsaville, 2002; Higgins, 1999; Higgins, Wong, Badger, Ogden, & Dantona, 2000; Tidey, O'Neill, & Higgins, 2002). Token economies and voucher systems, in which clients earn vouchers by exhibiting treatment compatible behaviors, have been widely used in inpatient or residential settings to reinforce abstinence, clean urine screens, and progress toward treatment goals. The vouchers can later be exchanged for desirable commodities or privileges. Applications to outpatient treatment have also been successfully utilized.

Evidence indicates that voucher systems are generally successful in reducing substance abuse during treatment, but that these gains tend to drop off relatively soon after treatment ends (Epstein, Hawkins, Covi, Umbricht, & Preston, 2003; Rawson et al., 2002). This finding may be related to the problems many substance abusers have rewarding themselves based on contingencies that are less immediately salient than the reinforcements provided by consuming their drug of choice. When the reward (token, privilege, etc.) is under the control of a party external to the client, such as the therapist or treatment provider, clients do not have access to that reward until they perform the contingent response. In contrast, when it is up to clients to reinforce themselves for actions that are consistent with treatment or after-care objectives and incompatible with continuing substance abuse, the conflict with competing rewards emerges. This is crucial to address in outpatient therapies where the client cannot rely on external parties for much of the time that the client's response and reward contingencies need to be managed. In the less controlled environments where nonresidential therapies play out, the client must learn to control her or his own rewards and responses to the extent feasible.

B.F. Skinner wrote that the greatest flaw in human nature is the tendency to prefer easy, immediate, but potentially harmful consequences over rewards that take more time and effort to obtain, even if their overall benefits to the individual are greater. For substance abusers, making choices to forego substance abuse and seek other kinds of reinforcement is indeed a challenge that must be faced to maintain changes initiated in therapy.

Thus, treatment planning in the action and maintenance stages of change introduces contingency management strategies of both types: (a) where an external party controls administration of the reinforcers for new behavior, and (b) where the client applies self-reinforcement. The former may be more useful in the early phases of action, when clients are more inclined to punish themselves for incomplete efforts or outright failures to reach target behaviors. The client may also struggle with inconsistent motivation to carry out a self-reward plan contingent on target behavior. An example would be the client who decided to buy herself a new garment after one full week of sobriety, but then went shopping before the goal was accomplished or talked herself out of the purchase even after successfully meeting the goal because she had struggled so much with cravings during the week that she did not feel she deserved the new outfit. The therapist can explain to the client that,

As you take steps in the direction we've agreed on, I'll do what I can to provide and point out rewards occurring along the way. I want to support your efforts. But another goal I have in mind is to help you develop a solid ability to reward yourself for positive steps you're taking and to recognize when you're getting some good results along the way to your ultimate goals. That way you can learn to keep progress moving in a direction you're satisfied with even when I'm not there to talk about it with you.

This therapist statement alludes not only to efforts to control the consequences on which the client's behavior is contingent, but also to the method of changing the client's responses to anticipated outcomes even when the circumstances cannot be influenced at the environmental level. For example, an alcohol dependent client in early remission cannot change the fact that many grocery stores include aisles displaying alcohol, which has in the past provided liquid reinforcement for shopping. However, the client can learn to modify the experience of grocery shopping in anticipation of the urges and cravings stimulated by a glimpse of that liquor aisle. Prochaska and Norcross (1994) referred to *reevaluation* as the method of changing reactions to expected outcomes when contingencies are not modified. For the client who is not in a position to entirely avoid grocery stores (or convenience stores, restaurants, beer commercials on TV, etc.) and the consequent cravings, the treatment plan could include time to discuss alternate interpretations of the circumstances and behavioral options the client has in response to those various interpretations. In the prior example, the client could reinterpret the urges incited by the liquor aisle as challenging but not compulsory, and grocery shopping could alternatively be viewed as an opportunity to demonstrate resolve rather than as an automatic "beer run."

Reevaluation and generation of alternative interpretations are interventions utilizing cognitive restructuring techniques. In the process of planning treatment, the therapist advises cognitive restructuring to analyze the client's motivations, behaviors, and their outcomes with objectives of identifying maladaptive thought processes and replacing them with messages that facilitate confidence, action, and growth. Research on cognitive therapies with substance abusers suggests that treatment effects show up later in treatment, but are maintained longer after treatment when compared with strictly behavioral treatments such as contingency management through token economies or voucher programs (Epstein et al., 2003; Rawson et al., 2002).

Although the research findings could be perceived as a horse race between behavioral and cognitive interventions, from a planning perspective it is more viable to think of building a structure for therapy using multiple available tools and offering the client a coherent blueprint (Onken, Carroll, Rawson, Higgins, & Marlatt, 2000). Giving the client compellingly integrated strategies as part of an action plan helps the therapist sustain motivated action toward treatment goals in the latter stages of change.

*   *   *

I described treatment planning as a continuous process of offering recommendations, negotiating strategies, and encouraging client choice. Through careful and collaborative planning, the therapist develops a meaningful structure for the course of treatment and promotes increased motivation and self-efficacy on the part of the client. This is accomplished by providing a rationale for goals and strategies tailored to the client's degree of self-efficacy and readiness for change. Because clients with substance use disorders often embody insufficient senses of structure, motivation, or efficacy to promote change (if not all three), effective planning establishes therapeutic conditions under which substance abuse can be potentially reduced and positive changes in behavior can be undertaken.

In this chapter, I focused on the rationale for collaborative treatment planning along with overarching goals and objectives of therapy to address substance use disorders. Note that the goals do not automatically prescribe abstinence from all substance use, but are designed for each client with that individual's interests, abilities, and motives in mind. The next four chapters cover specific forms of intervention used to operationalize treatment objectives.

Psychoeducation in Substance Abuse Therapy

Frequently, if not always, attempts to reduce the deleterious impact of substance use disorders involve new learning on the part of both the client and the therapist. Psychoeducation combines interventions that provide new information or refine the use of information a person already possesses with careful attention to the individual's cognitive, affective, and behavioral responses to that information. Consistent with an educational foundation and a process-oriented philosophy of psychotherapy, psychoeducation in the treatment of substance abuse disorders is a form of technology transfer—a means to teach important information along with means to apply it. Psychoeducation crafted to fit the client's interests and needs is a useful and often necessary component of therapeutic treatment plans for clients who abuse substances. This chapter outlines the types and methods of psychoeducation that may be relevant to addictions therapists, their clients, and their supervisors and trainers.

My premise in this chapter is that psychoeducation works most effectively when viewed as an interactive process. Clients learn much from their therapists, but they have much to teach as well. Similar learning potential exists in the interaction between therapists in training and their supervisors. The discussion to follow thus focuses on information about substance abuse and its treatment that both therapists and clients can share in a manner that will promote both client change and the therapeutic relationship. It is crucial not only to know relevant facts, but how to communicate them and how to engage others in dialogue about their relevance.

Psychoeducational interventions can teach a client powerful lessons about (a) how therapy works and what to expect, (b) what past or continuing substance use has meant to the client and how it is affecting the client, and (c) how to motivate efforts toward recovery from problems, minimize risks of continuing use (if any), and take active steps toward beneficial change. For the therapist, psychoeducational strategies provide tools for facilitating client insight and action. Furthermore, employing such interventions also can stimulate therapists to enrich their own understanding of substance use problems and their treatment. The intricacies of disordered drug or alcohol use encompass so many variations on biological, genetic, environmental, and psychological themes that all professionals involved in treating substance abuse retain room to expand their own knowledge in addition to educating their clients.

Supervisors and trainers of therapists can also utilize psychoeducational interventions to help trainees extend and apply their knowledge of addictions treatment. This form of intervention can also be used to encourage trainees to explore their own attitudes and conflicts regarding both psychoactive substance use and clients who abuse drugs and alcohol. Furthermore, psychoeducation in supervision can motivate supervisees to develop good clinical judgment skills and continue their own education and research beyond their formal training. Supervisors and trainers of therapists learning to work with substance use disorders will wield greater impact if they engage in their own ongoing education about the ever-evolving realm of substance abuse treatment.

Psychoeducation embedded in alcohol or drug therapy aims to provide the client with learning opportunities that are consistent both with the client's level of readiness and the phase of the therapeutic relationship. Over the course of treatment, therapists will educate clients about some or all of the following topics: (a) the processes of therapy and recovery; (b) the types, actions, and effects of psychoactive substances; (c) addiction and its behavioral, neurobiological, and health implications; and (d) means of counteracting addictive behaviors. Each of these topics in turn is addressed in this chapter in terms of what the therapist needs to know about the topic and what the therapist needs to consider in educating the client about each topic.

HOW THERAPY WORKS AND WHAT TO EXPECT

The preceding chapters have demonstrated that both the therapy process and the personal change process are frequently characterized as sets of transitions through definable and somewhat predictable series of stages. Effective therapists utilize the characteristics of the therapy relationship at each stage to navigate the course of therapy. The client's reactions to each phase of therapy depend in part on where the client stands in terms of the process of change. The therapist's choice of an appropriate psychoeducational strategy derives from the therapist's evolving understanding of the present stage of the therapy relationship and the client's point in the change process.

It is often constructive for the therapist to offer the client some explanation of how therapy works and how change occurs. The specific nature of this psychoeducation is shaped by the therapist's predictions of the client's response to particular information at that time. In the initial stage of therapy, psychoeducation about the nature of therapy can help clients consider the potential utility of therapy as an option. If the client chooses to continue, psychoeducation helps prepare him or her to use therapy to decide what problems are to be addressed. The assumption is that clients who have information about what to expect plus a chance to ask questions and express concerns, doubts, or hopes about therapy are in a better position to decide if and how they will engage in therapy.

To help the client learn where to start and how to move forward, therapists first need to determine what expectations the client has for therapy and to estimate the client's level of readiness to change. Some clients come with no prior therapy experience (although they may have some expectations, realistic or otherwise, about what therapy will be like). Other clients bring backgrounds of past substance abuse treatment or mental health therapy, which can vary from minimal to extensive and from beneficial to inert to detrimental experiences. In each case, the therapist helps establish rapport with a new client by finding out the client's perspective on therapy and by informing the client of the therapist's understanding of how therapy works. Clarifying expectations, rights, responsibilities, and possible tasks sets the stage for the work to follow.

Addressing Therapeutic Confidentiality and Its Limits

Early in therapy, clients are educated about confidentiality in the therapy relationship. Although it is, as a matter of course, crucial for clients to be clearly informed of limitations on confidentiality, it is equally important that the therapist emphasize the protections of confidentiality. Many clients who present for substance abuse treatment have encountered some kind of trouble that led to the referral, and these clients are understandably concerned about what the therapist will do with any information the client reveals. Sometimes this concern is quite overt, and clients will ask whether the therapist is going to talk to the client's spouse, parents, probation officer, or employer. Even if the client does not raise the question, the therapist has the responsibility to inform clients of their rights to confidentiality within ethical and legal limits. Ideally, confidentiality needs to be established with each treatment provider to promote rapport with that individual.

Therapists can add to rapport by expressing their own appreciation of the value of confidentiality. For example, the therapist can say,

I want you to know that what we say in here stays between you and me, except under a few conditions, which I will talk about in a minute. But first I want to emphasize how important I believe confidentiality is to the work we can do together, because I know it's hard to trust someone with personal information unless you believe it will be held in confidence. So I want you to know that confidentiality a professional value which I take very seriously.

Then the therapist can add information about situations in which confidentiality cannot be guaranteed, such as when the client reports intent to hurt her or himself or another person; when the client reports knowledge of abuse of a child, elderly, or disabled person; or if the client's records are needed for a medical emergency or subpoenaed by a court of law. The therapist also explains that if any third party requests information about the client outside of these limiting conditions or if the client wishes for the therapist to provide information to a third party, disclosure will be made only with the written, informed consent of the client. Questions the client might have about confidentiality and disclosure are invited and discussed as part of this psychoeducation about therapy.

The rights of minors in many states to seek substance abuse treatment without parental knowledge or consent has already been noted in chapter 5. If the client is a minor brought by the client's parent(s), the therapist first discusses confidentiality and its constraints with both the client and the parent or legal guardian. In the minor client's presence, the responsible adult is informed of existing rights, according to relevant state law, of parental access to the client's record and to consultation with the therapist about the nature of therapy sessions. The therapist can explain to the adult that the potential for therapeutic progress can be enhanced if the parent is willing to grant additional confidentiality so that the client can speak freely to the therapist without worrying that everything the client says will be automatically reported to the parent. This request can be delivered with the assurance that if anything comes up that the therapist feels the parent has the right to know, the therapist will work with the client to decide how to inform the parent. If the parent or guardian agrees, and after that adult leaves the session, the therapist goes over confidentiality again with the minor client to be sure the client understands, to see how the client reacts without the parent present, and to address any questions the client might have.

Setting Realistic Therapy Goals

When clients enter a new therapy relationship with unrealistic or demoralized expectations, the therapist addresses these directly by specifying the importance of creating realistic goals and objectives. The therapist tells the client that therapy ideally involves the two of them working together to come up with goals that are meaningful to the client and appear feasible to both participants. Also, as goals are established, they will identify and choose workable strategies for attaining the therapy goals.

In the process of deciding and approaching the client's goals, the client can expect the therapist's nonjudgmental attention and support for a specified period of time on a regular basis. The client can also expect that the therapist will provide feedback and challenges to the client along the way. The therapist further requests that the client share thoughts and feelings about the course of therapy as it evolves, communicating the client's right to expect the therapist's responsiveness to the client's feedback. This explicit consideration of what the client can expect from therapy is especially useful with those substance abusers who enter therapy with some resentment at the prospect of being told what they must do.

Establishing Ground Rules

Along with educating clients about the value of exercising client choice and input in the therapy process, initial psychoeducation about therapy clarifies boundaries and ground rules of therapy. The therapist indicates what is expected of clients as well as what clients can expect in therapy. As soon as substance use concerns emerge as a focus in therapy, clear expectations should be communicated about reporting substance use. At a minimum, the therapist asks that the client refrain from coming to sessions under the influence, and that the client agree to respond honestly to the therapist's questions each session about any substance use since the last session.

The Abstinence Expectation.   With respect to the first expectation of coming to session clean and sober, therapists should be specific according to their personal stances on this issue, taking the client's response to this expectation into consideration. Some therapists require that the client abstain from substance use from the time they awake on the day of a therapy session. Others expect at least twenty-four hours free from substance use prior to a session to avoid the possibility that the client will be experiencing a hangover or acute withdrawal during a session. Still other therapists insist that the client completely forego recreational substance use during the course of therapy. The therapist needs to be clear about expectations in a manner that is true to the therapist's own beliefs and values, but the therapist is also exhorted to be responsive to the client's level of motivation to comply with the therapist's conditions.

Adequate psychoeducation does not mean simply informing the client of expectations, but also involves providing a rationale and being receptive to the client's reactions. The therapist explains that coming to sessions sober is expected for a few reasons. First, the client is less likely to effectively use and remember the time in session if he or she is under the influence. Second, the therapist believes that more productive work can be undertaken if the client's mental and emotional functioning are not chemically altered. Third, the client's travel to and from the session is risky if she or he has been using substances that day. The motivation of clients who willingly agree to this condition is typically reinforced by such rationale. For clients skeptical of the need to comply or lacking confidence in ability to comply, the therapist's stated rationale provides a springboard for further discussion.

Although the therapist is advised to converse with the client about reactions to this abstinence expectation, the therapist still holds to the expectation of the client's commitment. Clients may try to convince the therapist that being "high" is actually a normal state of mind for them, and thus is not a barrier to their functioning. Clients may also say they will try, but cannot promise, or may agree while nonverbally communicating that they do not take the requirement seriously. In these circumstances, the therapist asks the client to elaborate, showing interest in addressing barriers to compliance, and letting the client know what will happen if the client violates the expectation. If the client remains unwilling to commit to abstaining prior to session, the therapist can raise the topic of possible referral to more intensive treatment.

The therapist may wish to distinguish between expectation of client effort and insistence on outcome. In other words, the therapist communicates the expectations that the client will make a good faith effort to abstain from substance use prior to therapy sessions and requests that the client cancel the session if the client has been using drugs or drinking that day. However, the therapist who treats substance abusers will probably on occasion have clients show up under the influence despite stated agreements and perhaps the best of intentions. It is often useful, especially with clients who inquire directly, to inform them early in therapy that if the client is unable to make or maintain the commitment, it indicates something important is happening that demands immediate attention in the session. For the therapist, this is a primary reason for stating the abstinence expectation at the beginning of therapy, so there is a shared context for exploring the client's actual success or difficulty with compliance over the course of therapy.

Some therapists will decline to continue working with a client who continues drinking or using drugs, or will cancel the session on the spot if the client shows up under the influence. A more fruitful strategy with clients who do not demonstrate total compliance with the abstinence expectation is to maintain interaction as long (within agreed time frames and therapeutic boundaries) as the client is willing and able to talk appropriately about what is interfering with compliance and how compliance can be realistically enforced in the future. Clients who are too inebriated to converse in a reasonable manner can be referred for detoxification, but a client who had a drink with lunch or smoked one "hit" of marijuana before a session may be capable of interaction with the therapist. If the client shows up for session for the first time under the influence, the therapist definitely does not ignore this, but rather initiates candid discussion of what the therapist observes and what the client has to say about it. The therapist explains that although this incident gives the therapist a better understanding of what the client is like under the influence, the therapist adamantly asks that the client recommit to attending all future sessions sober, reiterating the rationale. The therapist informs the client that this agreement will be discussed again at the next session when the client is sober, and that if the client comes to session under the influence again, the therapist will refer the client for more intensive treatment.

As long as the client is capable of reasonable interaction with the therapist, meeting with the client who shows up under the influence also gives time for the client to "sober up" or "come down" from the substance. If the client is not able to engage appropriately in the session, the therapist may choose to end early, and may offer to follow up with a phone call in a day or two to see how the client is doing and to confirm the client's intentions to attend future sessions sober. Before the client leaves the premises, however, the therapist should also find out how the client got to the session. If the client drove and there is any doubt about the client's capacity to drive safely, the therapist asks that a third party be contacted to drive the client home. To the extent that the therapist has used psychoeducation to inform and discuss these potential outcomes with the client ahead of time, the procedures, if necessary, are less likely to elicit resistance from the client who knows about them. Advance notice probably also increases the likelihood that the therapy alliance can be maintained past this point of noncompliance.

Regular Report of Recent Substance Use. The second minimum expectation of the client is to honestly report any substance use between therapy sessions. The therapist educates the client about intentions to explicitly question the client every session about recent use, with the rationale that the therapist needs an accurate picture of what the client is doing to work effectively with the client on addressing therapy goals. If the client's response indicates the need, the therapist explains that the purpose of asking is not to shame or punish the client, but to create a climate in which the topic can be straightforwardly addressed. The therapist maintains the intervention over time by then asking the client each session in a nonjudgmental manner whether the client has used any substances between sessions. The therapist remains responsive to the client's questions or concerns about this procedure as therapy continues. The therapist should also be prepared to address and explore answers from the client that are vague or evasive in a manner that expresses interest and concern rather than suspicion or blame.

If the therapist has not established this ground rule at the beginning of therapy or at the point when substance use concerns are raised, and then later suspects that the client is using substances in a manner that is inconsistent with the treatment contract, it can be quite awkward to raise the question then. Therapists may wonder whether they are accurately interpreting indications at hand and worry about offending the client if the therapist's hunch is wrong. This fear can lead the therapist to avoid or minimize the question. From the client's perspective, such a question from the therapist can be off-putting if the therapist is incorrect and threatening if the therapist is accurate but has not provided a compelling rationale for the question. The client who is using substances, perhaps despite agreements to the contrary, but who has not agreed to regularly report any substance use to the therapist, may be inclined to deny the behavior or otherwise falsify information to protect from detection with unknown consequences.

Elaboration of the Treatment Plan

After mutual expectations and ground rules are established, psychoeducation about the process of therapy continues with specification of the goals and strategies to be employed. Chapter 6 already alluded to the use of treatment planning as an intervention with psychoeducational components. Through collaboration in developing or revising a plan for therapy, clients learn something about how the therapy process is conducted according to this particular therapist. The client must also decide whether addressing substance abuse concerns will be among the priorities of the plan. Discussion of possible objectives and methods provides opportunities for therapists to present their own perspectives on how therapy facilitates change and on the client's choice points in that process. The therapist raises the importance of creating realistic expectations about change, internalizing the client's own control and responsibility for outcomes of therapy, and making meaningful changes in the client's lifestyle to support efforts toward recovery or change.

Although giving the client some structure for expectations is useful for building motivation and rapport in the initial phase of therapy, psychoeducation about therapy also continues across the course of the client's work with the therapist. As therapy progresses and new interventions are utilized, the therapist pays close attention to the client's verbal and nonverbal reactions. When the client appears confused, skeptical, resistant, or reluctant, it is often useful to initiate a discussion of immediate reactions and observations. The therapist who offers an explanation and rationale to educate the client about therapeutic intentions and procedures may be able to enlist client efforts. Unless the therapist has a compelling reason for maintaining opacity, articulating what the therapist is thinking, doing, and anticipating helps demystify therapy so the client is better prepared and motivated to take next steps.

WHAT SUBSTANCE USE HAS MEANT TO THE CLIENT

No matter when concerns about the client's substance use emerge in the course of a therapy relationship, the therapist proposes the shared goal of learning more about the role of substance use in the client's life. If the client declines, the therapist can suggest revisiting the idea later if needed. If the client agrees, the therapist is then in a position to teach the client information about psychoactive substances and their many impacts, in addition to finding out more of the client's history and perspective. Furthermore, this type of psychoeducational intervention includes explorations of the interest and perceived relevance the client attaches to such information.

The therapist may wish to be explicit that one goal is to provide clients with a broader base of general drug and alcohol information that will assist the client in making better informed choices about substance use behavior. Learning more about psychoactive substances and how they affect human beings fits into conversations about what substance use has meant to the client and how continuing use may influence the client's future. Therapists will need to ascertain how much clients already know about the substances they have used, and to possess accurate information for validating and extending clients' knowledge. Discussions in session will compare general facts about substances and their effects to the client's own experience with using substances. Also the therapist should be open to learning new information from the client and from additional facts sought on the client's behalf when the therapist's own knowledge limits are reached.

Another major goal of psychoeducation about drug and alcohol effects is to sensitize clients to the conditions under which they have chosen and could choose to use substances, so that clients will become more knowledgeable about the implications of the factors and circumstances surrounding their own substance use. This goal is more personal than the general one described earlier. To help clients deepen their comprehension of the significance of their personal substance use, the therapist can make use of the emerging patterns described in chapter 2, particularly the meanings the client ascribes to substance use and the interpersonal messages expressed through the client's substance use. If the therapist is responsive to the client's reaction to this exploration, the therapist can guide the client toward taking more responsibility for personal choices about substance use or abstinence.

Psychoeducational interventions about the impact of chemical substances on the body and brain help stimulate consideration of both the risks and benefits of continuing use. Examining these trade-offs may motivate the client to reduce or eliminate the assumption of such risks. It is also worth mentioning that the vast array of information available about substances and their effects includes some controversial and contradictory positions. For example, some clients are familiar with literature and arguments in defense of the benefits of using marijuana (e.g., Conrad, 1997) or alcohol (e.g., Mukamal et al., 2003). From both educational and therapeutic standpoints, the client can profit from weighing competing perspectives with emphasis on mobilizing active client choice about how to use this analysis to meet personal goals.

Psychoeducation About Psychoactive Substances

As indicated in chapter 4, it is useful for substance abuse therapists to know enough about the pharmacological actions and behavioral outcomes of psychoactive substances that they will be able to describe these to clients in terms clients can understand. A legitimate question arises about how much the client needs to know about complex drug actions and effects to contribute to change in substance use behavior. Psychoeducation about actions and effects of drugs can help the therapist develop the client's sense of discrepancy between present behavior and future goals, which in turn can motivate behavior change.

Effects on the Brain. What therapists want to emphasize with clients engaged in risky substance use is that drugs and alcohol can modify normal functions of the brain in ways that can disrupt a person's abilities to think, feel, and act in response to immediate circumstances. Although some substance-induced alterations of baseline functions are certainly experienced as desirable, the substance abuser also invites consequences of impaired cognition, affect, and behavior that can be stressful and even dangerous.

If a client is interested in more detail about how drugs change brain functions, the therapist can provide it. As the therapist invites the client to comment on personal experiences of these general effects, the therapist should be prepared to address a few possibilities. Clients may report that before they tried drugs or alcohol, their own baseline functions were far from rewarding. Due to either environmental deficits or internal constraints, clients may believe that what was normal for them is different from average or better off persons. Such clients may be convinced that compromising some functions to attain higher pleasure is justified in light of personal circumstances.

In the spirit of avoiding argumentation (Miller & Rollnick, 2002), the therapist will want to empathize with the client's perspective and further explore its underlying basis. In addition, however, the therapist points out that, although the client's substance use has served an understandable function, the positive effects are temporary, whereas the less desirable ones are likely to persist. The user will need to keep consuming the drug to resume the beneficial impact, but repeated exposure actually induces changes not only in the functions, but also the anatomical structure of the brain, with potentially long-term detrimental impact as discussed in chapter 4. These structural changes compromise the user's experience of drug reward (if use continues), ability to function, and ultimately quality of life.

As the therapy dyad examines these considerations—that substance use seems justifiable in the short term, but risky in the longer term—the intervention focuses on what significance this observation has for the client. The reader will recall that the goal is to motivate the client to make conscious choices about future substance use or abstinence in the client's own best interests. For some with hope of avoiding or reducing debilitating effects of risky substance use, this intervention will stimulate insight or action toward change. Other clients, however, may argue that the damage has already been done or the alternatives to substance use are too difficult or too painful.

These clients might remain unconvinced that efforts to change are worth their time, or they could remain torn by indecisive contemplation. Even if such clients take action to reduce their risky substance use, they are likely to struggle with fears, anger, or sadness about the negative impact their substance use has already made. In cases like these, therapists can employ psychoeducation about the process of recovery from a substance's effects (to be discussed later in this chapter).

Effects on the User's Body.   To sensitize clients to the potential harm that abuse of substances can inflict on the human body, the therapist may also educate clients about actions the body takes to eliminate foreign chemicals capable of altering or damaging the body's equilibrium. As mentioned in chapter 4, the thrust of the psychoeducational message is that the intricate structures that can rid the body of hazardous substances may be injured by high levels of exposure to drugs and alcohol. The therapist can point out that the body functions fairly efficiently to rid itself of moderate amounts of psychoactive substances. However, excessive use can damage organs and their interacting functions to the point of contributing to major health problems, including cardiac and pulmonary effects, weight management difficulties, and neurological and psychological disorders, to name a few.

It is thus important for therapists to know and help clients consider what it means to the client that the experience of a favorite drug's effects requires some risk to the user's body. Again the client's interpretation of this trade-off may differ extensively from the therapist's, so the therapist intervenes most effectively when equipped with both an open mind and the ability to assert clear, accurate information. Also because clients are quite diverse in their opinions and analyses of the risks and benefits of substance use in light of psychoeducation about drug effects, the therapist remains attentive and responsive to the individual client's perspective and cultural norms.

As the therapy dyad or group studies both the general and specific impacts of drugs or alcohol in the context of the client's decision making and action plans, one theme often emerges. Even when the client acknowledges the risky nature of substance use, the client for whom substance use concerns have emerged in therapy also typically expresses some wish to continuing use to obtain the benefits despite the risks, even substantial ones. A psychoeducational stance permits the therapist to stay more neutral while still prompting examination of different angles on the topic. The inability to control substance use even in the face of debilitating consequences is one prominent feature of Substance Dependence. In addition to teaching clients about relatively short-term reactions in the body to the presence of a drug, the therapist also educates the client about the process of addiction that can occur with repeated drug use.

Chapter 4 illustrated that the human body has natural mechanisms for obtaining reward and minimizing damage from interactions with the environment, including the consumption of exogenous psychoactive substances. Together these two sets of biological functions reinforce the likelihood that an individual will continue using drugs or alcohol.

Psychoeducation About Consequences of Long-Term Substance Use

The therapist basically wants to communicate that if changes induced in the body by drugs are maintained over a long time by repeated drug use, the potential for detrimental consequences continues to increase. Not all of the consequences of continuing substance use are necessarily problematic. However, as detailed in chapter 4, the rapid actions and euphoric effects of drugs with high abuse potential provide strong gratification that can overshadow the user's interests in nondrug activities and awareness of delayed costs of substance use. Outcomes like tolerance and withdrawal can stimulate the user to engage in more frequent administration of greater quantities of drugs. In turn, this behavior can enhance the likelihood that the user will come to depend on drugs to feel normal because drug intoxication is becoming his or her typical state of being. Therapists can help substance using clients to identify the characteristics of withdrawal, tolerance, and dependence.

Substance Withdrawal. Regarding withdrawal, some clients may not be aware that specific symptoms they experience are attributable to the chemicals they are ingesting. Therapists can help educate such clients to the symptoms generally associated with the particular drugs the client has used (or is interested in using). Furthermore, therapists can guide clients' assessments of their own symptoms in comparison with a general withdrawal syndrome. Other clients are acutely aware of their substance withdrawal symptoms, but say they have learned to live with them or do not believe there is much they can do about them. Still others think they are funny—all just part of a good night on the town. Whatever the client's perspective, the therapist encourages the client to elaborate and then consider possible interventions to address the client's own symptoms.

Tolerance. With respect to tolerance, the therapist informs the client that just because the user's experience of a drug's effects is diminished as tolerance develops, it does not mean the potential or actual damage is reduced. In fact although tolerance does not guarantee problems, it may well increase the risk of substance dependence, especially in persons who are genetically, medically, or psychologically vulnerable. When tolerance leads to continuing use at higher rates and doses, the user also risks other delayed consequences, including health problems.

Some clients who abuse substances clearly take pride in their high tolerance for their drugs of choice. Trying to convince a client this is unwise will probably only raise resistance. But a psychoeducational intervention facilitates equal consideration of different viewpoints on the same topic, including awareness of reasons to feel nonchalant or smug as well as reasons to be concerned about clients' reported abilities to handle themselves when intoxicated. In the context of balanced review of relevant perspectives, the therapist can impel clients to think about choices they make about personal substance use.

Substance Dependence. Substance dependence can be an especially tricky topic in psychoeducational interventions for at least three reasons. First of all, there is great confusion in the general public, the media, and even among scientists and professionals about how to distinguish chemical dependence from normal substance use. Terminology, explanations, and implications vary widely across persons using them. The therapist models flexibility through willingness to openly acknowledge various, even conflicting perspectives as they arise. The additional ability to steer the client into discussions of personal understandings and questions can facilitate client choices about how to view substance dependence and its ramifications.

Second, many substance users fear or resent the label of Substance Dependence, and may have little wish to discuss dependence or learn about it. An advantage of a psychoeducational approach is the capacity to present material in an abstract or removed fashion, even with explicit statement that the information may or may not be relevant to the client. For example, the therapist might say,

> I'm not in the position to say you do or you don't have a problem with drugs (or alcohol). That is up to you to decide. But I can show you how my profession defines chemical dependence and the criteria we use to distinguish Substance Dependence from substance use and Abuse. Then if you're interested, we can talk about how those criteria relate to your own experience.

Otherwise reluctant clients are sometimes willing to review *DSM–IV* criteria or listen to third-party descriptions of substance dependence characteristics if they are assured it is their choice whether to talk about personal experience. Clients may offer comments about their own circumstances in response to learning generalized material, or they may absorb information the therapist shares without verbalizing a response.

The attentive therapist watches and listens for the client's nonverbal as well as spoken reactions to psychoeducational material. A facial expression, a change in body posture, or a wordless sigh or groan each serves as a cue for the therapist to invite comment. If the client has indicated willingness to explore personal relevance, the therapist can probe specifically for details about the client's personal experience that fit with the material in question. If the client has not agreed to delve into first-hand examples, the therapist can still ask in general terms, "Any thoughts or reactions to what we just covered?"

If the client says no, the therapist can point out the client's nonverbal cue that triggered the therapist's question (e.g., "I noticed you raised your eyebrows and sat back in your chair when I read the criterion of frequent, unsuccessful attempt to control substance use"). If the client still declines to elaborate, the therapist can offer the possibility of revisiting this information at a later time if the client is ever interested in doing so.

A third reason psychoeducation about substance dependence can be difficult is that even when clients are interested in learning about it, that interest can be accompanied by fear of implications for the client's own life. Clients who are engaging in risky use but do not meet Substance Dependence criteria may worry about becoming chemically dependent, especially if they have a family history of alcoholism or addiction. If they have experienced substance dependence in either the past or present, they may express regret about problems already encountered or fears about consequences, such as health difficulties, that may yet result.

Realizing that confronting such prospects can elicit the client's ambivalence and resistance, the therapist further pursues discussion of the client's feelings and perceived options in light of this information. If the client expresses the wish to avoid thinking about this or despairs of finding a way out of substance-related problems, the therapist can offer alternatives and hope. The therapist might acknowledge,

> That's one way to look at it, but I'm in this business because I believe many problems are worth confronting, and that people can learn to control how they deal with those problems. So are you willing to spend some time talking about ways we could proceed from here to address your own concerns?

Both the disease and the learning models of addiction reviewed in chapter 4 give reasons to expect progress toward change if the client decides to modify substance use patterns. From a learning perspective, maladaptive behavior that has been learned can be unlearned. According to disease models, some biological and neurological changes induced by drugs can be reversed, and some damages can be reduced if the substance user exerts control over risky or compulsive drug-taking behaviors. Such changes are neither quick nor easy, but recovery of more normal functions is possible with commitment and effort, and therapy can be one useful avenue on the map to recovery. The provision of psychoeducation about drugs and their short- and long-term effects thus leads back to further education about the process of therapy and other means of addressing problems associated with the client's own substance use.

HOW TO MOVE IN THE DIRECTION OF BENEFICIAL CHANGE

Ideally, learning more about the actions and effects of different types of drugs, plus having a caring therapist to help process this information, will stimulate the client to think about what it would be like to relinquish problems associated with her or his own substance use. Whether the client is considering this prospect only in hypothetical terms or is ready to take action, the therapist can offer additional psychoeducation about the process of recovering from any negative impact of substance abuse.

Although many clients in therapy struggle with tendencies to externalize their problems to sources beyond their control (Teyber, 2000), this inclination is even more pronounced when substance use concerns arise in therapy. Clients who abuse drugs or alcohol often report that their substance use actually helps or is good for them, and that anyone who cannot appreciate that is the real problem. Such clients may use denial of personal control or responsibility over problems to justify continued access to the desirable effects of drugs or alcohol. Even if the client expresses ambivalence, intoxication further clouds any needs to think about their own contributions to current difficulties. When these client dynamics are encountered, the therapist gently confronts the client with the ideas that (a) the only things people really can control are aspects of their own behavior, and (b) it is up to each person to consider what she or he is able to control and how much responsibility she or he is going to take for exerting that control. The therapist can offer support and encourage the client to mobilize other forms of social support. Ultimately, however, dealing with adverse consequences of past substance abuse or changing behavior to reduce risk of further consequences depends on the client's own initiative and effort.

Underscoring the importance of internalizing the rights and responsibilities to address one's own issues need not be purely a harsh or punitive lesson. In fact taking stock of what one can actually control also exercises the capacity to choose which efforts are worth making. The therapist can thus inform the client that the process of recovery typically involves looking inward to identify problems in need of attention as well as internal capacities and limitations pertinent to resolution of those problems.

Choosing Actively Rather Than Passively

Recovery from problems linked to a person's substance abuse rarely, if ever, happens by default. Clients for whom substance use concerns have been raised will need to decide whether these concerns are to be a focus of therapy. If so further choices are essential in addressing these concerns meaningfully and effectively.

Therapists educate clients about the importance of making active choices in the recovery process. Therapists assert their own willingness to guide and support the client's decision process, but also clarify that, in the end analysis, the choice rests with the client. The therapist explains that even if it were possible for the therapist to choose what focus or approach is best for clients, the therapist would decline because that could block clients from learning how to choose for themselves.

The assumption here is that clients who have problems with drugs or alcohol use have, to some extent, come to rely on default or delayed decision making. This can occur with respect to how the client copes with stressors (e.g., "I don't know what to do about this issue, so instead of worrying about it, I'll have a drink [or substitute drug of choice] to get my mind off of it for a while"). Passive decisions may also be made about substance use (e.g., "I can always quit tomorrow, so why not indulge one more time today?"). This passivity may fluctuate, as in the example of the heavy drinker who wakes with a hangover and vows not to drink again that day (or that week, or ever), but ends up reaching for another bottle later that same day.

Interactive psychoeducation about choice in recovery, then, involves the therapist learning how the client feels about the prospect of choosing more actively, as well as how the client has tended to make decisions in the past. Motivational interviewing strategies (Miller & Rollnick, 2002) can be usefully integrated into therapists' efforts to empower client choice activity. In therapy sessions, therapists encourage clients to choose the extent to which they want to concentrate on substance use concerns. Outside of therapy, clients are further urged to be aware of and take responsibility for the actions they choose.

Therapists should be prepared to address at least two common client reactions to a focus on active choice. First, clients may express or insinuate the wish that someone else (perhaps the therapist?) would fix the problem or tell them the solution. The therapist will probably want to point out possible resentment the client might feel if someone else did tell the client what to do, took credit for any beneficial outcome, or failed to provide resolution. The therapist might add,

> I don't see how either one of use would truly benefit if I tried to fix the problem for you, but I see real potential in us working together to help you decide what you want to do about it.

A second common client response to active choice involves statements of ambivalence, often peppered with low self-efficacy for making decisions. Client ambivalence is increasingly recognized as an inevitable factor in change and recovery (Kell & Mueller, 1966; Miller & Rollnick, 2002; Teyber, 2000). Therapists teach clients that mixed feelings are normal and even potentially useful. Then therapists help clients articulate and examine their own ambivalence with aims of developing decisions and coping skills to resolve it. Addressing a client's difficulties with decision making can be valuable even if the client's substance abuse is not the chosen focus.

Creating Realistic Expectations

As clients internalize responsibility for choosing the problems they will tackle and the strategies they will attempt, the therapist can help foster realistic expectations of both the process and outcomes of recovery. Difficulties in maintaining focus can arise when the client expects too much or too little. However, it is not unusual for clients to entertain idealistic hopes or nagging doubts about recovery. Sometimes clients waver between the two.

Therapists directly address their clients' expectations by inquiring periodically, and also by sharing views from theory and experience about the process of recovery. The therapist offers confidence that the client will see genuine improvement so long as the client makes a good faith effort, taking manageable steps with good chances of success. The therapist emphasizes in addition that recovery is typically a gradual process, and change is rarely total or absolute. Many small steps taken over a long period of time are usually necessary to build toward sustained improvements in the client's circumstances and well-being. Furthermore, the therapist admits that the gradual progression of recovery usually encounters some setbacks along the way, but such relapses can be reframed as additional sparks in the stalled engine of change. Of course the therapist also points out that it is realistic for the client to expect the therapist's close involvement and support with negotiating the unfolding recovery process, including the setbacks (more on relapse prevention in chap. 8).

Clients are asked to share their reactions to this presentation of recovery as a slow procedure requiring concentrated effort with probable bumps along the way. Some clients will express relief and gratitude for the therapist's forthrightness and support. Others will talk about frustration, disappointment, and maybe hopelessness. Not surprisingly, perhaps, still other clients will vacillate among these sets of feelings. When the client is opposed to the prospect of longer term commitment to therapy and recovery, the therapist can offer the possibility of a time-limited contract, suggesting that it is reasonable to expect progress in that time frame with the understanding that the contract can be renegotiated if needed. The therapist's job as psychoeducator continues with empathic exploration of whatever reactions the client reveals, both verbally and nonverbally.

Developing Recovery Plans

Already this recovery section has implied the need for clear, workable tasks to direct client energies toward recovery goals. Either directly or indirectly, the therapist teaches the client the potential value and utility of defining one's goals and choosing activities designed to move closer to those goals. This piece of psychoeducation links to the concepts of ongoing treatment planning (chap. 6), relapse prevention planning (chap. 8), and after-care planning (chap. 10). Because each of these topics is covered elsewhere in this book, a few simple points are highlighted here.

Helping clients to internalize their focus, exercise active choice, and create realistic expectations for recovery all involve developing a plan that is understandable, meaningful, and motivating to the client. In short, recovery usually requires some structure that the client helps to determine based on the client's own inclinations.

Substance abusing clients sometimes come across as having or wanting minimal structure in their lives. Other times it is evident how thoroughly their lives are structured around getting, using, and recovering from their substance. Typically clients have strong, often mixed, emotions about altering the structure by which they are accustomed to living, even if they wish to recover from negative consequences of a substance abusing lifestyle. Therapists can work with clients to assess the viability of restructuring the client's activity in light of emerging goals. They can also consider the client's feelings about doing so.

Obtaining Support

Certainly the therapist can provide steady support for the client's recovery. The therapist's genuine expression of support can be a powerful interpersonal reinforcer of the client's commitment to therapy. Psychoeducation about recovery also includes exhorting the client to cultivate additional sources of social support.

For clients whose social networks primarily include people with whom they use substances, this can be a daunting task. The therapist can inform or remind clients of general options, such as friends or relatives who do not abuse substances, or who have successfully recovered from a substance abuse history; therapy or self-help groups; or other interest groups centered around hobbies, sports, religion, politics, charity, or whatever interests the client. If desired, the therapist can coach the client on articulating requests for support and negotiating interpersonal processes that follow. With selected clients, the therapist may choose to introduce consideration of the two-sided nature of communication and relationships to help build the client's social skills. As before, eliciting and processing the client's responses are crucial.

Reinforcing Progress and Coping With Regress

To facilitate recovery, clients learn the importance of rewarding their successes and accepting their setbacks. Therapists not only offer this insight at the beginning, but often reiterate this component of recovery at various points along the journey. Clients may agree with the general principle, but still run into difficulties applying it in practice.

Therapists can help resume realistic expectations when the client is disillusioned by slow progress. By educating the client of possibilities for reframing small changes as deserving active reinforcement, the therapist can teach clients to reward themselves more effectively. The therapist can also teach clients alternative ways to deal with regress, so that instead of self-punishment, the client takes useful lessons from lapses.

* * *

In this chapter, I demonstrated the essential nature of psychoeducational interventions in therapy with clients who abuse drugs or alcohol. In teaching new information to the client, the therapist is encouraged to discuss not only the facts at hand, but the client's overt and subtle reactions to the information. Furthermore, the chapter advocates for therapists to engage in active interpersonal dialogue exploring the various interpretations of material at hand and the relevance of that material to the client's own decisions. In addition, bibliotherapy can extend the impact of psychoeducation. Recommending relevant books or other media for the client to consume helps keep clients actively involved beyond the therapy session, and therapists and clients can later discuss the content of such reading materials in session. The goal of psychoeducation is to expand the client's potential for critical thinking and active choice regarding personal substance use by providing broad-based information and a relationship in which to consider its import.

The therapist should also take account of the following possibilities in the context of psychoeducational interventions about mind-altering substances and the processes, including therapy, of recovery from their abuse. First, clients are most always in possession of information on these topics provided by sources other than the therapist. If the client is or has been involved in other sorts of treatment or education regarding drug and alcohol use, the therapist may not need to give all the types of information covered here. The therapist will still need to assess what the client knows, how that knowledge meshes (if at all) with the therapist's own knowledge, and how thoroughly to pursue psychoeducational approaches given the client's presentation.

Second, the vast literature on substance abuse and addiction extends into fields that may lie far from the therapist's own expertise. When the boundaries of the therapist's own knowledge about drugs, alcohol, and related problems are reached, the therapist is strongly advised to make appropriate referrals or, if plausible, to seek out information or consultation. Especially because there are health and legal consequences of substance abuse for many clients, therapists should be careful to refer clients as needed to professionals with the requisite credentials and expertise.

Finally, therapists frequently work with substance abusers to facilitate communication between the client and third parties. Disordered substance use, frequently associated with recurrent problems or outright failure to fulfill important roles or activities, creates interpersonal responsibilities for clients to address those problems with other involved persons. However, clients may have limited understanding either of what is expected of them by invested third parties or of necessary steps to satisfy external requests or incurred obligations. Therapists can help clients clarify the nature of the problem and the expectations that need to be addressed to resolve the problem. This may include coaching the client on what to say and how to talk to a relative, employer, judge, doctor, or other party to elucidate obligations and communicate effort. Therapists may also teach clients how to assess and implement their options and likely consequences for promoting interactions that will permit the client to resolve current problems and avoid future similar troubles associated with psychoactive substance use.

Chapter 8

Relapse Prevention Strategies

Jeannie stopped smoking pot for the past three weeks as part of the goals she set for herself in therapy. She is pleased to find she coughs less often and seems to concentrate better, but she frequently misses getting high. She tells her therapist the temptation to smoke has been especially strong in the past few days since her best friend returned from a vacation and has been inviting Jeannie to come over and get stoned like they used to do. Jeannie is still unconvinced that her decision to refrain from marijuana use is a permanent one.

Barry has successfully abstained from drinking for three months after completing intensive outpatient treatment (IOP). Barry came for therapy when his wife expressed doubts about staying married if Barry continued drinking himself into a stupor every other night, using the alternate days to recover from massive hangovers. (An earlier version of Barry's written treatment plan, as he was deciding to enroll in IOP, was already described in chap. 6.) Barry now tells his therapist that he feels physically healthier in recent weeks, and that urges to drink do not plague him as much as they did in the first month or two sober. However, he is now flooded with excruciating memories and feelings he had been blotting out about his painful childhood with an alcoholic mother, and he is beginning to despair of ever finding a less depressive outlook on life, even without the burden of his drinking.

Nathan has expressed great motivation and enthusiasm for continuing the progress he has made toward establishing more satisfying relationships and identifying new occupational options since he quit using cocaine, marijuana, and alcohol with the support of intensive outpatient therapy. He has recently remarried and is considering pursuit of a career in healing ministries. As he approaches the six-month marker of staying clean and sober, however, Nathan confides to his therapist that he has lain awake several nights in a cold sweat, using every ounce of his will to resist gut-wrenching urges to seek out some crack cocaine.

Viola just began her term of parole after serving time for possession of heroin. She got clean in prison by studying any available literature on treating drug addictions and promoting health and healing. By the end of her three years inside, she was co-leading workshops on healthy lifestyles for other inmates. Required to obtain drug therapy as a condition of her parole, Vi now reports to her therapist that she doesn't see herself going back to using heroin, although she now drinks alcohol on occasion. However, she admits that moving back to her childhood home to care for her terminally ill, formerly abusive father after twelve years living out of state poses significant stresses, and she would appreciate some help with coping.

Each of these clients has taken important steps toward reducing the negative impact of substance abuse on their lives. Each too faces new or continuing challenges that threaten to disrupt their progress and could potentially trigger a relapse into less healthy behaviors. Working with clients to develop their skills to prevent relapse is an integral component of substance abuse therapy. The cases described earlier will be referred to again throughout the chapter to illustrate the establishment of relapse prevention and coping strategies.

The discussion of *relapse prevention* in this chapter employs broad definitions of both *relapse* and *prevention*. Relapse can refer both to a resumption of problematic substance use (however defined for a particular client), and also to recurrence of other maladaptive behaviors that have in the client's past been associated with substance abuse as a coping strategy. For example, if Barry again started to withdraw from his family after recent attempts to mend fences, even if he is not drinking at present, he is relapsing into problematic behaviors that are tied into the impact of his own and his mother's alcohol dependencies on his life. Prevention of relapse includes both warding off the resumption of problematic behaviors and building additional skills for coping with any episodes of substance use or related problems that do occur.

Therapists can help clients learn how to keep from falling back into old habits they are working hard to overcome by generating and implementing relapse prevention strategies. In this chapter, useful components of comprehensive relapse prevention strategies are emphasized, with attention to the utility of embedding relapse prevention planning across the entire therapy process. Marlatt and Gordon (1985) presented relapse prevention as a program by which individuals learn to manage their own behavior and change maladaptive habits by acquiring behavioral skills and cognitive strategies based on deliberate awareness and responsible decision making.

Marlatt (1985a, 1985b, 1985c), one of the early proponents of relapse prevention strategies, underscored the crucial nature of the maintenance stage of the change process in determining long-term outcomes of treatment. Although motivation, commitment, and action are all considered necessary components of changing problematic behavior, the gradual process of learning new coping strategies to replace former maladaptive coping mechanisms is essential in preventing and dealing with relapse. From this perspective, occasional mistakes or lapses in implementing therapy goals are to be expected, and can be viewed as opportunities for strengthening newly learned strategies rather than as indications of treatment failure.

Marlatt (1985a, 1985b, 1985c) promoted relapse prevention training as a self-management program with goals of anticipating and coping with high-risk situations. Based on a social learning paradigm, relapse prevention efforts take an optimistic view of potential therapy outcomes, assuming that substance use disorders are characterized by behaviors that are learned and can be unlearned. In combination, efforts to increase self-efficacy and self-control are foundations for the maintenance of change in substance use behaviors.

Substantial research on relapse prevention has been conducted since the publication of Marlatt and Gordon's germinal book. In a 1996 review of this literature, Carroll concluded that the evidence suggests that relapse prevention has the greatest potential to reduce the severity of client relapses, sustain the effects of treatment over time, and be more effective with more severely impaired substance abusers. A meta-analytic review conducted by Irvin, Bowers, Dunn, and Wang (1999) further supported the general effectiveness of relapse prevention. The cognitive-behavioral relapse prevention model was recently reconceptualized to facilitate extended research (Witkiewitz & Marlatt, 2004), and a long-awaited revision of Marlatt and colleagues' relapse prevention text is soon forthcoming (Marlatt & Donovan, in press).

Tools that clients generally need to develop to prevent relapse and maintain progress toward change include: dealing with factors that could trigger relapse, substituting healthy activities for formerly problematic behaviors, learning from relapse if and when it happens, and reinforcing successful relapse prevention efforts as they happen. In combination, these four objectives move the client toward the goals of mastery and confidence in their own relapse prevention skills. Individually, each objective can be approached in a course of therapy by employing methods selected to move clients from points at which they are presently struggling to points where they feel better able to cope.

DEALING WITH URGES, CRAVINGS, AND TRIGGERS TO RELAPSE

Marlatt (1985a) defined *addictive behaviors* as "compulsive habit pattern[s] in which the individual seeks a state of immediate gratification" (p. 4). Throughout the substantial course of recovery from disordered substance use, individuals face moments of temptation to fall back on drugs or alcohol for an easy boost of mood or a quick escape from stressors. Factors that can trigger a relapse may be fleeting or pervasive, occasional or continual. While they are salient, they typically require the individual's vigilant exertions to resist temptations to stray from recovery goals. Therapists can help strengthen clients' skills for preventing relapse by paying attention to clients' most likely barriers to treatment goals and by guiding clients toward planning and practicing effective strategies for responding to such barriers.

Potential Barriers to Therapy Goals

The first step in dealing with barriers to progress is to clarify what kinds of situations, events, feelings, and thoughts have been associated with the client's tendency to use substances inappropriately, and which of these will probably continue to prod the client to want to use again despite treatment goals. In much of the substance abuse treatment literature, these factors are subdivided into urges, cravings, and triggers, with the advantage that such descriptive terminology helps clients sort out multiple factors contributing to their relatively undifferentiated experience.

Cravings. Cravings are experienced as somatic pangs, like hunger, created by depletion in the body of a substance required to maintain homeostatic functioning. As an individual develops a tolerance for exposure to larger or more frequent doses of a psychoactive drug, the tissues and cells adapt their operations to the presence of the drug so that withdrawal of the drug creates imbalance in the system. Initial withdrawal of a heavily used substance is often associated with intense physical craving, but the experience of craving a favorite substance can continue or recur long after the substance has been completely flushed from bodily tissues. Cravings are thought to result from both conditioned learning and cognitive expectancy processes (Marlatt, 1985a, 1985b, 1985c). Part of relapse prevention thus involves helping clients to anticipate, recognize, and react more adaptively to their cravings.

Urges. Urges are intense, pressing desires to consume a substance and to bring on, as quickly as possible, the immediate gratification the substance promises to provide. Like cravings, urges are compensatory responses a person makes when external cues trigger anticipation of the effects of substance use (Lewis, Dana, & Blevins, 2002). The impulsive nature of urges can lead to snap decisions to ignore long-term consequences of use. Strong urges can push a client down the slippery slope to a relapse unless the client learns to prevent relapse by deliberately engaging in planned alternative behaviors. For example, Nathan learned in therapy that, when struck by urges to seek out cocaine, he found it helpful to write in his journal or practice relaxation and meditation techniques instead. When reporting the results of these techniques to his therapist, Nathan also came up with the idea of reminding himself in those difficult moments of the several painful results of past use that he had to face over many years of heavy drinking and smoking. He confided later that this turned out to be his most effective strategy for dealing with his intense urges.

Triggers. Triggers refer to situational factors that cue individuals with substance abuse histories into remembering the pleasurable aspects of drinking or taking drugs. By signaling the possibility of re-creating that pleasurable state, triggers prompt the individual to use substances again. For the individual in recovery, classically conditioned triggers continue to operate, stimulating desires to resume use and paving the road to possible relapse. For Nathan, seeing a recent news report on crack cocaine use that included footage of silhouetted figures smoking a crack pipe triggered unexpected urges and cravings to use crack again, even after several months of abstinence. Jeannie, the client in the early recovery example, found that a strong trigger for her was spending time with her best friend on the patio where they used to get high.

In relapse prevention models, persons who abuse substances are presumed to exhibit maladaptive skills for coping with high-risk scenarios and with cues they have been conditioned to associate with substance use (Rawson, Obert, McCann, & Marinelli-Casey, 1993). Relapse prevention planning helps countercondition individuals who have decided to quit abusing substances by extinguishing the old learned response and consciously replacing it with a new and incompatible one.

Methods for Responding to Potential Relapse Factors

Changing conceptions of cravings, urges, and triggers as well as modifying behavioral reactions to them are gradual learning processes. Although clients cannot implement a relapse prevention strategy until they have taken action to modify their substance use and are in the stage of maintaining behavior change, they can begin to plan a strategy even as they are contemplating or preparing for action. Early in therapy, therapists can explain the rationale and procedures for planning how to prevent relapse to acquaint clients with the concept. They may focus on harm reduction. Then once clients agree they are ready for the next step, the therapist can structure a discussion of the personal triggers, urges, and cravings of which clients are already aware or coming to recognize. As clients list the factors that contribute to their own substance use behavior and describe how they have reacted to urges, cravings, and triggers in the past, clients can be further encouraged to consider possible different responses to such factors in the future. Finally, the therapist invites the client to practice these new response options when encountering triggers, cravings, or urges in present daily life, and to report back to the therapist about how these efforts are experienced.

In addition to talking about relapse promoting factors in individual sessions, clients can also be invited to explore related experiences in a group therapy context. With other clients sharing perspectives, clients can gain insight into experiences and barriers common to many recovering substance abusers, as well as into more rare or unique aspects of one's own situation that will require individualized attention in planning relapse prevention strategies. Therapists can also suggest homework to keep clients involved in therapeutic planning or implementation in between sessions. Clients can try methods like generating or expanding lists of personal triggers to drink or use drugs, or they can use logs to monitor the occurrence of urges or cravings during the time between sessions. They may be willing to keep a journal, either by writing about barriers to goals as they are experienced or setting aside a regular time to record thoughts and feelings about the barriers the client is identifying. The specific methods to promote identification of a client's relapse triggers are best negotiated from the therapist's observations and the client's preferences.

Along with listing specific factors potentially promoting relapse, clients also need to sharpen their awareness of the situational contexts in which these relapse triggers are most likely to be salient as the client works toward initiating and maintaining change. For example, Viola's return following years of incarceration to the community where she grew up, combined with her new caretaker role for a father who treated her poorly during childhood, will together present her with a variety of situations that strongly elicit her anger or sadness. If Viola already knows that feelings of anger and depression can tempt her to relapse, she will also need to clarify the aspects of her new circumstances that may bring up sad or mad feelings. Her therapist can better prepare her to confront these situations in a manner that prevents relapse by talking about and recording the particular events that Viola anticipates will be most stressful. The more the client can anticipate such situations and their potential impact, the better prepared the client can be to deal with them without giving in to temptations to relapse into old coping mechanisms associated with abusing drugs or alcohol.

Developing and practicing strategies for overcoming identified potential barriers to treatment goals is the crucial next step in helping clients prevent relapse. Often in the client's past, cravings, urges, and triggers have been associated with problematic cognitions, emotions, and behaviors, which the client must now learn to manage to avoid relapse. Therapists can provide methods and clarify procedures by which clients can actively engage in deliberate change processes. Clients frequently benefit from a therapist's guidance regarding identification and weighing of options, selection from among options, and implementation of new strategies through regular practice. Especially because many substance abusers have overlearned expectations of immediate gratification, therapists also need to emphasize patience with the gradual, approximate nature of change. Therapists must pay attention to the client's fluctuating motivations to comply with the relapse prevention plan or remain committed to therapy goals. A therapist can reinforce the client's commitment to decisions to avoid relapse by generating alternative perspectives and strategies to promote healthier coping activities.

SUBSTITUTING HEALTHY ACTIVITIES FOR FORMERLY PROBLEMATIC BEHAVIORS

After clarifying potential barriers to treatment goals, the client and therapist expand the relapse prevention plan by specifying new ways of thinking about issues and concerns, new approaches for managing difficult emotions and disruptive behaviors, and new ways for the client to occupy time. Therapists can employ cognitive restructuring and emotional and behavioral management training to assist clients in replacing substance abuse as a coping mechanism with healthier alternatives. Engaging clients in new leisure activities and helping them develop occupational options are important in planning to prevent relapse.

Reframing Maladaptive Cognitions

The therapist first encourages the client to identify typical thoughts the client entertains about personal substance use, related stressors, and coming to treatment. Then the therapist teaches the client to challenge and replace self-defeating thoughts with more productive cognitions. Extending the example of the client in early recovery from marijuana abuse, Jeannie tells her therapist she thinks her friends are going to laugh at or reject her when she tells them she recently quit smoking pot. She is also convinced it is no longer possible for her to have fun if she is not high. Jeannie says she is still not sure she wants to quit totally or forever; she says she is only abstaining for now to avoid further trouble.

Generating Alternatives. Without invalidating Jeannie's original comments, the therapist points out that there are probably other ways to think about her situation that are worth considering. Although it is certainly possible that Jeannie's friends might give her a hard time for not smoking with them anymore, it is also plausible that at least some will be sympathetic with her situation and understand her choice. Some friends might even respect and admire Jeannie's new stance. The therapist can introduce questions of what Jeannie thinks about friends who would reject her on such a basis, about what Jeannie would think of a friend who confided in her of a similar decision, and about how much Jeannie thinks it matters what other people think of her personal choices.

Regarding Jeannie's doubts about why she is quitting and whether she can still enjoy herself, the therapist can offer the perspectives that it is Jeannie's prerogative to decide what she wants, that it is possible to find activities that are satisfying even when she is not under the influence of marijuana, and that it could be interesting and even exciting to discover these possibilities.

Stopping Self-Defeating Thoughts. Once the client agrees to try out new cognitions, the therapist can teach and reinforce thought-stopping techniques. Clients learn to mentally catch themselves entertaining a self-defeating thought. Then they are instructed to practice consciously letting go of that thought, deliberately replacing it with a more affirming or realistic thought. The therapist can also instruct the client to pair a specific behavior with the mental exercise, such as the classic snap of a rubber band against the wrist, to serve as both a symbolic gesture and a visceral reminder of the cognitive modification. Continuing the earlier example, Jeannie decided instead of wearing a "tacky" rubber band around her wrist, she will move the clasp of her favorite necklace, which she wears every day, around her neck whenever she stops and replaces a self-defeating thought with the concepts that she can meet her goal, and that she wants to do it first and foremost for herself.

It is crucial to emphasize that cognitive restructuring works best when the client believes the therapist understands and accepts the client's starting cognitions and when the client generates and chooses personally meaningful replacement messages and gestures. If the client feels either criticized or coerced by the therapist, the client is much less likely to take cognitive reframing seriously. Furthermore, the therapist can enhance results by clearly explaining that lasting change in cognition will take time especially because the client has had a long time already to establish the original self-defeating thoughts. By encouraging patience and regular practice, and by asking the client to reflect in therapy sessions on the efforts to reframe cognitions, the therapist teaches the client not only how to better regulate the content of the client's own cognitions, but also to formulate realistic expectations of personal change. This of course means that the therapist must also be patient with the slow nature of change and the negotiation required for effective relapse prevention planning.

Limiting Beliefs Encountered in Cognitive Interventions. Two limiting beliefs commonly expressed by clients with substance abuse histories are worth further mention. Tendencies to externalize problems to sources outside of personal control or to maintain ambivalence (at best) about the existence of a problem or the need to change are both cognitions that impede efforts to prevent relapse. When restructuring cognitions with a client, the therapist should work explicitly with the client's attributions of both ability and responsibility for addressing problematic substance use and related barriers to treatment goals. Some clients may believe they could but do not want to make certain changes to maintain therapeutic gains. For example, some alcoholics in early remission believe they can still go to bars while choosing not to drink alcohol. Such clients may prove reluctant to discuss risks or shoulder responsibilities for the possibility of relapse under such circumstances. Some may turn out to be capable of doing so; for others the temptation to resume problematic drinking turns out to be too great. Other clients are willing to accept responsibility, but are unconvinced of their ability to bring about desired outcomes.

Take the extended example of Barry, whose depression intensifies despite months of newfound sobriety. Barry commits to removing all alcohol from his home and driving past all liquor stores without stopping, but still is not sure that at the end of each day he can make himself leave the grocery store where he works without buying a bottle off the shelf. In each case, the therapist can help the client clarify, challenge, and balance beliefs about the extent to which the client possesses and takes control of factors that can influence his or her progress.

As the therapist and client together plan ways for the client to prevent relapse, the client learns to first recognize thoughts that interfere with making healthy decisions. Next the client develops alternative beliefs to counter self-defeating cognitions, and then she or he is challenged to deliberately notice and replace maladaptive thoughts with more productive ones. As the client practices and refines these cognitive restructuring skills, he or she wields new tools for resisting relapse. The client comes to believe that there are options besides drinking or using drugs for eliciting pleasure and satisfaction from daily life, that these options are in many ways preferable to former substance abuse behaviors given their relative consequences, that the client is capable and deserving of these more beneficial options, and that the client is willing to undertake the responsibility for making the effort to establish and reach personal goals.

Managing Negative Affect

Helping clients learn to manage difficult affect is essential in preventing relapse. In addition to self-sabotaging thoughts, limited skills for coping with negative affect—especially intense anger, sadness, or anxiety—frequently pose complications for clients recovering from substance use disorders. In many cases, clients were using drugs or alcohol as their primary mechanism to blunt difficult emotions or blot out guilt for affect-induced behaviors. After a client takes steps to reduce or abstain from substance use, strong feelings often emerge. A good example is Ricardo, who told his therapy group about a recent incident in which Ricardo's son was surprised to see his father crying for the first time and curious about why. Ricardo told the group he had explained to his son that, "It's okay. It's just that Daddy is starting to have feelings again now that he's not using drugs anymore." Unless the client develops effective new strategies for coping with rage, depression, disappointment, or fear, the risk is high for relapse to substance abuse as a means of shutting off such bad feelings.

Relapse prevention plans should thus include steps for helping clients learn to manage their own inevitable negative affect. Affect management training refers to techniques by which therapists teach clients first how to recognize, acknowledge, and accept their emotions, and then to make informed and wise choices about how to act on their feelings, taking appropriate responsibility for the outcomes. Anger management is one well-known specific form of affect management training because anger issues are evident among many individuals mandated to obtain substance abuse treatment, and relatedly because the term has caught the attention of the popular media. However, all forms of negative affect can be exceedingly hard to experience and manage.

Identifying Affective Themes. Although a client's perceptions of past, present, and future can each be associated with a range of difficult emotions, often a client will exhibit some characterological affect (Teyber, 2000). For Barry, profound sorrow is prevalent; for Viola, the predominant affect is anger. In Nathan's case, guilt over past transgressions and mistakes is a recurrent theme. The therapist begins training the client to better manage affect by starting with the characteristic affective theme evident in the client's presentation, with the therapist's understanding that other forms of affect with which the client also has trouble coping are sure to surface once the primary affect is addressed.

Distinguishing Alternatives for Expressing Emotions.   To incorporate affect management training into a client's relapse prevention plan, a therapist first points out the evident affective theme and the apparent or likely difficulty of managing volatile emotions. Once the client agrees, the therapist then helps the client distinguish between "having a feeling" and "acting on the feeling." The therapist validates the client's feeling and the client's right to feel it. The therapist also helps the client explore and understand the reasons for the feeling and the ways the client has coped with the feeling in the past. This analysis of coping may yield discussion of feelings that trigger the client's urge to use substances, of emotions about the consequences of the client's substance abuse, and of feelings about the process of change. The therapist communicates the messages that emotions are neither wrong nor right, they are simply but inevitably what a person feels in reaction to a thought or an event. However, there are good and bad ways for people to act out or express their emotions, and examining different possible reactions and their probable consequences can help clients make better choices about how to manage their own feelings.

The client is invited to discuss these ideas and consider both effective and less effective options for expressing emotion. The therapist further encourages discussion of the probable consequences of choosing to express feelings one way compared with another. Role-play exercises can be used for the therapist to model and the client to practice new forms of affective expression, with minimal interpersonal risk to the client. Through these activities in session, the client learns to isolate the experience of affect from a behavioral response. In addition, the client begins to consciously generate options to an identified emotion, rather than acting according to a familiar, automatic impulse.

The therapist also asks the client to name specific situations and general contexts in which the client anticipates being confronted with negative emotions. Journaling or logging homework often helps clients focus in on people, events, memories, times of day, and the like that pose particular challenges or threats to the client's therapy goals. The therapist can guide the client in session toward deciding how the client plans to respond to those challenges. With an articulated plan, the client should become better able to consider and eventually employ new strategies for managing intense affect in the heat of such a moment.

Implementing New Affect Management Skills.   When the client is ready, steps can be taken to transfer these behavioral strategies for managing affect beyond the therapy session. Before discussing these steps, however, it is crucial for the therapist to remember to continue assessing and validating the client's experience of emotions as they are learning to behaviorally manage them. Understandably, some clients interpret the goal of affect management as eliminating negative affect. Even clients who endorse the distinction between the experience of emotion and a response to that emotion can be sideswiped by unanticipated feelings when methods that seemed clear in a therapy session turn out to be harder to implement than the client hoped or expected. Less than ideal outcomes can yank to the surface old impulses to escape bad feelings with drugs or alcohol. Clients typically need the therapist's continuing help and support as they learn to tolerate and manage their emotional reactions to ongoing issues and changing circumstances.

As new concepts and skills for managing the client's affect are developed in therapy sessions, the client and therapist further address the client's readiness to implement changes outside of the session. The therapist can ask whether the client has noticed any differences in how she or he has been feeling and how she or he has been acting on those feelings. The therapist should also inquire about any consequences the client has encountered in response to new forms of expression with which the client is experimenting. If the client is not reporting any changes, the therapist can suggest more directive homework. The client can be asked to try a specific strategy when the client experiences negative affect, and then to notice the results and discuss the experiment in the next therapy session. For willing clients, it will probably be useful to keep a journal to record impressions or a behavioral log of occurrences.

Clients often need guidance to structure their efforts to be meaningful without being overwhelming. Building on earlier planning efforts, the therapist can help the client select one particular type of affect eliciting stimulus with which to practice managing responses. Preferably, the situation, person, or issue selected should be one the client is likely to encounter, but not one of highest stakes to the client. By beginning with salient but less threatening stimuli, the client can practice and achieve some success or at least meaningful insights that will reinforce willingness to make additional efforts to try new management strategies in increasingly challenging contexts. The therapist can help the client make informed choices about where to focus efforts, what new approaches to try, how to interpret outcomes, and next steps to successively approximate affect management goals.

Developing Occupational and Leisure Options

As the client learns to substitute productive thoughts for former self-defeating cognitions, and to generate healthier responses to difficult emotions, the need to develop alternative vocational, educational, or leisure activities emerges. To promote treatment goals, the client must not only reduce reliance on old habits of coping, amusement, or involvement; the client also needs to replace habitual activities with other intrinsically satisfying means of occupying the client's time. Clients who have been using drugs or alcohol to entertain themselves, to keep busy, or to deal with (or avoid dealing with) issues will have to establish new activities as part of their relapse prevention plans.

The activities in which a client engages are intricately tied into the client's thoughts and feelings. Again recalling earlier examples: Barry's days have for decades revolved around procuring liquor for his fifth-per-episode binges, alternating with time spent sneaking into the garage to consume and store his supply. Although he claims he never drank at work, Barry does admit that much of his time at work and home was occupied, when he was not drinking, with severe hangovers compounded by brutal self-recrimination. Since he has been sober, he has vastly more time on his hands with which he would like to concentrate on improving family relationships. However, distressed by the barrage of depressing memories now crowding his existence, Barry voices doubts that he is capable of engaging in the activities he deems necessary to connect with his wife and son.

Nathan, for another example, sold drugs for years before his most recent arrest, his new wife, and his renewed faith all convinced him to clean up his act. As he worked with his therapist to identify new income-generating options, Nathan flirted with the idea of entering the ministry to share what he has learned and to help others in need. However, he feared that other people would not take him seriously or believe his sincerity considering his criminal past. Meanwhile, as he weighed the strength of his newly inspired convictions against his anticipated vows of more education and relative poverty, he could not help missing the quick money he made selling drugs. Furthermore, his current construction job is physically taxing, not to mention boring.

To prevent relapse for both Barry and Nathan, their therapists can direct these clients' attentions toward choosing productive activities and building involvement in those occupations, be they leisure or vocational. The development and subsequent revisions of a client's relapse prevention plan can usefully include discussions about how the client has been spending time along with alternative activities in which the client would like to participate. These alternatives may reflect interests the client has never pursued, former activities the client has given up to engage in substance use, and new options the client has never considered.

From the list of activities generated in this discussion, the therapist asks the client to prioritize and then select a highly ranked activity for concentrated focus. The therapist explains that other activities on the list will receive attention later, once the client has begun to achieve progress toward the initially selected priority activity. When the client is ready to commit to a particular pursuit, the therapist guides the specification of a target goal and helps break the goal down into attainable steps. The therapist will need to adapt the emphasis depending on the client's particular difficulties with the approach. Some clients, like Barry, will have trouble identifying alternative activities or setting priorities. Others, like Nathan, are able to articulate clear goals, but have little understanding of how to formulate a workable plan to move from where they are to where they want to be. The therapist can utilize psychoeducational and motivational strategies as needed to flesh out options, rankings, goals, and objectives for enhancing the client's vocational and avocational activities, thus reducing the risk of relapse.

After the therapy dyad has negotiated activity goals and objectives, the therapist assists in putting the plan into action, step by step. The therapist is advised to recall the four components of fostering a client's efficacy expectations, detailed already in chapter 6. Objectives aimed toward developing new client activities to replace potentially destructive behaviors should be carefully implemented by accounting for the client's performance accomplishments, emotional arousal, and exposure to vicarious successes and failures. The therapist also selectively offers verbal persuasion to support the client's efforts at attempting objectives that both agree are reasonably within the client's grasp.

The therapist's persuasive efforts are most needed when the client's confidence or commitment to relapse prevention activities starts to waver. Often after acknowledging the value of an objective or indicating willingness to take a step toward occupational goals, a client's ambivalence resurfaces. For example, now on parole, Viola has expressed excitement about enrolling in university coursework during early conversations with her therapist about relapse prevention activities. However, when the time came to comb through the schedule of courses and complete admissions forms, Vi questioned her own interest in hassling with such complicated, time-consuming paperwork when she had other necessary things to do. In addition, she complained to her therapist that earning a degree would take more time than she was able to give at her age.

Viola's therapist employed persuasion at this point, not to convince Vi that she really did want to commit four or more years to achieve a bachelor's degree, but rather to take the extra step of reconsidering her relapse prevention plan before abandoning this objective. Viola's therapist told her,

> Last week I heard the part of you that felt inspired to pursue your studies and expand your career options, and now this week I also clearly hear your doubts and concerns about whether that goal is feasible. If we pay attention to both competing sides of this issue, it looks to me like it's worth talking more in here about the pros and cons of school versus giving up on the idea of school, so that whatever you decide, you'll be satisfied that you thought it through carefully.

Viola agreed to further discussion and ended up deciding that she did want to take some courses, but not immediately because her dying father's care required so much of her time and attention. Vi and her therapist revised her relapse prevention plan to include one hour per week, subdivided as necessary and convenient, to study the university catalog for interesting courses while postponing plans to enroll.

Vocational counseling becomes an essential part of many relapse prevention plans as clients seek to determine what to do with their time and energy once they limit investment in excessive substance use. Categories of goals that may be relevant include: addressing problems that have arisen at a current job setting due to the client's substance use, pursuing educational or career goals that have been sidetracked or underdeveloped because of the client's substance use, and coping with occupational stressors without resorting to excessive use of psychoactive chemicals. Related vocational counseling applications are discussed more extensively in chapter 9.

In summary, over the course of addictions therapy, a therapist can help clients develop skills to avoid relapse by learning to substitute positive cognitions, emotions, and behaviors for former drug-associated tendencies. As the therapist supports the client in the gradual process of strengthening these skills, the client will typically experience some gratification that further reinforces the client's commitment to avoiding relapse and replacing substance use with newly valued alternatives.

ADDRESSING RELAPSE IF AND WHEN IT HAPPENS

Despite valiant efforts and best intentions, clients sometimes relapse anyway. The literature cites many indicators of the likelihood that the majority of substance abusers will engage in some substance use or misuse following treatment (Tucker & King, 1999). Especially in early recovery or at times of stress or crisis, clients continue to encounter strong ambivalence about changing addictive behavior. Urges and cravings to again experience substance-induced pleasure can become excruciating, thus exaggerating the relief the substance promises to provide. Even when the urges subside and the client has successfully resisted the temptation to relapse, additional cravings frequently follow within days or hours. For clients whose desire to use substances fades over time, the risk of relapse remains high as long as other problems remain salient yet the client has few or poorly established coping skills aside from escape through substance use.

To work effectively with the high probability of relapse during addictions therapy, therapists are advised to accept the likelihood of relapse, address negative thoughts and feelings about relapse, and utilize client relapses as windows of opportunity to further therapeutic change. This section outlines means of building these interventions into plans for preventing client relapse. Emphasis is placed not only on the impact of relapse on the client's recovery process, but also on the therapist and the interpersonal therapy process.

Accepting the Possibility of Relapse

By acknowledging up front that relapse can happen, a therapist presents the client with a realistic picture of the recovery process. Early in the development of a client's relapse prevention plan, the therapist explains that, although the potential long-term benefits of addiction therapy are highly worthwhile, the pull of old habits is likely to be strong and hard to resist at times. The therapist offers viable hope of progress and eventual success through the therapy collaboration, but also informs the client that some frustrations, setbacks, and possibly episodes of relapse are inevitable along the way. The therapist lets the client know that anticipating these eventualities will allow the client to be better prepared to deal with them if they occur. Furthermore, the therapist invites the client to specify—as part of the relapse prevention plan—objectives and strategies for coping with both potential and actual incidences of relapse. The therapist assures the client that if relapse happens to occur, it can be used in therapy as a chance to learn more about personal strengths, limitations, and needs.

To maximize client involvement, the therapist needs to take steps beyond simply stating this acknowledgment to the client. The therapist should further inquire about the client's reaction to the perspective on relapse just described. Sincere consideration of any miscomprehensions, disagreements, or doubts will facilitate the elaboration of a plan that is most personally relevant to the client.

Note the importance of the therapist also accepting the probability of client relapse. The helping professions are rife with unfair sentiment that therapy for substance abusers is largely fruitless because such clients cannot or do not want to change. Some other professionals who reject this pessimistic outlook and believe that relapse does not equal failure of treatment still may encounter their own feelings of disillusionment when a client succumbs to temptations to fall back into old behaviors. Therapists need to be aware of their own attitudes and feelings about client relapse, and to carefully pick and choose how to utilize as therapeutic tools their own reactions to the sensitive issue of relapse. Supervision can assist newer or struggling therapists in working through their own resistances and in working effectively with the difficult dynamic of client relapse.

By encouraging the client to report relapse incidents or other considerations of acting counter to therapy goals, the stage can be set for using therapy sessions to promote learning from setbacks as well as from successes. The therapist reassures the client that,

> If you choose to share a relapse experience with me, I won't think it means you've failed, nor will I think any less of you. What I will do is help you understand what happened and to explore what the experience teaches you so we can use that awareness to strengthen your skills to prevent future relapses.

The therapist may also ask for or reassert the client's permission to inquire at each session about any recent substance use.

Dealing With Feelings About Relapse

Once the possibility of relapse is admitted and an agreement to examine any relapse episodes is in place, the therapist remains attentive for emerging needs to address negative thoughts and feelings about relapse as they arise.

The Client's Perspective.   From the client's perspective, anticipatory feelings range from excessive fears to arrogant overconfidence about abilities to resist relapse. When the therapist hears extreme or unrealistic anticipations of relapse potential, the therapist intervenes by reflecting back what the therapist is hearing and by challenging the client to explore those thoughts and feelings in greater depth. Regarding a relapse that has already occurred, clients may feel anything from intense guilt and shame to relief or resignation associated with resuming substance use.

Some clients openly acknowledge a relapse, whereas other clients who have agreed in advance to report a relapse still hesitate to confide about an incident once it has actually occurred. An attentive therapist can often detect changes in client mood or attitude that hint that something has happened. Being careful not to assume a relapse has in fact occurred, the therapist can notice aloud the difference in the client's presentation and express curiosity, inviting the client to elaborate on its meaning.

As discussed in chapter 7, the therapist who regularly checks in with the client to inquire about any substance use since the last therapy session provides a context in which a client who is reluctant to bring up the topic can be prompted to share information. Also such inquiry during each session gives the therapist a baseline against which a client's atypical response more clearly signals the need for greater investigation. As the therapist explores client material that appears vague, evasive, unusually emotion-laden, or cryptic, it is important to remember that pushing clients to admit relapses they have not yet acknowledged rarely helps. Using open questions that avoid presumptive wording is more likely to elicit relevant content from the client.

When a client reports a relapse, either by self-initiation or in response to the therapist's exploration, the therapist first offers support by reiterating unconditional acceptance of the client along with curiosity about what can be learned from the incident. Then the therapist asks both about what happened and how the client is feeling about it. Empathic listening will help the therapist maintain rapport at such difficult times, and it also helps assess how the client is actually reacting to the relapse. Relapse prevention planning continues from this point to incorporate analysis of the relapse experience and to apply findings toward treatment objectives. Analysis of the lessons learned from a relapse is most useful when the therapist can get an accurate reading of the client's emotional state following relapse.

Whatever feelings the client expresses, the therapist both validates that affect and encourages the client to generate or review options for acting on that feeling. A shame-ridden client can be reminded that, although his feelings are understandably painful, it is important not to lose sight of progress he has already made, as well as the remaining potential for additional progress. The client wrapped up in anger that she bothered to try therapy when this relapse proves she was just setting herself up for yet another failure can be prodded to recall her reasons for seeking and attending therapy prior to this relapse. If the client indicates indifference to the occurrence of a relapse, the therapist can acknowledge that sentiment at face value, but also ask the client to remember and comment on stated treatment goals and rationale. In each case, the therapist will most likely suggest a review of the treatment plan, especially the provisions for relapse prevention. The therapist further determines with the client whether some revision of the plan is needed based on incoming information.

The Therapist's Perspective.   In addition to helping the client address feelings about a relapse and its impact on treatment motivations, therapists also experience their own strong affect at points of client relapse. It is one thing to anticipate the possibility of client relapse, but a report of the actual event can send a therapist reeling with intense emotion. Among the feelings the therapist may need to deal with are feelings of responsibility for the relapse, guilt for not doing enough to prevent it, anger or disgust with the turn of events, or sadness or fear regarding consequences the client now faces. Such emotions on the therapist's part can be as hard to experience and as influential on the therapy process as the client's reactions to relapse.

The therapist should not try to ignore or deny these feelings, but must also consider what it would be like for the client to hear about the therapist's reactions to a relapse and what the client is likely to do with that information. The therapist chooses to share those thoughts and feelings that the therapist has justifiable reason to believe will be therapeutic. This means that any frustration or disappointment the therapist reveals should be closely linked with the therapist's continuing hope and support for the client's ongoing progress. Such messages are often also combined with challenges to the client. Explicitly or otherwise, many clients will want to know what the therapist truly thinks of the client. Thus, at the critical juncture following a recent relapse, the therapist's ability to offer honest critique paired with sincere faith in the client's potential is paramount.

Personal feelings about the client's relapse that the therapist cannot justify telling the client should be kept private. These may still be useful as sources or tests of a therapist's hypotheses. Such feelings can potentially also become problematic if they interfere with rapport in session, with the therapist's ability to offer support and hope, or with the therapist's well-being outside of session. Confidential consultation with a trusted supervisor or colleague may be useful or even necessary for a therapist burdened by negative feelings toward a client relapse that the therapist cannot quite put to therapeutic use.

By fairly addressing negative affect and disruptive cognitions as they arise in session, therapists guide clients toward accepting the reality of personal experience. Just as important, examining relapse episodes moves the therapy process toward using the experience to gauge the barriers and assets weighing against and for the client's recovery. The therapy dyad admits the downside of relapse, but in equal measure acknowledges the opportunities for learning and growth presented by the relapse episode.

Learning From the Experience of Relapse

Exploring a relapse creates chances to strengthen the clients' understanding of the processes of relapse and recovery. Furthermore, the therapist can seize opportunities to reassess and reassert the client's goals in therapy. The therapist asks the client what factors led up to the relapse and how this episode was similar to and different from other times the client has run into problems with drugs or alcohol. Clients are encouraged to articulate what they know now that they did not know before about personal vulnerability or resistance to relapse. Therapist and client together consider what they like and dislike about the way the relapse has been handled, and the therapist invites the client to talk about what the client can do differently in the future to better ward off another relapse or to minimize its negative impact.

This kind of discussion can be punctuated with a review of the client's extant relapse prevention plan. Insights gleaned from conversational analysis of the relapse lessons are then underscored by building them into a revision of the client's plan. The therapist can write these revisions in a format that can be offered to the client, with a copy maintained in the therapist's records to be consulted later by each as needed.

Thus, relapse prevention planning continues in the face of a client relapse. Instead of assuming treatment failure or using a slip as an excuse to give up, the therapy dyad can investigate the lessons inherent in the experience of relapse. Directly addressing relapse incidents teaches clients to better recognize and manage factors that could threaten their progress in therapy and recovery.

REINFORCING SUCCESSFUL RELAPSE PREVENTION EFFORTS AS THEY HAPPEN

Therapists reinforce clients' efforts to prevent relapse by emphasizing progress and rewarding client success. In addition to expressing praise, admiration, and appreciation of steps the client takes toward established goals, the therapist also instructs clients on how to reinforce their own skills at relapse prevention. The therapist accomplishes this through a combination of treatment planning, implementation, and outcome evaluation tasks.

Expanding the Treatment Plan to Promote Evaluation and Reinforcement

First, the therapist helps build evaluation and reinforcement into the client's relapse prevention plan. When clients identify strategies for avoiding barriers to treatment goals, or they choose new activities to substitute for substance abuse, therapists ask clients how they can reward themselves for attempts to implement these alternatives. Therapists also prompt clients to consider ways they can reinforce themselves for successes in meeting treatment goals or in resisting temptations to relapse.

For clients who in the past have used alcohol and other drugs to reward themselves, finding equally satisfying reinforcers is no simple task. As already noted, psychoactive chemicals have strong, inherently gratifying properties, and can furthermore blunt the brain's response to otherwise pleasurable stimuli. Therefore, it is often hard for clients who have excessively used alcohol or other drugs to identify and experience other reinforcers.

Therapists may thus need to generate ideas with clients about types of reinforcers both available and meaningful to the clients. Once a therapy dyad has developed a list of plausible ways for the client to reward progress, the therapist gives the client the list (retaining a copy for the therapist's file) and suggests that the client reread the list and apply a suitable option whenever the client notices indications of progress.

Some clients will also need help with evaluating progress that deserves reinforcement. The therapist can ask, "How will you know, outside of our sessions, when you have taken a step that's worth a reward?" For clients who have trouble answering this question, the therapist steers the conversation toward objectives specified in the treatment plan to highlight desirable outcomes. In terms of self-evaluation criteria, clients can be encouraged, especially in the early phases, to apply reinforcement for genuine efforts, partial successes, and small but still salient indicators of change. Therapists can implement cognitive restructuring and behavioral management of affect in facilitating discussions of client self-evaluation and reward.

Responding to Positive Results of Efforts to Modify Substance Use

As clients learn the concept of self-reinforcement, they also benefit from guidance in recognizing and responding to positive outcomes of their change processes. A client who grasps the idea of rewarding progress may still lack motivation or understanding of how to make it work for her personally. Jeannie, the client who has been abstinent from marijuana for three weeks, initially scoffed at the suggestion that she had made a good choice that merited some reward by deciding not to attend a party in the past week where she knew marijuana would be offered to her. "All I did was stay home, bored out of my skull and feeling sorry for myself. And I'm not sure I'd make the same choice if another opportunity comes up this weekend," she complained to her therapist. "You call that progress?" Her therapist admitted she could empathize with Jeannie's frustration, but also pointed out that the episode proved Jeannie was capable of exerting more control over her substance use and over staying out of trouble than she had expected. In addition, the boredom and self-pity she had encountered could be viewed in the more positive light as good indicators of the importance of finding alternative means of fun for Jeannie on those weekends that she does choose not to smoke pot. Reframed in this way, Jeannie came to see some advantages to the outcome of her choices, even if they were not entirely satisfactory. Along with recognizing desirable outcomes, clients can learn to find something desirable in many outcomes of their efforts, even the less obviously positive ones.

Substance abuse clients also need to practice responding in a reinforcing manner to indicators of their progress. If clients minimize or devalue steps they have taken, the therapist can encourage application of a different client response that supports relapse prevention efforts in a realistic context. For example, Barry notes that he is feeling physically healthier since he stopped drinking, but he also tells his therapist, "Not that it matters when I'm either depressed or just numb all the time." His therapist reflects the disillusionment she hears from Barry, but also points out that it is worth something that his headaches and stomach problems have abated, his hands are steadier, and his thoughts clearer. She asks him, "How about telling yourself that it is nice to feel healthier even though you realize there are still important emotional concerns to work on?" The therapist invites Barry to talk about how he could make some time in his sessions or in his daily routine to appreciate the physical improvements he is noticing.

Some clients like Barry have difficulty applying self-reinforcement. Aside from the gratifying effects of using psychoactive chemicals, they may have limited experience and few skills at responses that promote positive outcomes. The therapist can help clients learn to reinforce their own relapse prevention efforts by reflecting and interpreting signs of progress toward treatment objectives, and by prodding clients to think through how they can choose to react to situations in which a potential relapse was prevented or managed. Clients who are not convinced of their need or ability to reinforce themselves can be asked to experiment with new options for purposes of comparison. The therapist can recommend that the client try to "act as if" outcomes of their relapse prevention efforts are positive or worthwhile. Sometimes such experiments or exercises will surprise the client with the result that the new responses to recovery efforts and outcomes actually make the client feel better, stronger, or more competent. Gradually, recognizing and responding to positive outcomes of relapse prevention efforts become their own reward.

From the therapist's perspective, it can be enormously gratifying to hear the client's report of new behaviors and to see the client demonstrating expanded skills at preventing relapse and promoting progress. These are times when it is easy to help reinforce client initiatives, and the client will be wonderfully responsive to therapist feedback. There are moments of doubt and frustration for the therapist, too, when clients are not changing as much or as fast as the therapist had anticipated, or when the client does not acknowledge or maintain new behaviors that the therapist sees as signs or positive change. Thus, the therapist will need to stay attentive both for indications of small but still meaningful successes, and to find ways to productively discuss these with clients. A therapist's own frustration can serve as a signal that something is occurring in session that needs to be discussed.

If therapists decide to reveal their own feelings to their clients, it is strongly recommended that the therapist's expression of frustration be solidly paired with expressions of hope that sharing impressions will lead to reactivated momentum in therapy, along with genuine interest in the client's reactions to what is occurring in session in that moment. For example:

> I'm starting to feel like a cheerleader, like I'm trying to get you to admit that what you did is an important step, but the message I'm getting is that you don't see it as any big deal. Let's talk some more about what it means that we're looking at this so differently. What is your reaction to me saying this?

Or,

You're telling me you don't think it's worth trying anymore since this just feels too hard. I have to admit, that is hard for me to hear, but I'm also hoping that if we keep talking about it some more we can find ways to make this worth your while. Are you willing to talk some more with me about what is working and what's not and what we can do differently in here?

In essence, getting the client to stay involved in the therapy process and to keep coming to sessions until the work is satisfactorily completed is, in itself, a positive outcome and a step toward preventing relapse. As these moments occur in session, the therapist is in a position to provide immediate reinforcement to the client's engagement in continuing to sort out the advantages and difficulties of working to prevent relapse. In other words, when the client accepts the therapist's invitation to keep talking about what progress means and how to make it happen, in addition to the client's report of what the client is doing outside of session, steps toward relapse prevention are occurring directly in session. The therapist can acknowledge and praise all these client behaviors as they happen, thus utilizing the immediacy of the therapy interaction.

Just the fact that you're telling me this is new, and I want you to know I appreciate your willingness to explore this even though I know some aspects of this discussion aren't easy for either one of us. The fact that we can talk about it, even though it is hard, is part of what seems important about it, at least from my vantage point. So I hope to see you stick with it.

Revising Treatment Goals to Build on Client Progress

As the therapist and client together reinforce the relapse prevention strategies that the client is learning to implement, clients are likely to experience increasing success and satisfaction. As objectives are met, therapists can further develop clients' relapse prevention skills by expanding treatment goals to build on client successes. Earlier this chapter described the idea of using a relapse episode as a window of opportunity to clarify the client's abilities and limitations to deal with temptations to drink, take drugs, or engage in related problem behaviors. Episodes of client success at deflecting a relapse also provide parallel opportunities. When the client has met a relapse prevention objective or demonstrated a new skill at coping with a potential problem, the time is ripe for reviewing goals, articulating accomplishments, and clarifying new priorities and next steps. This process of revising the relapse prevention plan can itself be rewarding as the therapist encourages the client to use what the client has already learned in taking strides toward further skill development.

*   *   *

The changes a client begins to make through addictions therapy need to be planfully maintained and reinforced to prevent client relapse into formerly problematic substance use and related habits. Therapists can facilitate beneficial outcomes of treatment and help clients learn skills for preventing relapse by teaching clients to (a) cope effectively with urges, cravings, and triggers; (b) substitute healthier cognitive, affective, and behavioral strategies in place of old habits; (c) realistically address the possibility and actuality of a relapse during the recovery process; and (d) productively reinforce ongoing relapse prevention efforts. By gradually learning the logic and implementation of relapse prevention strategies, clients can expand their ranges of options and their senses of control over decisions they make regarding substance use, coping mechanisms, and productive activity.

Chapter 9

Interventions to Address Problems Linked to the Client's Substance Abuse

Because substance use problems are so often entangled with other difficulties exhibited or experienced by clients, a therapist will be in the frequent position of designing interventions to address complex problems in an integrated manner. Chapter 5 considered how both initial and ongoing assessments can reveal symptoms of co-morbid psychological disorders, health complications, relationship difficulties, vocational problems, and legal or ethical concerns. In chapters 6 to 8, planning and implementing treatment to directly address substance use concerns were discussed, acknowledging the importance of accounting for associated problems. This chapter focuses more explicitly on interventions undertaken to deal with contextual factors that may be contributing to, resulting from, or interacting with a client's substance abuse.

For present purposes, *intervention* is broadly defined as anything the therapist says or does during the therapy transaction that reflects a therapeutic intent generated from the therapist's understanding of the transactional dynamics of this particular therapy relationship. *Therapeutic intent* is further defined as an undertaking aimed at using the therapy interaction to improve the client's well-being through eliciting the client's critical thinking skills and empowering the client's conscious choices to the extent possible with regard to the client's circumstances. Thus, intervention includes ongoing assessment, planning, psychoeducation, treatment implementation, and evaluation. As emphasized in prior chapters, these processes may each take precedence at different points in the therapy process, but they are not discrete, exclusive categories of intervention. Ideally, they are interwoven, continuous aspects of an evolving course of therapeutic change.

Individuals who heavily consume drugs or alcohol are often using substances to replace something that is missing in their lives or to cope with troubles that are otherwise difficult to address or hard to eliminate. Attempts to escape from or altogether avoid negative affect have been posited as the primary motive for compulsive substance use (Baker, Fiore, Piper, McCarthy, & Majeskie, 2004). It cannot be emphasized enough that meaningful change in substance abuse behavior depends at least in part on helping clients learn to fill the gaps, resolve the difficulties, and deal with their feelings some other way besides seeking a chemically altered state of mind. Marlatt (1985c) highlighted the importance of lifestyle modification interventions to promote balance between the individual's sources of stress and resources for coping with that stress.

PHYSICAL HEALTH AND MEDICAL PROBLEMS

As mentioned in chapter 4, chronic excessive use of drugs or alcohol can trigger a host of negative health consequences, and even occasional risky use can threaten an individual's health and well-being. Chapter 5 underscored the importance of assessing the need for medical attention right away on detection of substance use concerns. If relatively high levels of severity are indicated on either Dimensions 1 (Withdrawal Potential) or 2 (Biomedical Conditions and Complications) of the ASAM Placement Criteria (Mee-Lee et al., 2001), the therapist should find out whether the client is receiving medical care. If not, the therapist advises the client to see a doctor and explores the client's reaction to this advice.

Marlatt (1985c) emphasized the likelihood that clients exhibiting substance use disorders, particularly more chronic patterns of abuse, will merit medical attention. With clients who express negative attitudes or report reasons against seeking medical help, the therapist intervenes by addressing these barriers. Indications of health problems or risks associated with a client's substance abuse may be evident during initial intake or may be revealed as therapy proceeds. In any case, the therapist can play an important role in referring the client for appropriate medical attention and facilitating the client's connection to health care providers.

Intervening When the Client Neglects Personal Health

Individuals who expose themselves to high doses of psychoactive chemicals also tend to engage in other behaviors that are hazardous to their health. This may include the tendency to ignore physical complaints or at least to neglect adequate attention to health problems. Repeated substance abuse can provide enough relief from discomfort to push off dealing with aches and pains until later. Individuals can easily redirect money for covering a doctor's fees to the purchase of more alcohol or drugs. Hearing a physician recommend that the substance abuser should give up substance use to feel better is not likely a desirable outcome. Even when the substance abuser is concerned about health consequences of continuing use, there are often fears about admitting illegal or otherwise sanctioned behavior to a medical professional, especially one with an impersonal or judgmental manner.

For any or all of these reasons, clients who abuse drugs or alcohol often do not immediately act on the therapist's suggestion to schedule a doctor's appointment. The therapist's intervention is thus likely to involve repeatedly raising the topic, following up on previous discussions. The therapist balances the presentation of concern about the client's related symptoms and behaviors with genuine interest in the client's rationale plus respect for the client's right to decide how to care for his or her own health.

The therapist can take the stance that future therapy sessions are contingent on the client obtaining medical consultation. The problem with this position is that if the client declines medical attention and consequently loses access to this therapist, the therapist has given up leverage to maneuver the client. The therapist who can maintain a continuing alliance with the client through communication of concern and respect, including the agreement to disagree about the relevance of medical consultation, is in a much better position to gradually sway the client toward articulating and addressing health conditions.

Once the therapist has discussed a medical referral with a client, the therapist asks in the next session whether the client has taken any steps or thought further about medical attention. If the client answers no, or resists further discussion, the therapist need not assume failure or irrelevance. Instead the therapist can say,

> Well, I get the sense this isn't something you want to talk about right now, but before we change the subject, let me just reiterate my concern about the symptoms you've told me about, and I'd like us to stay open to the possibility of discussing that further at some point down the line.

Afterward the therapist raises the consideration of seeking medical attention any time the client makes additional mention of health-related complaints. The topic may also come up at the therapist's initiative in reviews of the treatment plan.

Working With Client Ambivalence About Health Care

Related to earlier discussions of client ambivalence, clients can waver for some time between intentions to pursue and avoid health care. Miller and Rollnick (2002) wrote that, "change is motivated by a perceived discrepancy between present behavior and important personal goals or values" (p. 39). The therapist cannot make clients take better care of their health, but can employ interventions that accentuate the discrepancy between the client's future well-being and present tendencies to use recreational substances excessively and ignore health-related consequences. Interventions include conducting psychoeducation with the client about the long-term health outcomes of chronic substance use, incorporating conversations about the client's reaction to the material presented. The therapist may also ask the client to reflect on extreme case scenarios or hypothetical future outcomes of attending or failing to attend to current health factors.

Even when a client's initial stance is to dismiss health concerns or medical care, there is some part of the client, however repressed, that cannot deny outright the health risks embraced by the substance abuser. Clients may say they do not care, are not worried, or will not be affected. The therapist can acknowledge and validate both sides of the client's ambivalence. When applied consistently so that the therapist helps clarify the components of the client's complicated perspective without taking responsibility for the client's decisions or behaviors, the client often comes over time to make the argument for change.

Supporting Client Efforts to Address Health Concerns

At the point where the substance abusing client takes steps to seek medical attention, the therapist continues to offer support and guidance, and to identify other sources of support in the client's environment. The therapist can help prepare the client to maximize the utility of any medical appointments, and can help weigh options and implement decisions for acting on a physician's advice. The therapist can help monitor and enhance the client's compliance with treatment procedures, encourage additional medical consultation if treatment problems arise, and motivate the client to seek a second opinion if dissatisfied. Later this chapter expands on interventions for facilitating a client's medical consultations and decisions.

Before moving on, however, it is worth notice that concerns about a client's future health status can arise before the client experiences physical symptoms, especially with younger substance abusers. Clients may report anxieties about anticipated health problems for themselves or their offspring resulting from the client's past substance use. Therapists can provide opportunities for such clients to express their worries. Discussions can explore the possibility of accepting the past without staying mired in fears or self-recrimination. Therapists can help clients consider how to engage in active coping and decision making for the future. Alternatively, a therapist may become concerned about potential health consequences of the risky substance use a client is recounting in sessions, even if the client denies any current symptoms. With clients like this, the therapist wants to avoid alienating the client and yet cannot responsibly neglect to raise the concern. To walk this fine line, the therapist might say,

> I can hear that you are having fun with this. I'm also glad to hear you haven't run into any problems yet, and I hope you never do. But when you tell me stories like that I can't help but think there's a chance that you could end up with some real damage to your health if you continue using alcohol (or any other drug) that way. I bring this up because I care about what happens to you, and I wonder if you'd be willing to talk about this some more.

Physical health issues are intricately tied to the use of mind-altering substances because taking a substance clearly affects the body as well as the mind. By letting clients know that they are interested not only in what the client does to influence personal health, but also how the client thinks and feels about health care or neglect, therapists can intervene to promote client choices about substance use and related health issues. The process of therapy provides a context in which the client can work through doubts, fears, skepticism, wavering motivations, and frustration about health and medical issues.

EMOTIONAL DIFFICULTIES

As a therapist listens to a client's stories about substance use, themes of negative emotion and disruptive behavior are not unusual. Clients will report that they reach for their substances of choice to take the ache out of their sadness, the edge off their anxiety, or the sting from their grief. Others drink or take drugs in attempts to counteract their frustration or apathy. Sometimes clients abuse substances to escape from or even magnify their feelings of anger, rage, or hatred. The repetitious use of drugs or alcohol to dull dysphoria becomes a problem to the extent that the temporary relief provided by the substance also precludes the individual from taking productive steps to address the causes of the difficult emotions. Substance abuse can further exacerbate distressing emotions by putting the individual at risk for engaging in other potentially destructive behaviors or incurring damaging health consequences. Thus, interventions to unravel the knot of substance abuse and corresponding negative affect are essential tools in therapy for substance abuse.

Interventions to Promote Insight Into Co-occurring Affective Problems

In theory, the therapist teases out the causal relationship between problematic affect and excessive substance use. If the evidence suggests a substance-induced disorder of mood or anxiety, a recommended strategy might be to assist the client first in getting his or her drug or alcohol use under control. An assumption of this approach is that once substance abuse has been satisfactorily reduced or stopped, the therapist can help the client assess whether the symptoms of the secondary disorder have abated or still require therapeutic attention. If initial assessment instead indicates that the client's substance abuse developed as a strategy for coping with a primary disorder like depression or anxiety, the treatment plan might aim to address the symptoms of the primary disorder first and then determine whether the alleviation of depression, anxiety, or other disorder has reduced the client's need to self-medicate.

In practice, however, establishing primary and secondary relations between co-morbid disorders is both complex and controversial. The treatment plan should encompass the full, complex picture of the client gleaned from ongoing assessment of the client, rather than starting only with the first in a presumed temporal sequence of symptoms. A client who had formerly been drinking to mask depression might still feel strong urges to drink even after the depression has been lifted to some degree. Another client might continue to struggle with panic attacks after a substantial period of abstinence from cocaine, even if the original attacks were substance-induced, possibly in response to the continuing financial or social difficulties caused by the client's former habit. Even if it does become clear which disorder emerged first, that problem may not presently be the more glaring one, nor be the problem the client is willing to discuss. Substance abuse and associated problems typically chase each other in a vicious circle.

Several interventions are described next, with a preliminary reminder to the therapist to pay as much attention to the client's response to each intervention as to the therapist's plans and intentions underlying the choice of intervention. Often new information surfaces about a client's history or change process during an intervention that touches core emotions.

Extended Assessment. The first intervention involves additional, in-depth assessment of the interplay between the client's substance use and troubling feelings. Clients often drop vague or disjointed hints about use of drugs or alcohol to blunt painful feelings or to accentuate feelings in the face of numbness. They sometimes minimize the link with jokes or changes of subject, or they dismiss the relevance of their substance use with respect to problematic emotions. Alternatively, clients may be preoccupied in therapy sessions with the stress of feeling trapped in their own webs of poor coping as they sway between feeling bad and getting drunk or high. When clients present problems of negative affect tied up with habits of excessive substance use, therapists cannot assume they comprehend the problem without further assessment. The client is unlikely to trust a therapist who jumps to conclusions and offers solutions without taking the time to gather extensive personal information, including the client's own perspective on the problem.

To clarify the individual client's experience, the therapist probes for details, steering with a curious, caring approach and open-ended questions. The therapist paraphrases and reflects any hints the client has offered about using substances to cope with bad feelings and then invites the client to elaborate. The therapist also poses questions to assess further the specific nature of the problematic affect, the pattern of substance use as a coping strategy, and the perceived causal relationship between them.

The therapist asks for examples of recent situations during which the client experienced the problematic affect, inquiring about how the client remembers feeling and thinking. In addition to listening to the stories, therapists watch how clients tell those tales in session and invite clients to comment on how they feel in the present moment. Using neutral, nonpresumptive wording, the therapist asks how the client coped with those feelings at the time the story occurred. If the client does not mention substance abuse, and after the therapist has explored the coping mechanisms described by the client to the client's satisfaction, the therapist asks whether the client was using any substance at the time of the story. Any acknowledgment the client makes of drug or alcohol use can then be more pointedly investigated. The therapist will want to ask what reasons in that instance led the client to drink or take drugs. At what point in the incident did the client use substances (e.g., before, during, or after an event occurred or an emotion surfaced)? How did the client feel before and after consuming the substance(s)? Did the substance play any role in the problematic affect the client has already described in association with this situation? And so forth.

Analyzing a few examples provided by the client in this minute detail gives the therapist a sharper view of the connection between the client's substance use and the client's struggle to deal with negative affect. The therapist can use this enhanced knowledge to clarify the diagnosis by either identifying or ruling out comorbid disorders. This focused ongoing assessment may also help determine whether symptoms of affective disorder are primary or substance-induced.

Often the client will have her or his own ideas about causal impact (e.g., "I drink to medicate my depression" or "Smoking pot makes me paranoid"). Although the therapist should certainly take the client's rough theories into account, careful assessment is obviously in order. Adequate analysis of substance use concerns requires a thorough assessment of the client's history of symptoms, including the recollected timing of appearance and the duration of each relevant symptom. At what age did the client first drink or try drugs? When and under what circumstances did the client's substance abuse become regular? Become heavy? For how long has the client maintained the current level of use? What is the client's first memory of depressed (or anxious, or raging) feelings? How frequently have such symptoms recurred in the client's experience, and how long has each episode lasted? What does the client believe are the connections between his or her substance use and other symptoms of distress or dysfunction? Acknowledging that client memory is potentially limited to some degree, it is also useful when possible to ask such questions of family members or other involved parties to whom the treatment provider has legitimate access.

Psychoeducation About the Link Between Substance Use and Affect Management. The therapist further intervenes by providing psychoeducation about the overlapping mechanisms of chemical and emotional influences on the brain. Psychoeducation about stress management is another useful intervention. (A worksheet to facilitate stress management intervention with substance abusers is reproduced in Appendix B.) The therapist can also initiate discussion of the value (from both the therapist's and client's perspectives) of expanding the client's range of options for coping with anxiety, sadness, anger, and the like. This will include exploring the methods the client already knows and uses, and by distinguishing those that are conducive to healthier functioning from those that are not. The client may have already mentioned some of these coping strategies in earlier phases of assessment. A client's mode of reaction to uncomfortable feelings may include other problem behaviors, such as excessive gambling, stealing, disordered eating, interpersonal violence, and so on.

The client is then encouraged to consider how risk-taking and impulse-control problems can increase the client's potential for experiencing uncomfortable emotions in the future. The therapist prompts the client to think about the utility of exercising a broader set of alternatives for acting on feelings of anger, guilt, frustration, or whatever other emotions are troubling the client. The therapist points out that having a wide range of options puts individuals in the position to choose how they want to respond to a situation, rather than reacting reflexively or compulsively.

The client who agrees with or comes to agree with the value the therapist places on expanding options for emotional expression is ready for interventions designed to promote emotions management skills. Before these interventions are discussed, however, it is important to recognize that many substance abusing clients will not readily or favorably respond to the therapist's recommendation. Some clients will say that drinking or using drugs does a fine job of shutting off bad feelings, so why should they bother learning other coping strategies? Others argue that their negative emotions are so deeply rooted in good reasons that they cannot be removed, so why try? Such clients may even admit that substance use adds to their bad feelings in the long run, but given their dismal outcome expectations of any efforts to change, attempts to better manage emotions are not perceived as worth their effort. Still others will tell the therapist they like engaging in impulsive, risky, or disruptive behaviors, so they have no interest in changing something that makes them feel good or serves their own interests.

The therapist encountering these types of resistance can further intervene by nondefensively reflecting the client's point of view, expressing curiosity and interest in the client's stance. Additionally, therapists can share their sincere reactions to their clients' statements. In doing so, the therapist emphasizes that this is the therapist's own opinion and that clients are entitled to their own stated opinions. However, the therapist further asks the client to at least consider the therapist's vantage point just as the therapist is trying to understand the client's perspective.

This combination of empathic validation and gentle confrontation can be interspersed with interventions of continuing assessment of the client's history and perspective. Together these interventions with a client who resists affect management approaches may help reveal the client's ambivalence about current coping strategies. When clients acknowledge mixed feelings about the roles substance use plays in their lives, the therapist can comment on both or all sides of the evident ambivalence while still encouraging resolution on the positive side. For example, the therapist might say,

> I hear the part of you that tells yourself therapy is a waste of your time because you don't believe anything will (or needs to) change. But just the fact that you keep coming back to see me each week tells me you have at least some hope that your depressed feelings could get better with time. I can understand the doubt; from what you've told me, you have good reasons for it. But I also want to make sure we don't lose track of that part of you that believes things could get better, because I think it's possible that things will get better if we pay attention to your feelings and how you're dealing with them.

Identification of Hypothetical Options. If and when the client reaches the point of agreeing to consider other ways to manage affect besides drinking or taking drugs, the therapist guides the client in generating options. With clients still in the insight phase of therapy (precontemplation, contemplation, and preparation stages of change), clients are likely to be unconvinced that they can or will have to actually change behavior. The therapist may thus opt to discuss affect management options in hypothetical terms or as adjuncts (rather than alternatives) to the client's present habits.

For example, Randy says that, given his history of growing up with an alcoholic father who eventually died of liver disease, he should probably quit drinking altogether. However, he further states that his social life at this stage of his young adulthood rules out abstinence as a viable option. Still he concedes to his therapist that drinking when he is already in a bad mood has, on several recent occasions, led to his involvement in bar fights and arguments with his girlfriend. The last such argument halted abruptly when he hit her for the first time ever. Randy is not willing to completely stop drinking, but he is willing to talk about how he could better keep his anger under control even if he does still drink.

An intervention generating hypothetical options permits the therapist to explore with clients what they could do to promote healthy and responsible control of their expression of volatile affect regardless of whether the client chooses to use substances. In Randy's case, when his therapist asks about his options, Randy comes up with the ideas of monitoring the amount he drinks and refraining from drinking when he is already in a foul mood. The therapist suggests making those coping strategies even more specific, and together they generate a list of things Randy could do, such as checking in with himself to assess his mood prior to an outing, alternating alcoholic drinks with water or soda, ensuring he eats along with his drinks, and leaving the drinking establishment when he reaches his preestablished limit. Randy's therapist writes the list on a card Randy can carry in his wallet, and the therapist asks Randy to consult the list before he goes out drinking. In subsequent discussions, Randy and his therapist expand the list to identify things he can do (e.g., exercise, watch a favorite comedian, talk to a friend) besides drinking to cope with a bad mood. These ideas are added to Randy's wallet card.

Acknowledgment of Emotion.   Generating options for dealing with strong affect sometimes yields the discovery that the client rarely takes the time to recognize or even "feel" her or his own feelings. At the earliest signs of pending difficulty or annoyance, some individuals launch right into substance use to ward off the anticipated distress before it can take hold. With clients like these, the therapist can employ interventions to help clients experience and accept their own emotions. Once clients are able to do so, they can then be encouraged to pay attention to what the emotion is telling them, which can help generate additional options about how to deal with the emotional state and the factors contributing to it.

To increase awareness, the therapist can invite the client to experience and "sit with" a troublesome emotion in the therapy session. The client may be asked to describe the emotion and its impact: Does the client feel a reaction anywhere in the client's body? What does the feeling make the client want to say or do? Do any images or colors come to mind? What do those mean to the client? What is it like to experience this in the present moment with the therapist? In addition to listening empathically and responding in a reflective, affirming manner, the therapist advises the client to experience feelings in session without judging them, to accept that the feelings are there for some reason, and that experiencing negative feelings does not make the client a bad person. The therapist can initiate discussion of the ideas that a feeling can be expressed (or suppressed) in a number of ways, and that each person has both the right and the responsibility to choose how they will act on their emotions. This discussion often leads to additional conversations about how appreciating one's own emotion and possible reasons for it can help clarify the individual's options and decisions about how to act on that emotion.

With those substance abusers who tend to use drugs or alcohol to avoid having to feel, guided interventions to attend to emotions and expressive options teach the client to take time to think before using substances impulsively. With clients like the stereotypical "sloppy drunks" who use substances to permit expression of too much feeling, promoting acceptance of the authentic experience of emotion is also important. Counteracting the inclination to chemically alter one's state of mind to dampen (or accentuate) affect is typically neither quick nor easy. Therapists should be prepared to revisit and revise this intervention on several occasions over a course of therapy.

Elaboration of Expressive Options. It is probably obvious that helping substance abusers experience their emotions more deeply and fully is hardly sufficient by itself for managing emotions, especially if the disturbing emotions make the client want to drink or use drugs. As the therapist leads the client to explore the reactions and motivations stimulated by the experience of emotion in session, the conversation can be steered toward this question: "When you have this feeling, what are different ways you could choose to express it?" The therapist could add, ". . . instead of using your substance of choice," but this is recommended only if the client has already indicated interest in changing personal patterns of consumption. Until the client is ready to commit to action, the therapist who appears to rule out substance use as an optional response to difficult emotion is likely to encounter client resistance.

Both the client and therapist can make suggestions as the list of expressive options is generated in session. For highly motivated clients, this exercise could be done as homework, but solitary activity focused on bad feelings when available substances and established habits remain seductive may not yield the desired, completed results. Instead of homework, developing options in session, during time the client has set aside free from substance use to concentrate on therapy goals, capitalizes on the availability of support and suggestions from the therapist.

Once a set of expressive options has been generated (with the shared understanding that the list can be revised as needed), the therapist helps the client evaluate the personal viability of each option. For each identified form of expression, the therapist asks questions such as: Is your reaction to this option positive, negative, or somewhere in between? Why? Can you imagine yourself doing that option? Would drinking or using drugs be compatible with that form of expression? Why or why not?

Consideration of Specific Situations. The therapist asks the client to describe situations, either past or present, that are associated with emotions the client is learning to manage. Clients can then be guided in using mental imagery to visualize themselves using personally viable options to manage the feelings. Marlatt (1985b) referred to this intervention as *covert modeling*. The therapist probes for the client's reaction:

> How do you feel right now imagining yourself doing that strategy? How do you feel about trying it in an upcoming situation? What do you imagine are the likely outcomes? What would you do if things didn't turn out as you're expecting? What are the pros and cons of trying this in "real life"?

Guided imagery helps teach clients to elicit internal responses that are incompatible with their problematic affect. Intervention may emphasize relaxation strategies for emotion management when the client is overaroused (e.g., anxious, rageful). Teaching clients to consciously relax gives them greater control over their reactions to stressful circumstances (Benson, 1975; Marlatt, 1985a, 1985c). For underaroused (e.g., bored, apathetic) clients, imagery focusing on activating strategies present intriguing possibilities. Marcus, for example, has been drinking more since his wife got pregnant, and he tells his therapist he drinks to fill time he used to spend mountain biking. Now that his wife wants him home as her delivery date approaches, and in the future when they have an infant to care for, Marcus can bike much less frequently. He looks forward to being a new father, but he says he misses the sun on his back, the wind in his hair, and the adrenaline rush of pumping over rocks and ridges. His therapist initially tries relaxation training to help him manage his frustration, but her careful attention to his lukewarm involvement leads her to modify the intervention. She suggests to Marcus that together they develop a guided imagery exercise in which he mentally races his bike, imagining all the vivid sensory and affective detail he has provided in session. Marcus resonates to the idea, mentioning that he never drinks when he rides his bike because it would be too dangerous. Once they develop the imagery and practice it in session, with much more favorable client response compared with the sedate relaxation imagery, Marcus agrees to practice using this activating imagery outside of session when stressful emotions arise about his pending fatherhood.

Interventions to Promote Client Action to Manage Affect

Practice With the Therapist.   Role play, psychodrama, and rehearsal in session are profitable steps in affect management interventions. Clients can better assess personal viability of a new option for acting on emotion when they walk through it with their therapists. In addition, the therapist's direct observation of the client's performance of an affect management strategy puts the therapist in the position to offer feedback.

An example is Julian, who tells his therapist he has lately been trying deep breathing to calm himself down when he is angry instead of automatically reaching for a beer. On one hand, he says, it seems to help, but he is perplexed by a recent situation where he was refused service at a bowling alley after he complained about a cashier error. Julian reports to his therapist that, although he had been angry at the cashier, he had actively calmed himself using deep breathing, and still the manager had kicked him out. The therapist asks him to demonstrate his deep breathing technique. Julian stands up to his full height of six foot three inches and paces the therapy room, inhaling sharply and exhaling with deep heaves throughout his two hundred twenty pound frame. The therapist asks how he feels in this moment. Julian says already he was feeling better after noticing he had been getting mad again just talking about the incident.

The therapist praises his efforts and agrees it is great that he feels more in control of his anger. Then the therapist says, "Can I also offer some feedback on how I reacted to what you just showed me?" When Julian consents, the therapist tells him that, although she knew from what Julian had said that he was trying to calm himself, seeing such a big man huff and pace with a commanding presence appeared from the outside as someone whose temper could be about to explode. The therapist explains,

> I know enough about you to realize that you were actually maintaining control, but if somebody, like those bowling alley employees, didn't know you, they could perceive you as working up for a fight, or verging on losing control.

Seeing Julian's startled, skeptical face and stiffening posture, the therapist adds,

> I can imagine that's hard to hear, but I'm not saying it to make you mad. I want to get you to think about how the way you come across to others might not match how you feel inside. What's your reaction to everything I'm saying?

Julian makes it clear he does not like the therapist's interpretation, and he resolves to prove the therapist wrong by surveying his friends and girl-friend. He returns the following week, subdued by his findings that when he asked point blank his friends admitted that Julian comes across as a hot-head. Julian agrees with his therapist to work on refining his self-calming and anger expression techniques as a next step in his therapy. At the end of therapy, Julian brings his girlfriend, to whom he has recently become en-gaged, and both the client and fiancée thank the therapist for the positive changes evident in Julian's mood and self-control.

Practice Outside of Session. As the client learns and practices in session expanded options for expressing and coping with emotional difficulties, the therapist will eventually recommend trying identified means of manag-ing emotions in contexts outside of session. This is certainly part of the preparation and action stages for the client who is ready to change sub-stance use behavior. It is also worth noting that clients may be ready to take action on dealing with emotional difficulties while they are still just contem-plating or even before contemplating alteration of substance use habits. By later processing client's efforts, experiences, and outcomes, a therapist can tailor interventions so that outcomes of affect management strategies are brought to bear on considerations of substance usage goals, or vice versa, depending on the individual client.

Medical Referral. When the substance abuse client exhibits symptoms of a diagnosable mood, anxiety, or behavioral disorder, especially if the cli-ent is not improving in therapy over a reasonable time span, the therapist can refer for medication consultation. However, with respect to emotional and behavioral disorders exhibited by the population of substance abusers, special considerations are in order when a therapist suggests the possibility of pharmacological treatment. First of all, therapists referring a client who abuses psychoactive chemicals for a psychiatric consultation are urged to avoid assuming or communicating that the client definitely needs medica-tion. The position advocated here is that clients should be encouraged to make their own informed choices about treatment, particularly what sub-stances to take into their own bodies. Furthermore, the therapist plays a role in helping the client seek and analyze knowledge that will allow the cli-ent to make well-informed choices. Rather than viewing medication as inev-itable or necessary, the referral for consultation can instead be treated as an opportunity for the client to collect information useful to be aware of treat-ment options and to make personally appropriate decisions about treat-ment. In addition to empowering clients to exercise their rights and re-sponsibilities for determining their own treatment, this approach allows exploration of the client's attitudes toward taking psychiatric medication.

Some substance abusers are willing and even enthusiastic about having legal access to psychoactive drugs. Others report prior experience with such medications, using drugs prescribed for themselves or abusing those prescribed for someone else. Such clients often have their own opinions about the value of future medication based on past experience. Still other clients are reluctant to consider psychiatric medication because they fear its addictive potential or side effects, because they are limiting or foregoing their use of all psychoactive chemicals, or because they are afraid being prescribed medication means they are "crazy."

Many therapists do not have the medical training or credentials to prescribe psychoactive medications. Therapists have nothing to gain and much to lose by telling a client with co-morbid substance use and emotional disorders that the client is being referred for psychiatric evaluation because the client clearly needs medication. Instead the referral can be presented as one additional treatment option. The therapist can explain that talking to a psychiatrist or other physician does not mean the client will or must take antidepressant, anti-anxiety, or other medications. Rather the medical consultation presents a chance for the client to obtain a physician's opinion and inquire about the advantages and disadvantages of using psychiatric medication in light of the client's substance use history. Therapy sessions can be utilized as a context in which the client can both prepare for the medical consultation and afterward weigh the resulting information in a manner most consistent with the client's values and goals.

If a client rejects a referral for medical consultation, the therapist can communicate respect for the client's position with an open invitation to consider the possibility again later if relevant. If the client accepts the referral or is at least open to the possibility, the therapist can help prepare the client to make the most of the consultation. The therapist can guide the client in generating lists of concerns the client wants to be sure to report along with questions the client wants to ask the physician. Equipped with written lists, the client is less likely to forget pertinent details.

In addition to reporting symptoms of mood or anxiety disorders, the client should be prompted to inform the doctor about current and historical patterns of substance use. The therapist explains that this helps a physician or psychiatrist avoid prescribing medications that may have dangerous potential for addiction, overdose, or biochemical interactions with recreational substances. In many cases, medical doctors can select from among several options those medications for mood and anxiety disorders that have lower risk factors for individuals with co-morbid substance use disorders. Any concerns clients have about disclosing substance use may also be discussed with the therapist.

In preparing clients for a medical consultation, therapists can let clients know that there is a reasonably high probability that medication will be prescribed (given the natures of both the client's complaints and the physician's profession). Furthermore, the time available for consultation with the physician is likely to be briefer and more tightly structured than a therapy session. Thus, the therapist can find out how the client feels about these probable outcomes, using time in therapy to help the client think through an approach to the consultation. The therapist asks clients what kinds of questions they have about medications, and the therapist may suggest some questions as well. Common questions include: Are there any side effects? How long after starting medication will it take to notice improvements? How long will I have to take the medication? Will I be on the medication indefinitely? What if I miss a dose? What if I decide I don't like the effects after I start taking the medication? What can I expect if I decide against taking the medication at this point?

Therapists can emphasize in preparation that asserting these questions not only elicits information about the prescribed medication, but also about the physician's stance and opinions. Therapy session time can be used to role play anticipated conversations with the physician. Rehearsal is especially important for clients who are low in assertiveness or self-esteem. The therapist may encourage the client to bring notes into the medical consultation to ensure important questions get addressed, and also to record information communicated by the physician. Although some clients are already thorough about such procedures, many substance abusers have poor memory and organizational skills. Thus, they in particular may benefit from preparation in therapy. The therapist asks the client in advance what the client expects to do if medication is prescribed. The therapist also asks the client to plan on spending some part of the therapy session following the medical consultation discussing the experience with the physician.

Follow-Up to Medical Referral. In the session after the medical appointment, the therapist asks the client how it went. In addition to factual information, the therapist inquires about the client's feelings and decisions about the physician's recommendations. Whatever the client has decided, or perhaps is still struggling with, the therapist asks the client to elaborate, voicing both affirmations and concerns. The therapist reminds the client who has decided to proceed with medication of the importance of compliance with the prescription and of reporting any problems.

The therapist inquires about the client's responses to the medication in addition to assessing other indicators of change in affective state or affect management. Should the client report difficulties with medication to the therapist, the therapist refers the client for further consultation with the prescribing physician. In some cases, obtaining the client's consent for the therapist to consult directly with the physician may be in order. Therapists will continue to employ psychological interventions as well, communicating to the client that behavior change reinforces and extends medication-induced emotion management by teaching skills that can ultimately reduce reliance on medication. As indicated earlier in this section, reducing or eliminating the client's inappropriate use of recreational substances and increasing the client's engagement in healthy, meaningful emotion management strategies remain essential objectives with or without concurrent medication.

COMMUNICATION AND RELATIONSHIP PROBLEMS

Difficulties with relationships or communication can motivate an individual to seek solace through substance use. Also for many drug and alcohol abusers, disruptions in social interaction and important relationships are among the consequences of their substance abuse. As noted earlier, other persons beside the client sometimes provide the impetus for the client to obtain therapy. Better communication or an improved relationship with the referring party, among others, is likely to be one of the treatment goals. Problems may be associated with relationships in the substance abuser's personal life (e.g., family members, friends, romantic partners, acquaintances), or they may involve more public obligations, such as transactions with employers, judges, caseworkers, probation or parole officers, and so forth. Some clients have concurrent difficulties in multiple relationships.

Interventions to Develop Communication Skills

Clients who report problematic relationships often blame the problem on the other person, especially when this person is viewed as responsible for the client being in therapy. When the client has a history of substance abuse, the client's use of drugs or alcohol is typically seen, either by the other party or the client (if not both), as a major factor contributing to the relationship problem. Therapists seek to understand the client's conceptualization of the problem by reflectively listening and obtaining the client's concession that the therapist understands what the client is saying. More specifically, effective therapists do not simply reassure clients that they understand; they probe, paraphrase, and summarize what they heard their clients say, and they ask clients for feedback on accuracy with respect to the client's own viewpoint. Thus, the therapist models empathic listening as a basic tool for good communication.

As the therapist comes to understand the nature of the problem, the therapist will want to emphasize that certainly it sounds like the client has good reason to be frustrated, upset, disgusted, or whatever with the other person. Still the therapist points out that there are two sides in any relationship, and the therapist asks whether the client sees any ways in which the client contributes to the relationship problem. The therapist is cautioned against taking the side of anyone other than the client, especially if the therapist has never met that other person. However, the therapist can beneficially tap into the client's perceptions of what the other person might say or do. The therapist can remind the client that it is incredibly difficult to control any person's behavior other than one's own, further advising the client also against taking responsibility for anyone else's actions. Likewise the therapist contends that the client is unrealistic to assume that any other person has control or responsibility for the client's behavior. Nor is it healthy for clients to permit anyone outside themselves to assume such control.

In this context, the client can be encouraged to internalize the focus in therapy. The therapist promotes the utility of working toward goals and objectives over which the client has real influence (Teyber, 2000). This includes decisions about when, if at all, and how much to use alcohol or drugs, and about how to interpret and respond to concerns communicated by others about the client's substance use or abstinence-related behaviors. This interpersonal emphasis thus spotlights both the client's choice of behavior and manner of communicating about the implications of that behavior.

Assessing the Role of Substance Abuse in the Client's Communication Patterns. Substance abuse can serve as a way to avoid the effort of communicating or to summon the nerve to say or do something the individual feels otherwise unable to produce. Therapeutic interventions for communication problems thus stem from exploring the aids and barriers to communication created by the client's substance use, as described in chapter 2. As clients articulate these advantages and pitfalls of communicating under the influence of psychoactive substances, therapists can create interventions to address individual issues.

For example, a client, Victor, tells his therapist he is often unclear of what his spouse expects from him. When he drinks, he says, it is easier for him to tune out that uncertainty and resulting anxiety. The therapist could help Victor generate ideas for asking his wife for clarification, such as making his requests specific rather than general or vague, asking when he is sober rather than intoxicated, and giving his wife feedback to let her know whether he gets her point, rather than walking out without comment in search of a beer.

Barriers to effective communication explored here are not unique to clients with substance use issues. Nor are they necessarily caused by abuse of drugs and alcohol. The promise or experience of chemically induced intoxication can, however, bolster reliance on maladaptive communication strategies. Among individuals whose communication skills are not well established, substance use may become a substitute for trying to do something the person feels inadequate or incapable of doing. Thus, substance abuse can easily reinforce poorly developed communication skills and further dampen motivation to improve them. In therapy, identifying a client's own habitual style of communication and intervening to develop alternatives can assist the client in reducing the perceived need to chemically lubricate social exchanges.

Increasing Clarity in Sending Messages.   A common barrier to communication is lack of clarity in sending messages. When therapists hear indications of these tendencies from clients, they intervene by investigating the client's perceptions of contributing factors. Clients may externalize the focus by attributing their lack of clarity to the effects of alcohol or drugs. Certainly the influence of mind-altering substances can reduce the coherence of a person's expression and the thought processes behind it. In addition, blaming the intoxication (or the withdrawal symptoms, or the preoccupation with cravings) gives the substance user a convenient excuse for communicating vague or obtuse messages. Therapists acknowledge the client's viewpoint, but also empathically challenge claims that either the drug or the distracting symptoms are entirely responsible for the client's lack of clear expression or intent. The therapist must of course be careful to avoid blame, but can prompt the client to internalize the focus from actions of the drug to actions of the client.

The therapist can investigate with the client why the client chooses to give psychoactive substances the power or credit for what the client communicates to others. Explicitly stating curiosity rather than judgment, the therapist wonders aloud what the client might have to gain and lose by attributing communication style to the impact of drugs or alcohol. As clients reflect on personal intentions and efforts to clarify or obscure their own messages to others (including the therapist), the client may offer examples. The therapist can also request specific instances of communication problems about which the client is troubled. Together the therapist and client can examine particular examples to distinguish how substance use has helped and hurt the client's efforts to deliver a message in each instance. They can sort out aspects of the client's delivery that the client can choose to control (e.g., choice of wording, goal of interaction, tone of voice, timing, posture, etc.) from those clearly beyond the client's control (e.g., how the person receiving the client's message interprets and responds to it).

Among the choices the therapist can illuminate is the contrast between taking responsibility for the clarity of one's own communications versus relinquishing that control to an external person or factor, including the effects of a drug. The therapist, without forcing a decision, invites the client to discuss the meaning and affect the client associates with this contrast.

Such conversations can uncover much ambivalence. Clients may both want to be more clear or better understood while also wishing to remain opaque and thus protected. They may believe they express themselves more effectively under the influence of chemicals despite the costs. They may desire to quit turning to substance use to avoid more straightforward communication, and still doubt their abilities to refrain from use or to be more straightforward.

As these interventions yield more shared understanding of the client's communication barriers and the supporting role of substance abuse, the therapist suggests ways of honing the client's skills. Clients are encouraged to give themselves time before speaking to think through what they want to say and how to say it. Knowing that breaking familiar tendencies will not be easy, therapists ask clients to notice any difficulties, such as distracting urges to drink or take drugs, when the client tries to clarify intended messages. Clients are invited to work through the inevitable difficulties (and share the successes and progress) in therapy sessions. This may involve considering alternative approaches to past instances of problematic communication, as well as development and rehearsal in session of upcoming conversations that are important to the client.

If the client is open to the techniques, role play and empty chair exercises create experiential contexts in which clients can enact different communication approaches, with therapists providing input and feedback. The therapist can also utilize the immediacy of communication patterns occurring within the therapy interaction. The therapist can model pauses to think, as well as metacommunicative expressions of intent, struggles to choose the words to use, and efforts to seek feedback on how intended messages are actually received by the client. In addition, the therapist can make process comments on the client's delivery of communication between the two of them, exploring apparent constraints, inviting client elaboration, and reinforcing clarity and progress.

Enhancing Attention to Receiving Messages. A second, often related barrier to effective communication involves lack of attention to messages received from other people. Again use of psychoactive substances can interfere with the motivation, effort, or perceptual processes required in the receptive phase of the communication cycle. Therapists can aid clients in articulating both difficulties and alternative approaches.

Therapists have to demonstrate good listening with sincere interest to work effectively to develop clients' attending skills. When a person neglects to receive messages communicated by another person, it can signify absorption in the first person's own perspective at the expense of another's, or it can indicate the first person's deliberate avoidance of dealing with the other person's perspective. Either if not both of these inclinations may become evident in the material a client brings to session. The therapist can help explore their cost–benefit functions (e.g., the extent to which a client, like Victor, finds it both desirable and problematic to tune out the client's spouse). To do this, therapists are likely to discover they have ideas about what the client should say or do. Therapists may also find themselves reluctant to hear clients' complaints.

If therapists can notice times in session during which they are not actively listening to their clients, several interventions are then possible. Therapists can internally ask themselves what is happening in those moments to elicit the therapist's tendency to talk rather than listen, or to discount the client's messages. Therapists can also observe aloud the patterns of communication they are noticing along with the content and ask the client to comment on the observations and experiences relayed by the therapist.

Often when clients exhibit deficiencies in listening skills, they also feel unheard by other people. The therapist obviously does not want to recapitulate that experience for the client, yet may still encounter moments in session of not hearing or wanting to listen to the client. These instances are a problem only if the therapist fails to acknowledge them with a curiosity about what they mean.

Interpersonal theory suggests that people who expect (based on interpretations of past transactions) their messages to be ignored or misinterpreted are likely to communicate in ways that elicit that behavior from other people. When their prophecies are fulfilled by others, such clients feel justified in declining attention to messages sent by others whom the client perceives are not listening anyway. Clients accustomed to this style of interaction tend to employ it with therapists, too. So when therapists catch themselves lecturing or changing the topic or otherwise not really listening, they can contemplate what the client is saying or doing that seems to trigger this reaction in the therapist.

The therapist probably should not comment the first time such transactions occur with a client, but are better served by making mental note and remaining observant for recurrences. If similar interactions transpire between therapist and client, especially if stories the client brings to session reveal similar dynamics in the client's communications with other people, the therapist builds evidence for a pattern. Once the therapist is fairly convinced that the pattern is meaningful, the therapist can point it out to the client.

The crucial aspect of this phase of intervention is to phrase the observation in a manner that the client will not only hear, but to which the client will actually listen and consider. This is no simple feat with clients who are used to limiting their attention to what others have to say. The therapist's phrasing needs to reflect accurate empathy for the client's perspective and likely reaction to the therapist's process comments. To accomplish this, the therapist must be actively listening to the client, including conscious efforts to reactivate the therapist's own listening skills if and when they lapse in session.

With clients who abuse substances, therapists may be distracted from active listening by their own beliefs and assumptions about substance abuse, or by attitudes the client projects about drug and alcohol use. Therapists who presume that clients do not actually want to talk about their substance use, are not taking therapy seriously, or have no interest in changing behavior may gloss over or miss altogether clients' messages to the contrary, however veiled. Clients who have encountered past reactions such as, "I'm not listening to you; you're drunk" or "You don't care about anything except getting high" may (not surprisingly) be reluctant to convey receptive attitudes toward anyone, including a therapist, on the topic of the client's substance use.

As therapists learn to detect and address barriers to active listening on both sides of the therapy relationship, they can begin to challenge the client to try out new modes of attending and communicating receptivity. If the client feels genuinely heard and respected in addition to the challenge, the client often develops willingness to meet the therapist's suggestions to work out expanded means of receiving messages from others. Useful techniques include further discussions of situations in which the client finds attending to others difficult or undesirable. The role of substance use in reinforcing or complicating the client's typical patterns of interaction can be analyzed in session. Clients, if willing, may be assigned "homework," such as looking for evidence of themes and patterns or experimenting with new behaviors in interactions with other people between sessions. Some clients will be open to writing about their homework observations and experiences. Others will prefer just to talk about them in sessions. Therapists can offer to write down suggestions or reminders for the client to consult between sessions. Therapists can also carve out time in session to enact and discuss actual situations and alternatives.

Role play in session can help identify types of interactions the client tends to tune out as well as reasons for doing so. For example, clients may stop listening if they do not understand what someone is saying, or if they do not want to hear it. Even when clients admit to problems resulting from this strategy, they may not know how to do otherwise. In a role play or empty chair exercise, the therapist can stop the action at that point and ask the client what else could be done at that juncture besides stop paying attention. The therapist inquires about what the client would like to say or do, how the client predicts the other person would react, and how the client could improve communication with this person in this situation. Rehearsal in session can help prepare the client to try the new approach outside of session. The therapist extends these interventions by checking back later to see whether and how the client has tried implementing new options. The therapist's active listening throughout this process communicates caring involvement that potentially motivates the client to pay more attention and get more involved in interpersonal transactions starting with the therapy relationship.

Expanding Motivation for Mutually Desirable Transactions.   A third type of barrier contributing to relationship problems is low motivation for mutually positive interactions. Relationship problems stemming from this barrier may be less about communication skills than about goals of interpersonal interaction. Some people engage in behavior that comes across as characteristically manipulative, self-interested or narcissistic, hostile, suspicious, detached, deceitful, or remorseless. By no means do all substance abusers exhibit low motivation for mutually desirable interactions, but those that do sometimes appear to have these tendencies emboldened or reinforced by their substance use. For example, some substance abusers are even more likely to initiate fights or make outrageous demands when they are drinking or using drugs. One memorable client told his substance abuse therapy group repeatedly, with a huge grin, "I like pissing people off. I think it's fun!" He offered numerous binge stories and in-session behaviors to demonstrate his point.

With clients like this, it is understandably hard for therapists to stay involved. Still if the therapist holds sincere convictions in the potency of the therapeutic relationship to access the prosocial tendencies believed to reside in most people by virtue of their humanity, the therapist will work to engage such clients even when it is difficult. The time may come where the therapist refers or declines to continue treating such a client, but ideally not before exerting legitimate efforts to increase the client's motivation for reciprocity in relationships. When a therapist gives up too quickly on making a positive connection with a client who appears disinclined, that therapist probably reinforces the client's expectations of relationships and view of self. Conversely, the therapist who works to establish some positive interaction even in the face of the client's negativity creates the possibility of expanding the client's interpersonal repertoire.

Widening a client's range of interpersonal behaviors takes patience and time on the therapist's part, especially when the client's behaviors cluster rigidly around hostility. According to complementarity assumptions of interpersonal theory (described in chap. 2), affiliative behaviors on the part of one communicator tend to elicit and reinforce affiliative behaviors from a second person. Likewise, hostile behaviors tend to invite and encourage another person's hostility in response. Tracey (1993) cogently argued that base rates for these tendencies differ in that typical interactants will meet another person's hostility with affiliative responses, at least for a while, giving the counteraffiliative communicator the benefit of the doubt and a chance to modify behavior to a friendlier stance. In a therapy context, the therapist tries responding to a client's noncommunal behavior not by responding in kind, but by declining to complement the client's behavior. The therapist may offer a more affiliative response in hopes of eliciting complementary affiliative behavior from the client. Even if the client continues to respond in a more hostile or detached manner (e.g., "You're just acting like you want to talk to me because you're getting paid to do it"), the therapist avoids reinforcing the expectation of reciprocal hostility (e.g., "I can imagine why you think that, but actually I do this job because I like it, and I am interested in what you have to say").

With some clients, this approach will nudge the therapy relationship in a more afflilative direction. With clients whose low motivation for affiliative interactions is deeply entrenched, the process is much harder. Some of these clients have extensive relationship histories of refusing to reciprocate others' attempts at affiliation until other persons finally give up the attempt and either reciprocate the client's hostility or end the relationship. Other clients have become skilled at reinforcing another person's friendly communications only so far as it serves some purpose for the client, and then the client shifts into more hostile gear. For example, some clients whose substance abuse has led to troubles with employers or legal authorities express willingness to comply with others' expectations, but only as far as required to get the client out of trouble.

In theory, clients have developed such interpersonal styles in response to early experiences and interpretations of important relationships, and have generalized them to subsequent interactions. In practice, the stories such clients tell about themselves in relationships provide validating evidence for therapists' emergent conceptualizations of clients' interpersonal behaviors. As therapists consult their own curiosity about functions accomplished by the hostile client's behavior, they make continual choices about how to respond to the client's presentation of self and expectations of transactions. With a client who seems to invite interpersonal conflict, the therapist will inevitably experience temptations to move against or move away from the client, in addition to more internally acceptable inclinations to move toward the client. Interventions are guided by the therapist's careful selections about when and how to act on those tendencies.

A real challenge for therapists working with clients like these is to resist responding purely defensively when feeling criticized, tested, deceived, hurt, or dismissed by a client. Consciously or otherwise, the client may be trying to elicit a reaction from the therapist that justifies (for the client) further discounting the therapist. Still the therapist faced with difficult internal reactions to a client cannot simply ignore them and respond in a friendly manner. To do so not only comes across to a client as insincere, but also potentially reveals weaknesses in facing interpersonal tensions that the the client might choose to exploit. Thus, the therapist aims to simultaneously acknowledge the client's counteraffiliative behavior and possibly the affective response it elicits in the therapist while also offering a noncomplementary reply along with therapeutic intent.

The experience and expectations of clients with counteraffiliative interpersonal styles are that other people will eventually capitulate into hostility or expose insecurities about doing so. Rather than validating those expectations, the therapist instead confronts the client's behavior while communicating respect for the client and belief in the resiliency of the potential for mutual affiliation in the therapy relationship. This difficult and sophisticated form of intervention requires therapists to be aware of the reactions stimulated in themselves by the client's counteraffiliative behavior as well as the potential consequences of possible actions on those feelings.

Case Examples

A couple of examples can help illustrate this approach to intervention. The first example involves a client's attempt to test the therapist's integrity by disclosing his own dishonesty. The second demonstrates a therapeutic response to a client's request for affirmation of interpersonal behavior the therapist finds offensive.

Chris laughs as he tells his therapist that he lied at intake about his employment status. He admits that he falsely claimed to be unemployed so that he would meet the income cutoff to qualify for subsidized therapy. He says he does not believe he should have to pay for mandated drug therapy because he is not the one who thinks he needs it, and he thanks the therapist in advance for protecting his secret.

Chris' therapist, Sean, replies that he hears Chris' frustration with attending therapy and paying for it against his wishes, but Sean explains that he cannot in good conscience pretend he has no problem with Chris' revelation. He adds that he appreciates that Chris trusted the therapist enough to admit his deception, but that in doing so Chris put the therapist in a difficult position because Chris is asking Sean to maintain the deception of the therapist's employer.

Chris rolls his eyes and predicts aloud that now Sean will break confidence and get Chris in trouble. The therapist clarifies that his intent is not to bring trouble, but that he is not willing to violate principles for the client because Sean does not believe it would be in anyone's best interest. However, Sean also assures Chris he would like to discuss this in greater detail before taking action outside the session.

Chris retorts that he does not care to talk about it anymore, that he should have kept his mouth shut, and doubts he will return for another session. The therapist replies that it is Chris' right to make those choices, but Sean still hopes Chris will reconsider the possibility of working together to come up with mutually agreeable alternatives.

Chris may or may not accept the therapist's proposal. But this extended example shows how a therapist can employ a continuously recalibrated balance between challenging and supporting the client.

The second example recalls Karina, the client from chapter 1 who flaunted her ability to drink twelve beers in two hours. Karina tells her therapist, Denae, that she knows she lashes out hatefully when she is drunk. She doesn't even remember some of the situations, but when friends repeat to her the nasty things she has said, Karina does not feel totally bad because deep down she feels the other people deserved it. In fact Karina likes being able to freely speak her mind when she is drunk. She describes a few instances in which she humiliated men who had flirted with her at bars. She asks Denae, "What's so wrong with that? Men are all jerks anyway; wouldn't you agree?"

Karina's therapist replies that in fact she does not agree, but she wants to better understand why Karina feels that way. Denae explains that there appear to be some difficult past experiences or at least risk of difficult future consequences behind Karina's statements and behaviors, and Denae is open to exploring those if Karina is willing.

When clients exhibit low motivation to relate to others in an affirming manner, or any of the prior barriers to communication, the therapist can express interest in hearing about the client's past and current relationships. The therapist can inquire about the client's related substance use. Conversations about the client's relationship history frequently yield clues about the purposes served by the client's interpersonal attitudes and behaviors, as well as any potential to motivate change. By engaging a client in a therapy relationship that provides experiences of supportive challenge, acceptance of interpersonal conflict, and mutually affirming resolutions and compromises, a therapist can generate possibilities and hope. If clients report substance use or confirm substance abuse in response to therapists' questions, consideration of the impact of substance use on the client's interpersonal motivations and behaviors is integral to therapeutic interventions.

Clients who present themselves for substance abuse treatment often report relationship problems, and clients who come to therapy to address relationship problems frequently reveal associated substance use concerns. Either way these topics arise, the therapist's knowledge of interpersonal constructs and interventions can activate the potential of the therapy relationship for addressing these commonly intertwined problems.

EDUCATIONAL AND OCCUPATIONAL CONCERNS

People engaged in risky use of substances may encounter conflicts between continuing substance use and fulfilling other occupational or leisure goals. Substance abuse often impedes the process by which a person occupies time and commits energy. Therapists often intervene by helping clients develop short- and long-term plans to involve the client in activities besides alcohol and drug use to accomplish some purpose, whether it is to find fulfillment, enjoyment, knowledge, self-expression, productivity, or generativity; to make an income or to keep busy. Many interests and activities developed in the process of recovery from substance abuse will accomplish more than one of these purposes.

Individuals' concerted efforts to occupy their own time in pursuit of chosen goals for substantial time intervals comprise vocations. The implementation of personal goals through vocational tasks sometimes includes education to learn necessary concepts and skills. Substance use that is frequent, heavy, or excessive can interfere with the user's interests or abilities to sustain other occupational activities, including educational and vocational endeavors.

As with other associated problems already considered, concerns about the impact of substance abuse on a client's occupational problems can arise either as primary or contextual issues in therapy. A client may present with worries about failing grades or substandard performance reviews at work, and only later acknowledge extensive substance use in response to empathic probes by the therapist. Other clients may be referred by the employee assistance programs (EAP) at their job sites following a positive drug screen or after being caught drinking at work. They may also come to therapy voluntarily because they want to change jobs or academic majors due to current dissatisfaction barely muted by substance use, and yet have only vague ideas about what else they would like to do. Substance users with occupational concerns may or may not readily admit their levels of substance use. They may or may not view their substance use as relevant to any educational or vocational problems they wish to address in therapy.

Thus, the therapist needs to assess and address occupational difficulties associated with substance use disorders. Vocational interventions for substance abusers specifically address the significance of clients occupying time and energy with substance use activities at the expense of other endeavors. Furthermore, therapists can help establish and clarify educational and career goals through explorations of the client's occupational interests plus the client's efforts to structure a livelihood around those interests (Savickas & Spokane, 1999). Viewed in the richness of their capacity to command an individual's attention, arouse feelings, and activate behavior in particular directions (Savickas, 1999), vocational interests can be specified and applied using a broad and flexible range of occupational counseling tools to address the tensions between a client's substance use and occupational goals. Therapists can help clients investigate both the compatibility and discrepancy between continuing substance abuse and career efforts.

Addressing Problematic Client Attitudes

Two important factors contribute to many clients' investment in substance abuse to a degree that compromises other occupational activities. First, self-administration of psychoactive chemicals escorts the user to an altered state that transcends normal consciousness, more often than not experienced as desirable. Second, substance use tends to achieve its euphoric effects quite rapidly and with minimal exertion. Transcendent states of awareness and experiences of absorption (Roche & McConkey, 1990) can potentially be produced through educational efforts and career pursuits consistent with the individual's interests, although typically not without devoting extensive time and energy to one's work. Clients for whom substance use has become problematic include those who perceive themselves as unwilling to exert the effort or unable to achieve the desired transcendence through work efforts. It is thus useful for substance abuse therapists encountering career concerns to explicitly address the client's attitudes toward exerting effort and toward altering his or her state of mind.

Attitudes Toward Alteration of Consciousness. The desire to modify consciousness, to reach a state of awareness that differs from normal thoughts and feelings, motivates a variety of behaviors. These generally aim to achieve an experience of transcendence, of surpassing the ordinary range of perception so that the individual feels above and beyond the intensity and power of regular sensation. Not all persons seek such experience as demonstrated by research on personality variables (e.g., Clark & Watson, 1999). However, many people actively quest for altered states of consciousness through various means (Weil, 1972; cited in Marlatt, 1985c), including excursions into nature, meditation, religious and spiritual practices, hypnosis, sexual activity, sleep deprivation, hypnosis, or psychoactive drugs.

Probably curiosity about altered states achievable through substance use stimulates much initial consumption of alcohol or other drugs, except in cases where initiation is coerced or deceptive. The promise of euphoria mixed with novel sensations and enhanced perceptions makes substance use an attractive route to transcendent awareness. In addition, the actual experience of drug-induced alterations of consciousness can be profoundly rewarding, to the point that many substance users prefer that over normal states of mind.

In other words, positive attitudes and expectancies toward seeking altered states of consciousness increase the likelihood that a person will use substances. In turn, pleasurable experiences of drug-induced states of ecstasy further strengthen a person's positive attitudes toward altering one's own consciousness (see Thombs, 1999, for a review of related research on alcohol and drug expectancies).

People who use substances without incurring problematic consequences are also capable of achieving transcendent or at least rewarding states of consciousness through activities and events unrelated to substance use. Although they may enjoy the alterations of sensation and perception brought about by occasional substance use, they also appreciate the reinforcing effects of certain nondrug experiences. They know how to relax without chemicals. They value the rewards they get from engaging in interesting activities without substances. They are also likely to believe that the transcendent potential of such activities would be diminished under the influence of drugs or alcohol. For example, taking care of one's children, completing a big project on the job, and performing well at an important meeting are all occupational tasks that can grant an individual experiences that transcend normal consciousness. Additionally, each example represents a work activity that would for many people be adversely affected by the simultaneous use of alcohol or drugs.

Sometimes a state of transcendent awareness encompasses a person swiftly, spontaneously, or even unexpectedly. Examples include hearing favorite music, spending time with a treasured relative or friend, or absorbing the intoxicating sensations of nature's splendor. In many cases, however, like with meditation or goal achievement, desired alterations of consciousness require concentration and effort. Ideally, people learn that work is worth the exertion because the effort creates conditions with inherently gratifying features and transcendent potential.

For many people, a vocation or career structures personal activity through concentrated effort to accomplish purposes consistent with the individual's particular interests. Work-related activities can sometimes yield altered states of consciousness, as when the worker becomes so engrossed that the activities seem to flow from a heightened state of awareness and competence. Even when work activities are not experienced in a zone of amplified perceptivity, the job may still offer opportunities to earn the income and buy the time to pursue leisure activities the worker associates with enhanced states of consciousness. Workers may love their jobs or love their hobbies and vacations (or all three if they are lucky), and in each case their hard work on the job is reinforced.

Many substance abusers with co-occurring occupational problems have learned instead that quick, substance-induced alterations of consciousness disrupt the connection between exertion and transcendent potential. Over time they come to expect the fast gratification and prefer the intense rewards offered by repetitive substance use compared with the delayed and less reliable benefits of hard work. The substance abuser's interest in altering consciousness with drugs or alcohol can foster a number of attitudes that compromise educational or vocational efforts. Therapists may hear variations on any of the themes listed in Table 9.1 from clients presenting with both occupational concerns and substance use issues.

The irony of these positions is that gradually the altered states achieved through repeated substance use become less intense and reliable. As the mechanisms of tolerance (reviewed in chap. 4) are activated, the substance user typically has to spend more time and energy obtaining and consuming substances in search of the alterations of consciousness experienced with past substance use episodes. Of course the more effort the client puts into activities related to substance use, the less time and energy he or she has available for other leisure, educational, or vocational activities. Still several biological and psychological withdrawal factors (also reviewed in chap. 4) reinforce continuing efforts to alter consciousness using the client's substance of choice.

Therapists can use vocational interventions to help clients consider the imbalance in relying primarily on chemical substances to achieve transcendent states of consciousness. In particular, therapists can help clients develop and expand their options for acquiring inspiration, satisfaction, and heightened experience through meaningful activities that do not involve

TABLE 9.1
Attitudes Toward Occupational Issues Among
Some Clients Exhibiting Substance Use Disorders

1. I am more creative, sensitive, and perceptive when I'm under the influence of drugs or alcohol, so I use substances when I'm working to enhance my potential.
2. Nothing is fun, interesting, or motivating to me unless I am under the influence of psychoactive substances, so I use substances during work or school to maintain my effort and energy.
3. I'll reduce my substance use as soon as I find a job, a career, or a course of study that gives me satisfaction that compares to what I get from drinking or using drugs.
4. Any satisfaction I get from hard work is much slower and not as intense as what I get from substance use, so I'll put minimal effort (or less) into work or school so I can spend more time getting drunk or high.
5. The job options open to me will never provide gratification that matches the transcendent states I experience when I'm drunk or high, so I totally devalue work and view any job I might have as a necessary evil.
6. I have no motivation to work hard toward goals that are not guaranteed pay off in the long run when I can feel so good right away just by drinking or using drugs.

substance use. Before outlining specific interventions, however, the reader is invited to consider a second attitude frequently contributing to occupational problems among substance abusing clients.

Attitudes Favoring Avoidance of Exerting Effort. Some people develop attitudes that view work as little more than drudgery, annoyance, obligation, agony, or futility. Although virtually everyone can relate to "work" as strenuous and "play" as preferable, persons with positive role models and desirable work outcomes tend to learn a work ethic that values hard work within a balanced lifestyle. With involvement and success, they discover that work can sometimes be productive and fun. For these people, work and play are not always mutually exclusive. Other people hear derogatory opinions about work from their role models, or they experience frustration or failure with respect to their own efforts. Under such conditions, a person may learn to despise and avoid doing work that promises no compelling benefits.

Not all people who learn to dismiss the idea of work become substance abusers, nor do all substance abusers avoid work. However, for some clients the vocational problems associated with substance abuse are compounded by attitudes that most work is not worth the effort and is to be avoided whenever possible. This attitude is reflected in some of the themes listed in Table 9.1, specifically Statements 4, 5, and 6. Notice that the other three themes (1, 2, and 3) indicate that the client is willing to work, but only under conditions where transcendent potential is actualized. Statements 4, 5, and 6 suggest that work offers inadequate compensation or gratification, so the client's stance is to dismiss exertion of effort to the greatest extent possible.

Clients who avoid what they perceive as work tend to pass time by seeking immediate gratification or by looking for quicker access to the experiences of pleasure and play. This is similar to one form of what Marlatt (1985c) called an "imbalanced lifestyle," in which external demands are perceived to outweigh pleasurable or fulfilling activities, leading to "a perception of self-deprivation and a corresponding need for self-indulgence" (pp. 290–291). Individuals motivated thus can find several other means of minimizing work and maximizing recreation (e.g., gambling, shopping, videogames, Internet use, pornography, exploitation of other people), but for many, drugs or alcohol pose enticing opportunities. While it lasts, the rapid bliss and relief from hassles attained through substance use can either justify evading work (e.g., "I don't want to do anything that would step on my buzz") or can make the necessary evils of work more palatable (e.g., "If I have to do it, at least I'll enjoy a good buzz while I'm at it").

In addition to providing instantaneous escape from the aversions of work, substance abuse can also further erode the user's expectations that any personal effort will yield worthwhile outcomes. Because excessive or compulsive substance use can decrease users' motivation, cognitive processing skills, and behavioral performance, substance abusers are increasingly likely to accumulate unsatisfactory experiences in work contexts. Viewing oneself or being perceived by others as uncaring or incapable of doing a good job results in feedback that further sours one's attitudes toward exerting effort. Under the influence of substances, the individual may have trouble thinking clearly or acting effectively, which can contribute to giving up the effort and turning instead to the relief provided by more alcohol or drugs.

Clients may exhibit understandable ambivalence regarding this attitude: on the one hand wanting to use substances to avoid work, and on the other hand wanting to reduce substance use to start getting things done. The cognitive dissonance created by these competing motivations often gets "resolved" by resorting to quick, effortless escape through additional substance use.

Interventions to Modify Problematic Attitudes
Toward Work and Substance Use

Therapists can empathize with a client's desire to avoid the frustrations of difficult work and to enhance her or his state of consciousness. These inclinations can even be normalized to a certain extent. At the same time, therapists can point out that indulging these human desires at the cost of ignoring or downplaying other important realities contributes to an unhealthy imbalance in one's life activities. Many clients suspect this already, but probably have had few opportunities to carefully discuss the implications. Some will deny the personal applicability of such interpretations, but then the therapist can explore the client's perspective. Engaging skeptical or dismissive clients in conversations about the beliefs and feelings sustaining their attitudes sometimes reveals discrepancies or ambivalence about which therapists can further inquire.

Articulating the Pros and Cons of Holding These Attitudes.   Once the client becomes receptive to the idea that using substances to alter consciousness or avoid effort cannot be constantly or indefinitely sustained, the therapist guides exploration of the ramifications of using substances according to these problematic attitudes. Conversation focuses on observations of how seeking intoxication and avoiding tasks and responsibilities have reinforced each other over time, and still how substance use gradually declines in capacity to reach either goal. The therapist can suggest considering what it would mean to acknowledge that effort cannot entirely be avoided, that some work can be worthwhile and even fun, that transcendent awareness is by definition temporary, and that interests and goals can be achieved through activities that do not involve substance use. As clients resonate with one or more of these suggestions and begin to examine personal significance, therapists can help focus on changing attitudes to include more balanced perspectives.

Exploring Alternative Viewpoints.   Clients who are coming to accept the importance of adjusting occupational priorities can be encouraged to articulate what kind of work is worth their effort and what kind of outcomes are realistic to expect. Vocational interventions, such as interest inventories (Spokane & Decker, 1999; Tracey & Rounds, 1996; Zytowski, 1999), card sorts (Hartung, 1999), and career exploration (Blustein & Flum, 1999; Prediger, 1999) can assist in clarifying next steps in the client's recovery. Addressing low self-esteem and low self-efficacy, which may block individuals from vocational pursuits (Betz, 1999; Lent, Brown, & Hackett, 1994; Tracey, 1997), is particularly relevant with substance abusers who experience shame, low efficacy, or low outcome expectancies in occupational endeavors. Expanding a client's options for relaxation and leisure activities, and for spiritual growth, can also be useful in balancing work and play, or in Marlatt's (1985c) terms, "shoulds" and "wants." Clients also need to assess the past and future impact of using or abstaining from substances on their abilities to develop their interests and engage in relevant vocational or leisure activities.

Changing one's attitudes and priorities is typically a challenging process. Therapists need to provide flexible structure and guidance in interpreting interest and values assessment results, choosing occupational goals and objectives, and planning appropriate educational and vocational strategies. Therapists should also listen carefully for client ambivalence and be prepared to support and challenge as needed

Developing Relevant Occupational Skills and Experiences.   Even when clients identify new occupational goals and strategies, they may lack the skills or confidence to implement them. Additional interventions can be used to give clients experience and practice. In therapy sessions, clients can thumb through school course catalogues or job listings, with adjunct homework, if relevant. They can role play interviews with feedback from the therapist. They can learn stress management and communication techniques for dealing with work-related tensions. Therapists can facilitate specific consideration of the overlap and possible inconsistencies between the client's relapse prevention plans and occupational objectives. Together therapy participants generate strategies for enhancing the integration of these recovery goals, including dealing with potential conflicts and barriers.

Addressing Vocational Obstacles Posed
by Past Substance Abuse

Many substance abusers in recovery face barriers to newly established occupational goals resulting from consequences of past substance abuse or dependence. The following examples illustrate a few common obstacles that a therapist could help anticipate and address.

Dustin has a record of arrests: one for drunk and disorderly conduct and another for driving under the influence of alcohol. He is concerned about how his criminal record will affect his prospects for future employment. Dustin has heard that many job applications ask about the applicant's criminal history.

Connie was planning to apply for federal financial aid prior to her senior year of college until she learned she would be asked to report any history of conviction for the possession or sale of illegal drugs. Connie was arrested and tried recently for possession of marijuana, and she is now attending the required substance use assessment. She worries that she will be financially unable to continue attending the university if she is denied financial aid.

Luis had ten years clean and sober, during which he effectively built a career as a physician's assistant. Prescribed pain medication after a sports injury, he gradually increased his own dosage until well past prescribed amounts. Luis was eventually caught diverting narcotic analgesics from the hospital where he works. He has for the past two months recommitted himself to abstinence and recovery, but he is anxiously awaiting the medical board's decision regarding possible suspension of his license to practice.

Elecia has decided to submit applications for a new job after successfully completing an inpatient chemical dependency program followed by weeks of outpatient aftercare. She was fired from her previous job for repeatedly coming to work under the influence of alcohol. She needs a supportive letter of reference, but does not know whom she could ask.

In each case, the client must confront the realistic complications resulting from past substance-related problems. Clients may need help clarifying both their perspectives and their options. Choices to be made among available alternatives may seem like deciding between the proverbial rock and a harder place. The frustration or despair clients feel about dealing with occupational constraints like these can also comprise relapse triggers.

Interventions to Confront Barriers Created
by Past Substance Abuse

The value of encouraging clients to take responsibility for well-informed, deliberate choices for action in situations like those just described cannot be overstated. The therapist can invite the client to elaborate on alternative courses of action and the feelings that each elicits for the client. Hypothetical consequences of different action options can be discussed, with the client encouraged to evaluate the viability and desirability of each.

The therapist may wish to prompt consideration of how much information a client is obliged to reveal in particular situations. The client can benefit from talking through the process of deciding when to share information and when to stay quiet. It is often useful to weigh specific factors relevant to such choices in the client's particular situation.

Also, once information about substance abuse history comes to light, by the client's choice or otherwise, how can the client discuss that information in ways that will impress the receiver with the client's honesty, responsibility, and maturity rather than create doubt? Clients with histories of using deception to hide their substance abuse will often be neither familiar nor comfortable with open acknowledgment of responsibility for past behaviors. A therapist can point out how evasive, dismissive, or minimizing responses can raise suspicions that past problems are good predictors of future behavior. The contrary approach involves articulating not only responsibility for past behavior, but also for successful behavior change and for positive learning from the process.

Therapist and client can analyze the applicability of these contrasting approaches and their variations to the particular occupational situation facing the client. To whom might the client request or be expected to talk? What approach does the client plan to take in consideration of the client's occupational goals? The therapist can urge the client to rehearse the speech, with the rationale that putting it into words will make the speech flow easier when it counts. The therapist can offer feedback on both the process and content of the client's speech. In cases where the client is having trouble generating an effective, compelling message, the therapist can offer a demonstration of what the therapist imagines saying in that situation. The client is then invited to respond to and refine the therapist's message as needed to fit the client's intentions. Additional rehearsal is recommended until the client expresses satisfaction and confidence in what the client plans to communicate.

The therapist further stimulates consideration of how the receiver of the client's message might react. Both desirable and undesirable outcomes can be identified to help the client prepare for different possibilities and think through what the client would do next. The therapist can also explore the client's thoughts and feelings underlying both these hypothesized transactions and the process of discussing them with the therapist. Ambivalent reactions should come as no surprise. A client might believe the approach makes sense, but doubt he can pull it off in an actual employment situation. Another client might express conviction in her potential to make good on the lessons she learned in treatment, but still suspect no one will give her a fair chance. Therapists can empathize with such concerns as understandable and normal, but also reflect the hopeful and confident aspects of the client's mixed feelings. Attention to relapse prevention in the face of occupational stressors remains essential.

Therapists bolster these interventions by emphasizing that even when situations do not unfold as practiced (which they rarely do), the client's efforts to clarify a position will inform future decisions about how to present oneself in occupational contexts. In addition, these exercises help clients clarify current attitudes, perspectives, and options for themselves as well as for explaining to others. This is crucial because, no matter how the situation of immediate concern turns out, the client will have additional choices to make in the future about what behaviors to exhibit in occupation contexts.

LEGAL AND SOCIAL JUSTICE CONSIDERATIONS

Substantial numbers of clients in treatment for substance use disorders face concurrent legal problems. They may have been arrested and charged with possessing illegal substances. Others have used legal drugs in circumstances that are against the law. For example, use of alcohol by a minor, driving under the influence of alcohol, smoking cigarettes in public places where a ban is in effect, or consuming high doses of pharmaceuticals that were obtained without legitimate medical prescription are all situations that could lead to legal trouble.

In other cases, the causes for a substance user's legal entanglements go beyond illegal consumption of drugs or alcohol to include criminal behaviors the client performed while under the influence of chemicals or withdrawal, or in attempts to gain access to substances. The client may have violated another's person or property. Some clients have participated in the manufacture, distribution, or sale of illicit substances. They may have provided alcohol to a minor or controlled substances to an adult who wants to use them for recreational rather than medical purposes. Sometimes the criminal behavior is not definitively linked to substance use, but the client has been referred for assessment to screen for possible substance abuse.

Possible Scenarios Linking Substance Abuse to Legal Complications

When legal considerations arise in assessment or treatment for substance abuse, the therapist aims to help the client sort through and address the implications for therapy. Substance abuse therapists should be prepared to work with the following general scenarios:

1. The client is not yet in legal trouble, but is aware of potential consequences of past or continuing illegal behavior. An example is Dahlia, a college student with limited financial resources further compromised by her drug purchases. Dahlia recently began supplementing her income by procuring marijuana, and occasionally ecstasy, for her friends in the dormitories.

2. The client has been formally mandated to attend treatment and required to abstain from substance use based on legal actions taken in response to the client's substance-related behavior. Examples are Ian, on probation for punching his girlfriend in a drunken, jealous rage; and Barbie, convicted for stealing money that she says she used to buy drugs.

3. The client is required to satisfy specified conditions to regain access to privileges taken away as a result of past substance-related violations. Examples include Linden, who lost his driver's license after multiple arrests for driving drunk. Another example is Frieda, who is required to complete substance abuse therapy plus parenting classes and submit to random drug testing, along with several other conditions, to regain custody of her children, who were removed from her home after an investigation revealed evidence that Frieda neglected her children while she was on methamphetamine binges.

In each situation, the therapist can help the client determine what can reasonably be done in the context of therapy to address the substance-related legal issues. This can include coordinating services and facilitating referrals. The therapist works with the client to clarify both the nature of the problem and any obligations or expectations placed on the client as a result.

This can be complicated by the client's anger, anxiety, defiance, or denial about the hassles or responsibilites involved. Clients are sometimes confused or overwhelmed by intricate procedures or legal language. They may need help figuring out complex documents. They may comprehend the consequences, but have little idea whether or how they can recompense the losses. Clients in (or anticipating) legal trouble tend initially to distrust the therapist and may withhold or distort information. Some will argue that possession of drugs for personal consumption should not be illegal, and so they resent or deny being bound by laws with which they disagree. They may also perceive therapy as yet another form of punishment for alleged crimes and accuse the therapist of making a living off of other people's misfortune. Some clients try to manipulate the therapist to tell them what to do or do their work for them.

Therapeutic interventions with clients accused of or involved in illegal behavior thus require the therapist to tolerate difficult affect, both on the client's and the therapist's parts. Therapists will need to ride the waves of interpersonal tension that mount with such clients. Skills at building working alliances and negotiating treatment strategies in the face of such tensions are crucial. Therapists may find themselves perpetually challenged to clarify their own attitudes and feelings about the intersection between substance use and legal entanglements. They must be able to manage and utilize their personal reactions and to persist with therapeutic intent when interactions get rocky. Above all, effective therapists learn to simultaneously communicate respect for the client along with clear potentials and boundaries of the therapy process.

Specific Interventions for Substance Abuse Linked to Legal Concerns

The following suggestions are offered in some semblance of the order in which their relevance might arise. However, therapists are reminded that specific client presentations of substance-related legal concerns will necessitate flexible approaches. Also, the utility of particular interventions may recur as therapist and client negotiate their relationship.

   Elicit Specific Information.   Obviously the therapist needs clear descriptions of the client's dilemma to be in a position to intervene. Getting this information is frequently easier said than done. Clients may give terse or vague accounts because they do not trust the therapist or they are tired of repeating the story. They may retort that the therapist should get a judge, probation officer, or some other third party to give the minutiae because apparently the client's opinion does not matter. If clients were under the influence of chemicals at the time of a crime or arrest, they may not fully remember the incident, or the details may be fuzzy. The client's emotional state, either under- or overcontrolled, may impede communication. A client with limited social skills may be hard for the therapist to understand, whereas a client who appears to be manipulative or antisocial can leave a therapist doubting the client's version of the incident in question.
   To clarify, the therapist sifts through the available particulars, probing to fill in gaps and address apparent discrepancies. The therapist will need to be patient and nonjudgmental with stories that are only gradually revealed. For example, the case of Jarvid from chapter 5 is revisited here. Jarvid was initially reluctant to give his therapist details of his arrest for trespassing while he was judged to be under the influence of alcohol. Over many sessions, as he came to trust his therapist with the full story, he reported that he had been working overtime painting apartments the day of his arrest. He swore he had not consumed alcohol for over a year in recovery, but be-

lieved he had been exposed to a toxic level of chemicals in the paint thinner he had been using. He recalled meeting a stranger at the grocery store after work and then regaining consciousness in that person's house hours later, in the presence of police officers and with no memory of the interim. Additional shared research into the chemical compound of the thinner plus the criteria for substance intoxication induced by toxic chemicals led to an adjustment of Jarvid's preliminary diagnosis.

The therapist should find out how the client was referred for therapy. When clients indicate a treatment mandate, the therapist asks whether the mandating party provided any documentation of terms, such as a court order or conditions of probation. If the client has the document in hand, the participants can read through it together and discuss terms, questions, and implications. If the client did not bring the paperwork, the therapist requests that they review it together at the next session. Sometimes clients are not sure whether they have any documents or whether paperwork they were given is still in their possession. Then the therapist persuades the client to identify appropriate contact persons and ask necessary questions to clarify the terms of the treatment mandate. Also the therapist determines whether the client will need to give verification of treatment attendance to a mandating party, and clarifies conditions and deadlines for its provision.

Many clients are not sure exactly what is expected of them or how they can fulfill their obligations. Therapists aim to increase shared understanding of the circumstances that led to the client's legal trouble as well as the terms imposed as a consequence. The therapist pointedly refrains from legal advice (a topic to be addressed in detail shortly), and may in fact wish to consult with third parties in search of clarification on the client's behalf.

Third parties directly involved in the client's case should be contacted only with the informed consent of the client. In many situations, the client or referring party will request verification of the client's compliance with the treatment mandate. Therapists need a client's written consent to verify attendance and should specify with clients who is to receive the information, what information is required, and by what deadlines. Documented consent permits the therapist to share only the specified information. Hence, if additional detail is desired, appropriate consents should be obtained and documented.

If the therapist seeks legal or related professional consultation with third parties not involved with the client's case, the therapist takes care to protect the client's anonymity. Both kinds of consultation (with professionals who are directly involved or not) can be important for several reasons. Consultation helps therapists solidify their understanding and responsibilities. Furthermore, it offers perspectives besides the client's to help interpret complicated situations. It puts the therapist in a better position to strategize treatment objectives based on a more comprehensive view of the client's interrelated issues. Also consultation often provides ideas for involving clients more directly in transactions with relevant third parties.

Facilitate Communication Between Clients and Third Parties. Promoting better communication between clients and other professionals with whom clients are obliged to interact frequently becomes a treatment objective. In the process of unraveling the client's problems, evidence often emerges that the client is having tense or conflicted transactions with a parole or probation officer, a case worker, or a judge. The therapist can point out that satisfying incurred obligations and removing related constraints depends, to a large extent, on the client's ability to effectively interact with those third parties. In kind, the therapist can propose interventions that range from coaching the client in session to mediating discussion between involved parties. Examples of each follow.

In therapy to address his alcoholism, Emory angrily admitted that his ex-wife has accused him of molesting their daughter. Emory argues that her unfounded charges were fabricated to keep him away from them and from the ex-wife's new boyfriend. At least until his case is decided in court, Emory is limited to restricted visits with his six-year-old girl, which are supervised by a male caseworker. Emory claims the caseworker has made several disparaging remarks implying that Emory is a pedophile. Furious, Emory tells his therapist he is almost ready to forego future visitation, although he desperately wants to see his little girl. The therapist recommends using time in session to discuss and rehearse ways Emory could address his concerns with his caseworker or, if necessary, his supervisors. Together they brainstorm means of helping Emory avoid relapse, keep his temper, articulate his contentions, and deal with anticipated responses.

Another example involves Casey, a diagnosed schizophrenic referred for substance abuse therapy after she was arrested for possession of methamphetamines and marijuana. Casey's oral expression is poor because her tongue protrudes, which she attributes to the side effects of long-term antipsychotic medication. Her speech is often tangential, but the therapist detects frequent reference to frustrations with a caseworker, Joan. Probing for details, the therapist learns that Joan drives Casey to and from therapy sessions, so the therapist asks Casey whether she would consent to Joan's participation at their next therapy session. When Casey agrees, the therapist gets Casey's signed release to contact Joan to invite her to the session. Casey and the therapist converse in advance about what they want to discuss with Joan. When Joan attends the following week, the therapist helps set the agenda and mediates the discussion. By the end of the collateral session, all three have better ideas of how they can work together to help Casey.

Therapists promote improved communication between clients and other persons so that clients can progress toward treatment goals. By clarifying problems and responsibilities in necessary relationships, therapists can guide clients toward action. In addition, therapists' interventions demonstrate the role they can play in facilitating clients' own efforts.

Clarify the Therapist's Role. Clients in trouble may expect their therapists to fix their problems, explain the solutions, or add more hassles. Some assume the therapist operates in league with law enforcement. Others insinuate the therapist's interests are purely selfish and that the whole treatment racket is just a money chasing game. Still other clients want their therapists to provide legal advice. It is crucial in each case for therapists to clearly explain the extents and limits to which they can go in legitimate efforts to work with the client.

This kind of psychoeducation about the therapist's role is important across the course of therapy. In the beginning, therapists assert client rights, especially confidentiality and its limits. Mandated clients in particular may have concerns, misunderstandings, or questions about the nature of therapeutic confidentiality. Therapists try to be straightforward and fair in answering questions and responding to comments. Therapists can explain that they work independently of law enforcement, and that their intent is to work in the client's interests toward goals negotiated with the client so long as the client makes parallel efforts. They inform clients that they will exchange information with third parties only as permitted by client consent and confidentiality regulations. When they do communicate with third parties, they attempt to advocate for the client to the extent that the therapist's perception of the truth will allow. Their role is to work with the client toward a shared conception of the client's issues that will widen the base on which positive change can be constructed in the client's life.

Therapists often revisit explanations of their own roles throughout therapy. Overwhelmed or cynical clients may not thoroughly attend to information the therapist provides early in the process. Therapists continue clarifying their roles as emerging dynamics or overt questions suggest the need. This may also include explaining to other people with a stake in the client's outcomes what the therapist can and cannot do. Of course this means that therapists employ psychological techniques and interventions addressing the intersection between the client's substance abuse and legal problems. It also means that therapists are careful not to work outside of their own expertise.

Acknowledge the Limits of One's Expertise. Angry, frustrated, or scared clients can exert pressure on the therapist to help resolve their situations even quicker than possible. Therapists will encounter questions about procedures or areas of knowledge outside their own field as clients grab at opportunities to relieve their concerns. In addition to acknowledging the limits of one's own expertise, a therapist can also demonstrate willingness to help the client find answers. Possible interventions include research by the therapist, homework for the client, or referral to an appropriate professional or resource.

One tricky aspect of such scenarios is that client questions are sometimes delivered with a challenge to the therapist's expertise. Clients trying to deactivate any potential perceived threat may phrase requests to deride, taunt, or dismiss the therapist. Those hoping for quick resolution may flatter or idealize the therapist. Therapists will need to recognize temptations to prove or exaggerate their expertise. They should find their own comfort level with responding to such challenges, admitting their range of knowledge, and intervening with therapeutic intent to help the client identify realistic alternative resources.

Emphasize Discrimination of Realistic Options. Legal trouble associated with substance abuse frequently results in requirements that the individual abstain from substance use for a specified period of time. Clients not yet in trouble may still talk about stopping or reducing substance abuse in hopes of avoiding legal entanglements. Many clients in either position find it quite hard in actuality to change their patterns of substance use. For clients mandated to abstain, this difficulty feels compounded by the fines, fees, and other tasks imposed by the courts, probation or parole officers, or child protective agencies. Clients often experience stress about fulfilling these obligations, which can tempt the individual to use substances. However, using substances under these conditions carries threats of additional sanctions. Clients frequently get discouraged or cynical about trying to meet such terms even if they admit their own responsibility. They may become hopeless about the possibility of ever resolving their issues.

Therapists intervene by helping to identify realistic approaches to addressing clients' complicated problems. They encourage clients to talk about manageable steps, workable time frames, and reasonable expectations of outcome. Careful treatment planning and patient implementation can assist clients in steadily working through objectives in a step-by-step fashion, rewarding progress and coping with setbacks.

Returning to the example earlier in this chapter of Linden, the client wishing to get his driver's license reinstated, the therapist helps generate a timeline that prioritizes the tasks Linden needs to accomplish and the documentation he will need to gather to meet his goal. The client sets targets of completing both the drunk driver victim's impact panel and the mandated visits to the morgue by the time the required number of individual and group therapy sessions are finished. In this case, 75 treatment hours are required because of the extreme nature of intoxication (blood alcohol content was 0.19) at the time of Linden's arrest for the most recent violation. Therapy participants determine a strategy by which Linden will pay the hefty fine. Plans are solidified to maintain necessary contact with Linden's probation officer. Periodic assessment of the client's relapse prevention efforts are built into the timeline. A date is established by which he aims to have all necessary documents ready to present with his application for reinstatement because Linden has admitted tendencies toward procrastination and disorganization. The therapist suggests he designate a secure place to keep all the paperwork until the application is ready to submit.

This timeline gives the client a realistic picture of what needs to be done and how long it is projected to take. It further structures ongoing therapy sessions as the dyad assesses progress according to intervals created by target dates on the client's timeline. The therapist can then increase the specificity of the intervention by reinforcing client actions and exploring emotional, behavioral, and interpersonal barriers to action.

Encourage Responsibility for Actions and Outcomes. A significant barrier to action is posed when a client shuns responsibility for behaviors that led to legal sanctions. A client's refusal to shoulder responsibility for addressing consequences of the client's behavior certainly also constitutes a major obstacle to treatment. Therapists try motivating clients to take appropriate responsibility for past, present, and future behaviors; to be effective, corresponding interventions must be empathic.

Clients accustomed to dodging hassles by attributing responsibility to factors outside their control do not respond well to sheer insistence that they now accept accountability. However, if such exhortations are accompanied by the therapist's curiosity about the client's perspective and willingness to openly debate implications of differences in perspective, the client can sometimes be engaged in productive conversations about the nature of personal responsibility.

One clinical example is Cody, a client mandated to treatment for a first DUI offense. Cody's initial treatment plan has already been described in chapter 6. Cody makes it clear for several sessions running that he feels he did nothing wrong, but the cops in his neighborhood were prejudiced against him. He tells his therapist he will come when he is supposed to come and say whatever he has to say to get through his probation requirements. However, once he is done, he has every intention of resuming former levels of alcohol use. His therapist agrees that is his right, but that he would also be responsible for the outcomes of those choices, just as he bears responsibility for driving while intoxicated. Cody shrugs, saying he doesn't care.

The therapist tries to explore and empathize with Cody's reasons for not caring and for believing he is a victim of prejudice. Receiving only brusque replies, the therapist then states,

> Well, we could continue to face off here while I quiz you, but I'm more inter-
> ested in seeing if there is something or someone you do care about enough to
> assume a commitment. Is there anything we could talk about in here that in-
> terests you beyond keeping the chairs warm?

The therapist laughs, but Cody barely acknowledges the attempt at humor.
"Not really," he says initially. The therapist proceeds with psychoeducation about drugs, to which Cody had agreed, but periodically she reiterates the probes for any sense of his interests or responsibilities. Two sessions
before their designated termination, Cody surprises her by mentioning an
elderly neighbor for whom Cody and his brother run daily errands. Cody
declines to give many details, but the therapist thanks him for showing her
another side of himself—one that validates her confidence that he does
take responsibility when he cares. She adds that she hopes he will keep
thinking about whether he learned anything from his DUI and its consequences, including therapy, that will affect his investments of interest and
responsibility. This leads to some discussion of assuming responsibility for
one's own behavior even as one holds others responsible for their actions.

If and when clients do increase acceptance of personal responsibility,
the therapist attends to feelings of guilt, shame, grief, or other emotions
that may arise. If clients continue to deflect responsibility, therapists invite
consideration of the fact that others will hold the client responsible for past
and future actions, with exploration of the client's response.

Minimize Hypothetical, Political, or Philosophical Arguments. Discussions
of options and responsibilities often slam into a client's objections couched
in terms of passionate convictions. Some clients absolve themselves by citing cases for the legalization of drugs, the failure of American drug policy,
the corruption of law enforcement, or the social injustice in application of
drug laws. Therapists can give clients room to air their personal views without getting caught in trying to prove the client wrong or change the client's
mind. Therapists do not have to agree with clients (although they may) or
withhold personal opinion (although they might choose to), but will want
to call attention to the process as well as the content of such discussions.

At points like these, therapists will reflect on the function served by the
client's argument. Is the client prepared to take action consistent with
stated convictions, or is the client avoiding talking about or doing some-

thing else? Can the client reconcile stated opinions with the practical constraints or obligations the client is facing?

As therapists make process comments and share interpretations, they should expect at least some clients to protest or resist. Therapists can then stay curious and involved in further elaboration. Therapists also need to clarify for themselves their own perspectives on controversies about substance use, legal status, and social justice considerations. This will help them choose when and how to utilize self-disclosure of personal opinions or experiences.

Tolerate Negative Affect and Negotiate Relationship Tensions. As the reader can imagine, these issues in therapy elicit much volatile emotion and interpersonal conflict. Thus, therapists learn to maintain their interventional stance with resilience and the expectation of mutual respect. Therapists demonstrate willingness and ability within reason to continue conversations and maintain contact even when situations are tense. They call attention to the distinction between the right to express opinions and the responsibility to deal with the consequences of one's choice of expression. The therapist clarifies consequences occurring in the therapy transaction by providing (and inviting) honest, tactful reactions. Process comments and affect management interventions (discussed earlier in this chapter) help negotiate interpersonal tensions with substance abusers in legal trouble. Many times a therapist who can stand up to a client's challenges or outbursts will earn the kind of respect that facilitates additional rapport and trust.

Advocate for the Client and for Social Justice. Tucker (1999) summarized literature indicating disproportionate negative impact on minority populations of criminal penalties for illicit substance use, as well as negative effects of current drug policies on civil liberties. For therapists, the complex interactions among substance abuse, criminal behavior, and drug laws and policies can manifest in complicated client presentations. In certain situations, the therapist may come to believe that a client deserves reconsideration or has been treated unfairly. Therapists may also be asked to write reports documenting a client's progress or testify in court regarding the client's case. Individual therapists additionally take into account the policies of their employers, the laws and regulations of their states, and their own personal and professional ethics in making decisions about how to advocate on their client's behalf.

Naturally, therapists are encouraged to take action supporting their clients within the realm of their professional expertise. Therapists are further advised to present information in behaviorally specific terms. Offering speculation or conjecture without supporting evidence compromises a therapist's credibility. When therapists advocate for clients, it is best to specify what the client actually said and did. Responsible therapists are prepared to justify their claims about client issues with reasoning that embraces both logic and evidence.

Realistic Therapist Expectations of Outcome

Legal problems and the behaviors that lead to them are often troubling and can be deeply entrenched. Some clients mandated to therapy sometimes view it as a blessing in disguise—a chance to get the help they already knew they needed, an observation corroborated by Thombs (1999). Others overcome initially bad attitudes to do good work in therapy. Therapists value experience with clients like these, but they recognize too that some other mandated clients will demonstrate little progress despite the therapist's best efforts. Still therapists try to motivate and assist each client as much as possible within the boundaries of the therapy relationship through an empathic, realistic approach to the client's unique circumstances.

Therapists who work with substance abusers should be ready to deal with a full range of issues and attitudes tied up in clients' legal issues. Despite frustrations and disappointments with some clinical situations, therapists applying consistent efforts will also share in meaningful, real growth among clients determined to put past troubles behind them.

*   *   *

Balanced, holistic therapy for substance use disorders addresses the aspects of the client's life that influence or are affected by the client's risky substance use. Diagnostically, the impact of substance use on personal distress or dysfunction distinguishes normal use from problematic abuse. Thus, addressing the contexts in which that distress or dysfunction is manifest constitutes some of the goals of therapy.

This chapter has surveyed possible interactions between substance use and other clinically significant problems, including health and medical issues, emotional problems, communication difficulties, occupational and vocational troubles, and legal and social justice concerns. For each context, possible interventions and related substance abuse considerations were presented. The process of untangling the knotty problems often associated with substance use disorders benefits from the therapist's skills at thorough conceptualization, careful clinical judgment, and collaborative interaction with clients.

Effective therapists help clients clarify obstacles to the client's prioritized goals, with emphasis as needed on the perceived contribution of substance use. Further intervention focuses on developing strategies and following them through the intricate maze separating the client from personal goals. For clients with substance abuse histories, therapists encourage making choices about how the client wants to interpret the role of past drug or alcohol use in shaping the client's present problems. Equally important, the therapist also guides the client toward decisions about future substance use or abstinence in light of personal goals for the client's own physical health, emotion management, relationships, occupations, and citizenship.

Chapter 10

Terminating Therapy With Substance Abuse Clients

As clients work through problems associated with their substance abuse and whatever other problems brought them to therapy, the time eventually comes when the therapy relationship will end and the client will move on to a chapter of life beyond the present therapy. Among professionals, therapists often use *termination* to refer to the process of wrapping up a course of therapy (although they may use terms like "ending" or "closure," which sound less severe to the layperson, when talking with clients about finishing their work together). Substance abuse treatment providers frequently use the term *aftercare* to refer to steps the client will take, typically including involvement in other forms of professional care or social support systems, to maintain and expand beneficial outcomes past the end of more intensive intervention (Brown, Seraganian, Tremblay, & Annis, 2002). An important task of termination is thus to help clients clarify plans for their own aftercare.

For clients, the challenges are to continue their progress, extend their work toward personal goals, and avoid relapse after therapy is over. For therapists, understanding the recurrent nature of substance use disorders emphasizes the crucial tasks of the termination phase. Termination tasks include consolidating the lessons learned in the therapy and change processes, plus careful planning to prepare clients to apply those lessons on their own. Ideally, these tasks are conducted over several sessions, but when necessary can also be implemented with shorter windows of time.

Gains in therapy may be modest or substantial, but of course they never completely remove the potential for later stresses or difficulties when therapy is done. Clients who have grappled with substance use concerns frequently have complex thoughts and feelings about the work they have done with their therapists, about the fact that therapy is coming to a close, and about the continuing subsequent challenges. Depending on the circumstances under which therapy is terminating, clients may be relieved, nonchalant, or apprehensive about termination. They may express confidence, insecurity, or forgetfulness about their abilities to carry the insights and tools gained from therapy into their lives beyond. More often than not, client reactions encompass a mixture of feelings, such as the client who is both sad to say goodbye but enthusiastic about future independence from therapy. Other clients may express sincere gratitude for all they learned, along with difficulty describing plans to apply their new knowledge and capacities. Frequently, too, clients entertain both realistic and unrealistic expectations about wrapping up therapy.

Primary goals of the termination phase, then, are for therapists to structure a context in which the client and therapist together can review their work, assess the point to which they have arrived, and make plans for the client's future. When substance use disorders have been a focus, therapy participants explicitly revisit the nature of the original concerns and the significant themes and changes that evolved over discussions of the client's substance use. Therapists can guide clients in articulating past and current attitudes and behaviors regarding the use of psychoactive chemicals. Therapists promote review of strategies the client has developed for preventing and coping with possible relapse. In addition, conversations during the termination phase concentrate on anticipating likely situations that may trigger urges or cravings to resume excessive substance use, with focus on planning aftercare steps clients can take to deal with such circumstances should they arise.

PLANNING FOR THE TERMINATION OF THERAPY

In a very real sense, termination planning is a component of treatment planning, with the focus on how to use the last session(s) of therapy. As participants come to acknowledge that the end of therapy is imminent, therapists actively plan strategies to use the remaining time most productively. Specific strategies for implementing the termination agenda will be sensitive to the conditions under which the pending termination of therapy is initiated.

When Termination Is Mutually Determined

The most desirable scenario is when the client and therapist both agree that the client is making sufficient progress toward treatment goals, and that the client is capable of independently maintaining progress and coping with future threats to continued well-being. General indicators of readiness would be the client's expression not only of the desire to end therapy, but also of a coherent and compelling rationale for termination. In some cases, the therapist will initiate the move toward termination when review of goals and assessment of progress indicate client readiness.

In therapy for substance abuse, the therapist watches and listens for specific indicators of termination readiness, including the client's report of either abstinence from chemicals or reduction of substance use over a duration of time consistent with the client's treatment goals. Also the therapist looks for expressions of the client's intrinsic motivation and pride underlying the work accomplished, plus realistic confidence in the ability to continue progress toward personal goals. In addition to refraining from excessive substance use, indicators of client readiness for termination include the capacities to recognize conditions conducive to relapse and deal effectively with both probable temptations and potential relapses.

When indicators of termination readiness are evident, the therapist proposes holding two or three additional sessions to review and reinforce therapeutic insights and to prepare the client for independent action. Therapists are prepared to negotiate the amount of time left according to the client's response. For example, the client may reply with satisfaction about current progress, but still request more sessions than the few proposed by the therapist to solidify aftercare plans. Alternatively, the client might announce that actually the present session is the last one the client plans to attend based on self-assessment of readiness and a decision made prior to the session. In either case, the therapist can engage the client first in negotiating a time frame for termination discussions, and then in using whatever time is agreed and available to address the termination agenda.

When the Client Initiates Termination Prior to Therapist Agreement of Readiness

Clients sometimes decide they are finished with therapy before they have met therapy objectives or demonstrated clear progress. This is especially likely for clients who have yet to internalize much of the motivation to attend sessions. Substance abuse clients are prone to so-called *premature termination* when they repeatedly express resentment toward external conditions and authorities conspiring, as they perceive it, to impose therapy on them. Also the client may choose to terminate prior to therapist agreement if the client gets frustrated dealing with the persons and other factors that reinforce continuing substance use counter to treatment goals, or if the client becomes disillusioned by recurrent triggers or relapses despite treatment efforts. Clients attending primarily to comply with a formal treatment mandate may well quit coming when the minimum required number of sessions is complete, even if other treatment goals remain unmet. Those clients persuaded by significant others to attend often lag in motivation when interpersonal pressures are reduced or inconsistent, unless the client has developed internal commitments to treatment goals negotiated with the therapist.

The attentive therapist recognizes indicators that the client is contemplating or already implementing what the therapist would consider premature termination. Then the therapist employs a modified termination agenda specific to the context shaped by those client indicators.

Response to Indicators Evident in Session.   When the client's behavior in session indicates that he or she may be thinking about discontinuing therapy, the therapist raises the topic explicitly and without judgment. If the indicators are subtle, the therapist might say, "I notice that you have said (or done) [specify behavior of interest], and I wonder if that's a way of telling me that you're considering the possibility of ending our therapy soon." With a client who overtly states intent to quit coming, the therapist could say, "I hear you saying you feel ready to wrap up our therapy, and I'd like us to spend some time talking about that possibility before you finalize any decisions."

In cases where the client acknowledges leaning toward imminent termination, the therapist still negotiates for a reasonable span of time to discuss the course of therapy and the decision to end it. For example, the therapist can request one or two additional sessions to explore options, evaluate outcomes, and collaborate on a decision. If the client declines to return for any subsequent meetings, the therapist can structure remaining time to concentrate on the client's decision to terminate and its ramifications.

The therapist also still leads the client through the termination agenda of review, evaluation, and preparation. Sometimes this process will permit resolution of barriers to continuing treatment, or may uncover new or clarified concerns that renew the client's interest in continuing therapy. For example, with mandated substance abusers, therapists initiate discussion of how to answer requests from mandating parties for verification of client participation. When the therapist explains what can be reported in good conscience, in light of the therapist's professional judgment and the information the client has consented to release, a client might reconsider the wisdom of ending at the present juncture. (It is also possible that this same client might now withdraw consent for the therapist to verify attendance, but the therapist can point out that, although this is within the client's rights, the client will still be expected to account for this decision.) Another example is the client who confides, during discussion with the therapist of unfinished business, a deep secret about her introduction to substance use in the context of an incestuous relationship. Once this secret is out in the open, if the client feels supported and validated by the therapist's empathic response, the client may decide she feels safe enough to stay in therapy to deal with the implications.

However, if the resulting conversations do not yield agreement about whether therapy should continue or terminate, the therapist can still use the termination discussions to therapeutic advantage by communicating both concerns and respect for the client. The therapist who can tactfully and straightforwardly identify unmet objectives and remaining concerns about the client's substance use and related issues helps the client clarify the impact of therapy, the work yet to be done if and when the client chooses, and some tools and strategies at the client's disposal.

Response to Client Absences From Scheduled Sessions. Clients do not always show up to announce or even hint at their intentions to self-terminate. Some simply fail to attend without notice or subsequent contact. Others leave phone messages to reveal their decisions to terminate, to offer apologies or excuses, or just to cancel without explanation. When cancellations and no-shows are repetitive, and especially if the therapist has detected other indications of wavering commitment to therapy, the therapist addresses the likelihood of client self-termination. In each of these situations, the therapist still makes reasonable effort to reestablish contact with the client. This includes extending the offer to meet for one more session to discuss the client's options of continuing or terminating therapy and, if the client remains interested in the latter, to decide how to bring the present therapy to a satisfactory close.

The therapist can make this offer immediately over the phone if the therapist has intercepted the client's call, or the therapist can follow up with a courtesy call in response to a client's message or absence. (Of course the therapist protects the client's confidentiality in leaving any phone messages.) If the client does not respond within a few days, the therapist may elect to place another call with a similar offer of a final session, adding this time a polite request that the client reply by a specified deadline or else the therapist will assume the client is no longer interested in continuing. The specification of a deadline gives both the therapist and client an explicit point at which the therapist will close the file.

For clients who cannot be reached by phone or who do not return the therapist's calls, the therapist has the option of a termination letter. The letter specifies any missed appointments, any efforts the therapist has made to contact the client since the missed appointment(s), the offer to hold a final closure session, and a deadline before which the client needs to respond to keep a place in the therapist's case load. In the case of mandated clients, the letter can inform the client if and how the therapist plans to report to the mandating party if the client does not reply by the deadline. Also the letter should include a rapport-building statement acknowledging the work done and the relationship shared so far along with best wishes for the client's future regardless of the client's response to the letter. A sample letter is provided in Appendix C, but the letter ideally reflects the therapist's own words and relationship with the client. In their clients' files, therapists should keep records of attempts to call and letters sent to clients.

For clients who accept the offer of a final session, the therapist collaboratively asserts the purposes of the session. Here again the therapist aims to nonjudgmentally recall with the client any significant aspects of their work together, to assess the client's current status including the apparent decision to self-terminate and its implications, and to address the client's options for the future. Among future options, the therapist may propose resumption rather than termination of therapy. Some clients can be motivated to reengage by this discussion and by the therapist's caring interest. When clients are set on ending, however, the therapist can guide this discussion toward shared recollection of their course of therapy with identification of efforts made, progress achieved, unfinished business, and plans for the client's future self-care. Clients with substance abuse issues are asked to specifically focus on past, present, and future efforts to address those concerns.

With clients who do not reply to calls or letters, therapists can at least take satisfaction in knowing that they made reasonable efforts to bring the therapy relationship to as much closure as the client would allow. At the very least, the therapist's phone calls and letters attempt to communicate continuing interest in the client, and to plant seeds of hope that the client will continue some efforts (whether in future treatment or elsewhere) to address the work begun in therapy. These forms of contact also give the therapist an opportunity to say goodbye, leaving a premature ending less ragged for the therapist than it might have been without the efforts at follow-up.

When the Therapist Must Terminate Before the Client Is Ready

On occasion, such as when therapists relocate residence, complete a phase of training, or change employers, the therapist is compelled to initiate termination before clients have reached their therapy objectives. Under circumstances like these, the therapist needs to give the client ample notice to provide time to discuss not only the client's progress and plans, but also the participants' feelings about the conditions forcing termination.

When possible, therapists can let clients know at least a few weeks before the latest available session date that, although remaining time is limited, there is still time left in which meaningful work can be accomplished. To give the client a better idea of what that means, therapists can summarize the tasks of the termination agenda, emphasizing the following points in particular. First, the therapist openly acknowledges the possibility that the client has reactions to the therapist initiating termination, with importance placed on discussing those to the extent to which the client desires. Second, openly recognizing the business left unfinished by the therapist's departure leads to discussions of necessary and appropriate referrals for continuing care and/or strategies for seeking support for the client's continuing efforts to address personal substance use concerns.

It is not unusual for clients who learn their therapists will soon be moving to another community or leaving a current agency to feel hurt, abandoned, angry, or disillusioned. However, over a few final sessions, with the therapist's willingness to hear and work through these feelings, such clients often come to accept the inevitable and articulate the value of the time spent with the therapist. In the course of discussing these complex and changing reactions, the therapist can encourage the client to remember valued insights and apply new methods to their lives after therapy terminates, particularly forming bridges to additional sources of support and reinforcement.

Mann (1973) wrote that placing constraints on time sets into action predictable dynamics of a therapy relationship. Offering hope for a meaningful outcome in a specified period of time often mobilizes efforts toward progress and change. Even if the client is not sensing readiness for termination at the time the therapist introduces the necessity of ending, the astute therapist can structure termination to promote some client improvement. By allowing at least a few sessions to instill hope, process mixed reactions, and generate plans for the client to take next steps, therapists can help their clients take as much as possible from their experiences in therapy.

IMPLEMENTING THE TERMINATION AGENDA

When it becomes evident that therapy is moving toward a close, therapists can pose suggestions for finishing the work they have done with their clients. They can offer topics to be discussed and prompt clients to bring up things they would like to say or do in the remaining sessions. The therapist can give a framework for the discussion by saying something like the following:

> Since our time together is coming to an end, I'd like us to spend at least part of that time talking about how we want to wrap this up. Let me share a few ideas about things I think are important for us to touch on, and I want to hear any thoughts or requests you might have.

The therapist gives the client the choice among options to speak first or listen first to the therapist's ideas.

At some point in the session during which termination is introduced, the therapist adds,

> I'd like us to take some time to review the course of our work together, assess the current outcomes of all the work we've done, and consider what you can do once therapy is finished to continue working on things that are important to you in ways that feel right to you. If you have reactions right now to what I'm suggesting, we can talk about those now [assuming available time], or if you want to think about this until next session, we can discuss it more then.

Proposing this agenda lets the client know what to expect, and inviting client input tells the client how to participate.

The therapist may want to amplify this basic termination agenda either by (a) giving the client more specific questions to think about (when the client has agreed to at least one subsequent session and the client indicates a wish to contemplate before answering), or (b) using the more specific questions and prompts described next to structure a present discussion (when the client is ready to talk about ending therapy or if the client reports intentions not to return after the present session). The willing client typically benefits from allowing a week or more to process the multiple or shifting responses to the prospect of terminating. Some clients, however, will avoid or dismiss the importance of extended termination discussions. Therapists can propose and encourage at least one additional session with the rationale of taking advantage of the opportunity to consolidate any lessons learned or insights gained in therapy, thus increasing the client's potential to recall and use those gains in the future. Even if the client makes it clear that the client will not be returning after the present session, the therapist can aim to touch on each aspect of the proposed termination agenda in the time left available. Thus, the therapist maintains greater flexibility by introducing the termination agenda earlier rather than later in a therapy session.

Focus on the Past: Reviewing the Course of Therapy

Collaboratively looking back over the time spent together in therapy accentuates the comparison between the client's past concerns and present coping. Joint review also can solidify memories of significant events (good and bad) that transpired between participants. It further creates opportunities to better understand in retrospect transactions that were troubling, confusing, or discrepantly perceived at the time they originally occurred.

Therapists can structure this review by asking the client to reflect on what she or he remembers about their first meeting. How does the client remember feeling at the time? What issues, concerns, or ideas were prominent in the client's thoughts then? How was the client trying to cope with stressors at the time, and how effectively? What were the client's reactions to coming to therapy? Other questions and recollections may emerge as well. If the client does not spontaneously make comparisons to the present, the therapist can invite it.

When therapy has focused on substance use concerns, the therapist prompts the client to specifically recall the nature and typical pattern of substance use at the beginning of therapy. What does the client remember about the attitude assumed toward personal substance use back then? How did the client's substance use play into the client's reasons for seeking therapy? How does the client remember interpreting that contribution at the time?

The therapist will undoubtedly also have memories and impressions the therapist believes are important and appropriate to share with the client. However, it is advisable for the therapist to give the client the first chance to comment so that the therapist can actively listen and respond to the client's perspective before imposing his or her own. Therapists' closing observations are likely to be perceived as more meaningful and influential when the client first feels heard.

As the therapy participants share their reflections of their early sessions, the therapist can guide the conversation toward comparison of where the client was then to where the client is now. In addition, the therapist facilitates explorations of ways in which therapy contributed to identified differences in the client from past to present.

In terms of the client's substance use or abstinence, the therapist asks the client to talk about ways in which substance abuse behaviors and attitudes have changed or stayed the same. The client is encouraged to talk about feelings and reasons associated with those comparisons. The therapist also asks what the client remembers as significant moments during the course of therapy, both favorable and unfavorable, that had some influence on the client's thoughts, feelings, or behaviors with respect to substance use.

The therapist furthers the termination review by asking the client to think back, over all the conversations, about any occasions that stand out in memory. For example, the therapist could say,

> As we both look back on the time we have known each other, what strikes you as memorable or important enough for us to talk about as we bring our work to a close? Are there things you especially liked or disliked about our sessions? I think it's valuable to talk about both the things that make a positive impact as well as things that may not have worked so well to fully capture the experience. That way we can both take more crystallized impressions of the significance of this therapy into the future after our time together is finished. I have

some thoughts to give you, but I'm interested first in hearing about what stands out for you.

By presenting the questions this way, the therapist potentially elicits a range of client responses that can be explored in a collaborative manner.

Many clients will be clear in their expressions of either positive or negative emotions at termination, but not spontaneously addressing both. If the therapist hears only one side of the presumed ambivalence about termination, the therapist can probe to permit expression of a fuller range of feelings where relevant. After validating and exploring whatever feelings the client raises initially, the therapist inquires about any other reactions, first in an unstructured mode (e.g., "Any other impressions you want to add?"). If the open-ended approach evokes little or nothing, the therapist can narrow the question to address any unspoken thoughts and feelings (e.g., "So it's great to hear you feel good about much of what we've done. Were there any things that weren't so great from your point of view?" Or, "I understand you're frustrated about not reaching that goal even though you are graduating and our therapy is ending, but are you aware of any benefits you'll be able to take from our sessions?"). With clients who were externally motivated to begin with, the therapist could say:

So you've made it through this, and you're glad it's finally coming to an end. I can imagine there is some relief that you're almost done with something you didn't want to do in the first place. But now that it's about over, can you think of any useful aspects?

Clients may or may not follow this prompt with more reflections; but however the client chooses to respond, the therapist accomplishes a few purposes. First, by asking, the therapist communicates that it is fine and appropriate to discuss any residual feelings the client has not yet mentioned if she or he would like to make them known before saying goodbyes. Second, the therapist can clarify and normalize the likelihood that participants in therapy will have some positive and some negative reactions to the therapy process, including termination, and that shared consideration of both can help accentuate the impact of a course of therapy. Together these two purposes establish a basis on which a hesitant client might become emboldened or a forgetful client might be stimulated to bring up additional impressions of their experiences in therapy.

A third purpose is also served by encouraging clients to voice both favorable and unfavorable recollections of therapy. Therapists are also then in a better position to share their own selected impressions of significant aspects of a particular course of therapy. The therapist, in preparation for termination, will have already taken time to think back, review notes, and identify points in the process that seemed especially meaningful in terms of collaboration or conflict, impasse or insight. Careful therapists will have formulated ideas about points they plan to emphasize in termination discussions with clients, and additional ideas may be triggered by the discussion.

When a client chooses not to elaborate on a therapist's request for review of therapy, the therapist can let the client know what the therapist is thinking. Again it is often useful in promoting discussion if the therapist starts with broad comments and narrows them only as needed to generate more discussion. For example, the therapist could say:

> At this point it sounds like you're focused on the positive [or negative] aspects of therapy, and that's understandable. It's also not unusual for clients to feel a variety of things when thinking back on therapy and getting ready to end. I know I can remember times I wasn't sure how to interpret what we were doing in sessions, and other times I felt we were really connected and making real progress. And it seems like all of it was important in bringing us to this point.

A comment like this might motivate new reflections from the client's perspective, or it may lead to questions from the client for more detail about the therapist's perspective.

When the client has been given ample opportunity to speak and respond to questions first, the therapist judges that the time is right to offer more specific input about events and insights that stand out in the therapist's memory. Some of these might be reflections on memories the client has already raised. Others will target moments the therapist recognizes as significant that have not been mentioned, and may not be remembered, by the client.

Of the many recollections and corresponding present thoughts and feelings the therapist entertains, the therapist chooses to reveal to the client those that can be offered with genuine therapeutic intent. At the close of therapy, this means that therapists select elements of therapy review with aims to clarify, resolve, and reinforce aspects of transactions between participants, with further goals of focusing the review on beneficial outcomes of therapy that clients can take with them.

Focus on Present: Assessing Progress, Accomplishments, and Unfinished Business

A review of therapy including comparisons of past and present naturally leads to examination of the current statuses of both the client's functioning and the therapy relationship. Termination of substance abuse therapy involves assessment of the length of abstinence from substances or the nature of any current use. Therapist and client together articulate the significance they associate with the client's current behavior with respect to psychoactive substances. Sometimes clients will express awareness of meaningful changes in their behavior and related attitudes or concerns. Other clients say they see minimal, if any, differences compared with earlier in therapy. Clients may be satisfied with or even excited about their present level of functioning, or they may be discouraged about progress that was less than they expected. Some who were attending therapy primarily at someone else's request or mandate indicate indifference regarding progress in therapy or the lack thereof.

Whatever the client's opinions about therapy outcomes, the therapist asks a variety of questions to encourage exploration of current assessments and evaluations. How does the client see him or herself at present? What is the client doing now to deal with the issues that brought the client to therapy or that have emerged over the course of therapy? Considering the goals established in therapy, have any been satisfactorily met at this point? How so? Does the client see any progress toward those goals that have yet to be fully met? How is that progress evident in the client's thoughts, feelings, or behaviors? What are aspects of the client's goals that still need to be addressed or areas of the client's life that still need work? How does the client feel about success achieved, progress recognized, and unfinished business remaining? Answering questions like these in the presence of a therapist who tries to understand and accept the client's present state can help the client more fully appreciate the point to which the client has come.

This clarification of the client's present state provides a firmer base of comparison both to the client's past functioning and future potential to promote personal well-being. The flexible structure of the therapist's termination agenda aids in differentiating and acknowledging both the nature of progress the client has accomplished toward therapy goals as well as concerns or problems still to be addressed. In addition to listening and responding to the client's replies to the types of questions just posed, the therapist can intervene by sharing the therapist's own impressions of the client's successes, meaningful efforts, and continuing challenges.

An additional intervention at this point involves reviewing treatment plans with an eye toward mutual evaluation of therapy outcomes. After the client has shared views on her or his present state, or if the client says little in response to the therapist's questions, the therapist suggests looking together at the goals formulated earlier and talking about both progress and any lack of movement toward those specific goals. Any goals associated with the client's substance use behaviors, attitudes, and emotional or interpersonal complications are explicitly pinpointed if they have not already been raised in preceding discussions. Reviewing treatment plans with the client can serve to confirm or reinforce assessments of outcomes already volunteered by clients. In other cases, this review expands the consideration of therapy outcomes possibly reminding participants of unacknowledged consequences or even altering assessments of where things stand at present. Review of treatment plans at termination is also consistent with the intent for which collaborative planning was introduced in the first place—to enhance the capacity for therapy participants to assess progress over time.

One more intervention therapists can employ to enrich awareness of the present state is to prompt discussion of feelings about therapy coming to a close. This includes the therapist sharing feelings as well to communicate the depth of human interaction that has occurred between participants. For example, the therapist might offer:

> Now that we're almost to the end of our work together, I have a whole bunch of mixed feelings. On one hand I'm happy about the progress we've identified, and I'm proud of all the good work we've done. I'm excited for you to be moving on with new skills and more confidence in using them, and I'm glad I've had the chance to know you. On the other hand, it's sad to see you go, and to know that we didn't get to everything we might have wanted to. I'll miss you, and I'll remember you even though we probably won't meet again. Even though there are things we didn't manage to resolve or even fully address in our sessions, I have faith in your ability to keep doing good work on those things in the future.

Obviously the specific content expressed by the therapist will reflect the therapist's genuine feelings toward ending therapy with the particular client. As clients hear these expressions and share their own immediate feelings, clients may more deliberately reflect on the complexity and significance of their present state of being as shaped in part by their experience of therapy. The therapist will need to be ready to respond genuinely to both positive and negative affect. Clients can come to more deeply appreciate gains they have made by comparing this enriched sense of the present to their past modes of functioning. Furthermore, they can use this honed awareness to prepare themselves to face subsequent challenges.

Focus on Future: Planning Next Steps to Promote Continuing Progress

The termination of therapy rarely, if ever, means that the client has nothing left to do. It often means that the client will have at least a few new ideas and improved abilities for dealing with future concerns and problems. During the termination phase, therapists can strengthen the client's readiness by guiding clients in identifying likely future tasks or interactions, and by specifying plans to confront those.

In the substance abuse treatment field, efforts or programs designed to help clients maintain treatment gains after more intensive treatment is complete are called *aftercare* (Brown, Seraganian, Tremblay, & Annis, 2002). In this section, the term *aftercare planning* is used to refer broadly to the therapist's efforts during termination discussions to help the client specify steps to promote progress and minimize the potential for relapse. Planning a client's aftercare includes:

1. identifying steps the client is willing to take to maintain gains;
2. clarifying possible steps to further the client's progress toward partially met goals;
3. considering steps the client may wish to take to work on the unfinished business and unmet goals of therapy;
4. preparing the client to anticipate, recognize, and cope with possible setbacks occurring after therapy; and
5. referring the client to appropriate sources of informal support or professional services as the need is indicated.

Aftercare Planning.   Clients with substance abuse histories benefit from aftercare planning during termination sessions because the chronic nature of substance use disorders and the prevalence of substance use and related cues in numerous social contexts combine to present substantial challenges to such clients as they complete therapy. As part of aftercare planning, therapists ask clients to anticipate probable situational triggers for relapse along with workable strategies for encountering those triggers without relapse.

Again the therapist will want to pose questions that spur the client to generate answers based on her or his own words and memories. What has the client learned in therapy that can be taken and used in the future? What kinds of issues or difficulties does the client expect to confront in the future, both short and long term? How might the client apply skills, tools, or insights derived from therapy and other change efforts to deal with expected complications? If and when unanticipated problems arise, what could the client do to mobilize resources? How confident does the client feel about abilities to maintain gains and extend efforts toward progress using lessons learned in therapy? Is the client ready to consider steps toward addressing issues not resolved or goals not met in the present course of therapy? How would the client recognize indications that seeking additional support or help would be in the client's best interest?

The more clients become able to supply their own answers to these questions, the more likely that clients will be able to recall, own, and utilize those answers under future challenging conditions. Thus, the therapist impels the client to speak first, although the therapist certainly offers suggestions to reinforce or expand on the client's comments.

If the client omits specific mention of substance use issues in answering the therapist's questions, the therapist makes sure to raise the topic. No matter who originates the topic, the therapist aims for thorough shared examination of possible complications and ongoing concerns, with concurrent development of aftercare plans that the client agrees are relevant and workable. The therapist can constructively assert the therapist's own residual concerns and recommended strategies if the client has not mentioned similar content. In such instances, the therapist provides opportunity for the client to respond to ideas voiced by the therapist.

Relapse Prevention Review. Relapse prevention plans are explicitly reviewed in the context of planning aftercare. As before, the therapist encourages the client to take ownership of relapse prevention in aftercare plans by asking the client first to articulate components of his or her relapse prevention strategy. Some clients already have their plans committed to memory or paper and are able to recite them in session. More commonly, clients generate partial or sketchy descriptions. When this is the case, the therapist reviews relapse prevention point by point. First the therapist names general components (dealing with factors that could trigger relapse, substituting healthier activities for more problematic behaviors, learning from relapse experience, and reinforcing successful relapse prevention) and then asks the client to give examples of each component that pertain to her or his own situation. If the client should have trouble generating personally relevant examples, the therapist can offer some based on the therapist's discussions with the client.

For clients preparing to end therapy without demonstrated ability to describe a personal plan for avoiding relapse (as often happens when substance abuse therapy is terminating without mutual consent), the therapist reemphasizes the value of well-defined plans. The therapist can explain that a plan need not be elaborate, but must be clear and specific enough for the client to remember and use as needed. Interventions that aim to improve client recall include asking the client to reiterate the plan in the present session after reviewing it with the therapist and again in subsequent sessions, if any. Giving the client a written copy of the plan and urging him or her to reread it regularly after therapy ends may be useful. Also therapists can engage clients in further discussions about thoughts, feelings, and actions regarding personal relapse prevention efforts.

Unfinished Business. With some clients, as seen in earlier chapters, substance use concerns are not evident in therapy until the later phases of the therapy relationship. It can happen that a client waits until the prospect of termination is close on the horizon before acknowledging problematic substance use. This could occur if a client feels safe enough to bring the subject up only when there is limited time left to address it, or possibly when previously unforeseen circumstances force a premature termination. Even under such constraints, however, the therapist can use at least some of any remaining time to discuss next steps the client can take to address newly revealed substance use problems. This is likely to include discussion of referral options for treatment services or support groups, along with consideration of the client's feelings and intentions about following through with contacting the referral.

The unfinished work identified in termination discussions creates opportunities to discuss options for things clients can work on in the future. In addition to continuing new behaviors that promote healthier functioning and help prevent relapse, the client will invariably also face challenges to confront residual problems or occasional setbacks. Therapy may come to a close before the client has faced or resolved issues associated with personal repercussions of substance abuse, or with other people who have been negatively affected by the client's substance use. To give a few examples, therapy may be scheduled to terminate before a client's court date to face charges associated with the client's substance abuse, or prior to a hearing at which the client's professional licensure could be revoked based on substance use violations on the job. Clients also might terminate therapy before talking to significant others about detrimental consequences of the client's substance use on their personal relationships or vice versa. The latter includes circumstances where problematic interpersonal transactions or perceived relationship pressures have served as triggers for the client's substance abuse.

During termination discussions, therapists help clients anticipate scenarios that are likely to arise or already definitely ahead. As clients talk about the thoughts and feelings they expect to have and the behaviors they intend to employ during those situations they expect to encounter, they prepare themselves to deal more effectively with those situations. Therapists can listen for potential difficulties and evident confusions and then guide clients toward brainstorming options for coping with related stresses should they actualize. Clients do not always need, nor may they even be in a position, to decide among future coping options. However, using the final phase of therapy to increase client's awareness of a range of options will hopefully expand the client's capacity for more flexible, satisfying responses to future stresses.

Active Client Choice. As in earlier phases of the therapy process, the therapist during termination discussions endorses and reinforces the client's own choices from among options for coping with the unfinished work of therapy. Therapists can certainly encourage clients to identify multiple

options, offer suggestions the client has not mentioned, and venture opinions about the options under consideration. Ultimately, however, the therapist acknowledges that the client will be the one choosing how to act and react to future problems, and the therapist can encourage clients to make
choices that capitalize on the insights, skills, and supports the client has developed in therapy. Emphasis on internalizing and initiating client choice is
especially crucial at the point of termination, after which the client will no
longer be consulting with the same or perhaps any therapist.

For example, recall Nathan in chapter 8, who struggled mightily with cocaine cravings that intensified after about six months of abstinence and
who developed a relapse prevention plan that included a new career path
toward the healing ministries. By the time he and his therapist agreed six
months later that he was ready for termination, Nathan had clarified strategies and taken significant steps toward his new career goals. He had successfully maintained his abstinence from all psychoactive substances for a full
year. In the meantime, he and his therapist had shared many details of Nathan's complicated life story. In termination discussions, Nathan said that
talking about his family history and comparing past and current relationships helped him better understand how substance use had come to play
such a huge role in his past, and how he planned to live his life without
drugs or alcohol in the future. However, when asked about unfinished business, he revealed that his new wife had been insisting that, to permit full
healing, Nathan needed to confront the stepfather who kicked him out of
the family home when Nathan was fifteen. Nathan confided his intense reluctance to reestablish contact with the stepfather whom he had not seen in
years, and he asked his therapist if such a confrontation were necessary.

At this critical juncture in aftercare planning, the therapist validated Nathan's conflicting feelings of wanting to promote his continuing recovery
and to respect his wife, as well as his wishes to avoid at all costs a painful encounter of unpredictable outcome with the man who had treated him badly
so long ago. The therapist further pointed out that directly contacting the
stepfather was only one of several options by which Nathan might continue
to work on his lingering concerns, and that it was necessary only if Nathan
believed that it was so. Through further discussion, Nathan clarified that
whatever gains he could imagine from encountering his estranged stepfather were far outweighed by the detailed risks he associated with a potentially hostile encounter. Together, Nathan and the therapist considered
other possibilities, like extending their work together for a few additional
sessions to address this concern, or having Nathan talk with his wife about
his reasons for choosing not to contact his stepfather. Nathan stated that he
felt the issue had already been sufficiently addressed in therapy, and he decided his primary task after therapy that day was to explain to his wife the
reasons for his decision not to pursue her recommendation.

The therapist not only validated Nathan's well-reasoned choice, but also encouraged him to reinforce himself for a decision carefully made. The therapist suggested Nathan role play options for communicating his decision to his wife, anticipating her probable responses and practicing Nathan's possible replies. The therapist pointed out that the process Nathan had used to make this decision could be used in the future. Finally, the therapist reminded Nathan that seeking additional therapy, information, or support were all options in the future if he ever felt his emotional state or temptations to resume substance use again became problematic. Nathan reiterated that he planned to continue attending a self-help group through which he had established strong social supports.

This extended example demonstrates that helping clients at termination specify multiple viable options frees them from the pressure of assuming one necessary, narrow path to progress. Increased awareness of options, careful consideration among available options, and empowerment to make decisions in one's own best interest are powerful tools the therapist can offer and discuss in the last sessions of therapy.

Referrals. Among the options therapists can suggest are specific referrals to additional sources of professional treatment, social support, or other means of client self-help. The client may request this information directly, such as when therapy must terminate before the client's confidence in controlling substance use is sufficiently strong, or when the client expresses readiness to tackle consequent legal, medical, occupational, or other issues once therapy is terminated.

In other instances, referral is based on the therapist's concerns about issues the client has not yet resolved or perhaps even admitted at the time of termination. Examples include clients who have reached the end of a mandated course of substance abuse treatment and then report that they "can't wait to start partying again" now that their obligations to abstain during therapy are satisfied, or the client who has tried hard to meet personal goals of abstinence but continues to relapse, or the client who has dismissed for weeks the therapist's suggestion that the client's physical symptoms—admittedly exacerbated by heavy drinking and smoking—are worthy of medical attention.

In such cases, termination is more than likely occurring without mutual agreement of completion. When the therapist is in a position to do so, offering the option of extending therapy and postponing termination until such concerns can be better addressed is therapeutically desirable (although the therapist may privately entertain conflicting wishes to let the client go). However, in many cases, continuing to work with the present therapist will not be an available option by the time termination discussion has been initiated. When the client declines or when the therapist is unable to offer continuing therapy at a level appropriate to the client's needs, the therapist can still provide referral information. The therapist ideally offers more than one type or source of referral (e.g., professional contacts plus self-help groups or relevant books or Web sites) and encourages clients to exercise both their rights and responsibilities to make active choices about how to decide among and utilize the options provided.

When time permits, the therapist can discuss with clients their immediate reactions and intentions regarding suggested referrals. For clients who are unwilling or uncertain about contacting referral sources right away, the therapist can still urge them to pay attention to indicators that additional help or support is advisable in the future, and to be open to contacting referrals or other sources should the need arise. The therapist can qualify that

> Maybe, hopefully, you won't run into the kinds of problems that could bring you to seek professional help in the future. But it's important to remember you have the option of therapy plus the other options we've discussed if you ever do find yourself in a position to want those resources.

Some clients will ask their therapists whether they think the client needs more therapy. Therapists are wise to answer these questions carefully, offering honest opinions without taking the power for the choice from the client. The therapist can tell the client,

> I'll give you my thoughts, but first you should know that it's up to you to decide the answer to your own question, since you know yourself better than anyone else does. I think it's good to know you have the option of additional therapy if and when you decide to take advantage of that option. In your case I can see some reasons why more therapy could be useful [and therapist lists reasons]. On the other hand, I could also make a case for taking some time off from therapy [again, therapist lists reasons] and working on other options. And now that I've given you my thoughts, I'm curious what you think of these ideas.

The relative weight of these considerations on the therapist's part will not always be equivalent at termination. In cases where the client's behavior, symptoms, or other obligations induced by substance use indicate higher risk of continuing problems, therapists make it clear that they recommend additional treatment. If the client, however, has exhibited sustained improvement and competent coping, yet lacks fully developed senses of confidence and independence, the therapist might recommend experimenting with a trial period without therapy during which the client can test newfound capacities, knowing further therapy is available if needed. Even when the therapist's leanings are strong and based on sound rationale, the therapist can validate that the ultimate choice rests with the client by covering alternative options and encouraging the client to explore, weigh, and evaluate them.

Focus on Feelings

Both the client and therapist have emotions at the termination of therapy that reflect the nature of the relationship that has transpired between them. As participants review and assess their time together, and discuss the gains or lack thereof to be carried beyond termination, feelings about therapy and its ending tend to be salient. The therapist can expand and utilize awareness of these emotions on both parts.

Allusions have already been made in this chapter to the importance of working with affect and reactions elicited in discussions of the termination agenda. The therapist working with substance abusers will need flexible abilities to acknowledge and respond to the specific types of predominant emotions evoked at termination for both (or all) participants, including the following:

1. A client who feels good about changes observed and progress made.
2. A client who is disappointed in slow or minimal progress, but hopeful about the potential for further improvement.
3. A client who is not only disappointed by lack of progress, but discouraged or hopeless about the future.
4. A client who is apathetic about outcome and relieved to be done with therapy.
5. A client who resents efforts to induce change and who intends to resume or continue substance use.
6. The therapist's own feelings of inspiration, with liking and admiration for the client, mixed with feeling sorry to see the client go.
7. The therapist coming to appreciate the client after intense effort at understanding, motivating, or liking the client.
8. The therapist's relief at ending with a client with whom therapy was an ongoing struggle, either internally or interpersonally, for the therapist.
9. The therapist's discouragement by the client's lack of progress with worry about the client's future.
10. The therapist's disgust, anger, or annoyance with the client's apparent lack of effort.

Of course gratification and reinforcement through the process of termination are most easily accessible when the client and therapist like each

other and feel good about their productivity together. Under those circumstances, exploration of feelings at termination is an inviting and rewarding
interaction wrought with meaning for both participants. The feelings associated with less desirable or less clear outcomes from either perspective are
harder to approach, yet potentially just as significant in determining the impact of therapy.

Probably as often as not, substance abuse therapy reaches its end without
definite indications of sustainable change and confidence in the client's
ability to avoid future problems with substance use. These "less finished"
terminations, however, are no less endowed with meaning and therapeutic
potential. To realize a greater influence of therapy even when outcomes are
not optimal, therapists need to be able to talk openly about more negative
feelings that arise when therapy is ending without resolution of the client's
problems. Imperfect resolution by no means implies that the therapy has
made no impact. If the therapist can engage the client in discussing the significance to each of them of the human interaction that has occurred between them, the participants can find something of value they will take
from the experience of working together.

In theory, facing the prospect of separation without resolution, and coming up with better responses in the therapy relationship to this inevitable
human condition, are curative components of the therapy process (Mann,
1973). In practice, however, both client and therapist will be tempted to distort, minimize, or avoid experience of uncomfortable feelings that emerge
when a relationship is ending with issues unresolved. Thus, as the therapist
leads a client through the termination agenda, she or he needs to be ready,
willing, and able to address whatever emotions surface, especially the more
negatively toned affect, in as direct a manner as the therapist deems appropriate and the client will allow.

The more the therapist can invite the client's expression and accept the
shared experience of difficult feelings, the more likely the client will sense
adequate even if incomplete closure of the therapy relationship. As these
emotions are vocalized and acknowledged, the therapist and client together can consider how to act on and cope with those feelings, both at
present and in the future. Equally important is the therapist's ability to
work with the therapist's own emotional reactions to the prospect of ending
therapy with each client. Therapists should be able to acknowledge and examine their feelings toward clients with deliberate choices about what to
share with clients based on therapeutic intents underlying therapist disclo-
sures. In other words, in deciding how to share one's own feelings about a
client, therapists can ask themselves what they really feel and how they expect it would be helpful to share or withhold those feelings from the termination discussion with that client.

Working with volatile emotions involves sophisticated skills that often take a while for therapists to develop. Clients who have abused substances to the extent that it becomes an issue addressed in therapy are often poorly equipped or lacking motivation to manage negative affect well. Even when such clients have made progress in therapy, they often display long-established, well-ingrained, and often maladaptive habits for dealing with the kinds of emotions stimulated by the termination of therapy. In turn, therapists find strong affect and their own characteristic coping mechanisms are triggered by clients who express themselves in less adaptive ways. As therapists are learning to work with these dynamics of termination, supervision can play a crucial role in facilitating the therapist's use of feelings in conceptualization and intervention. Even among more experienced therapists, stress can develop when working with difficult emotional reactions to termination with substance abusers who have made limited progress or continue to express bad attitudes. Consultation with trusted colleagues can be an important source of insight and support.

INSTILLING HOPE AND PRIDE

To briefly summarize, the termination of therapy can be approached as a planned but flexible process, during which therapists guide clients in reviewing the course of therapy, assessing its present outcomes, and planning steps for promoting additional client progress after therapy ends. For clients terminating a course of therapy concentrating on substance abuse issues, neither gains realized in treatment nor absence of observable change dictate the client's future motivation or behavior, so therapy closes with emphasis on the client's potential for future choices in the best interest of the client and others in the client's life. Throughout the termination process, therapists attend to and address the variety of emotions that accompany the process on the assumption that verbalizing the feelings and discussing appropriate ways to act on those feelings will best prepare the client to use what has been learned in therapy.

Before saying goodbye, the therapist tries to reinforce pride in the client's efforts as well as hope for the client's future. The nature of this communication must be genuine, realistic, and responsive for clients to take it seriously, particularly for clients who express fewer benefits or demonstrate less progress at the close of therapy. Even when feelings of disappointment, frustration, or resentment about therapy outcomes and fears or doubts about the client's future potential are evident, however, therapists can acknowledge and work with those feelings and still search to identify and emphasize a basis for some simultaneous optimism. One of the therapist's goals during termination is to help the client formulate a more clearly specified perspective on both the strengths and challenges available to the client.

At termination, clients who have abused psychoactive substances may, to some degree, still question their abilities or desires to refrain from future risky substance use. Ideally, therapy helps shift the client's perspective from greater weight placed on reasons to use excessively to increased weight placed on reasons to moderate or abstain from use. However, even clients who have made commitments to change their substance usage or who have developed good relapse prevention and aftercare plans may admit that some part of them has been wondering if their changes in substance use behavior will be permanent, or if they might go back to former levels of use some day. They might indicate that, although they enjoy many aspects of the changes they have already implemented through therapy, and although they wish to avoid accumulating further negative consequences, they sometimes miss the effects of their drug of choice or their episodes of extreme substance use. In other words, the characteristic ambivalence about engaging in chemical alteration of one's state of mind may resurge or intensify for some clients at termination when they are contemplating their futures beyond the end of therapy.

Therapists can help clients recognize and normalize any ambivalence if they anticipate its likelihood and acceptingly encourage clients to talk about their mixed feelings, if any. If clients focus only on intentions to moderate or abstain from substance use along with convictions in their own ability to carry out those intentions, any niggling doubts that remain unexpressed may later pose struggles to clients who have not prepared themselves to deal with those doubts. The therapist who reinforces the client's pride, intentions, and convictions can still also inquire about any concerns or questions the client might have or imagine having in the future. The therapist thus communicates that combinations of confidence with some residual doubt or internal debate are understandable phenomena and acceptable topics of conversation in the remaining session time. Given the opportunity during termination to discuss mixed feelings about future substance use or abstinence, clients can clarify and validate their complex thoughts and feelings so they can more thoroughly prepare to deal with any future conflicts about drug or alcohol use.

The therapist's efforts during termination to reinforce pride and instill hope remain essential in this context. Certainly this means noting progress toward healthy, satisfying lifestyles and in avoiding and coping with detrimental consequences of substance abuse. But this is not all it means. Communicating pride and hope also includes realizing with the client that future challenges and setbacks are inevitable, but that the therapist trusts (and encourages the client to trust) the client's growing capacities to assess such circumstances and to make good choices for dealing with challenges and setbacks. Therapists prompt clients to recognize that, although they may run into problems or complications in the future, they now have more options and skills for dealing with those stressors.

Thus, the termination process aims to close the therapeutic relationship in a manner that equips the client to make better choices and cope more effectively without resorting to risky abuse of psychoactive chemicals. A word about *closure* is in order here because the term is frequently misused and overinterpreted in the popular media. Closure of a therapy relationship or a course of substance abuse treatment virtually never implies that the client is free from problems or that the therapy has left no loose ends. Effective closure of therapy openly admits that no resolution of human difficulties is perfect, and few interpersonal transactions completely address the interests of all participants. The termination of therapy instead concentrates on achieving a closure that offers a greater sense of insight and resolution than the client has experienced in the past, providing tools for application through deliberate choice, including realistic awareness of unresolved issues and unknown future complications yet to be addressed.

*   *   *

Therapists bring their relationships with clients to a close by creating opportunities to ensure that important things do not get left unsaid. Depending on the stance of the client, the format of the treatment, the circumstances of termination, and the nature of the therapy relationship, the therapist carefully considers what appears essential to talk about in the final contacts with each individual client. One major aspect of this determination involves asking the client to say what in particular seems important to cover, but often clients are not sure about how to identify or raise crucial points for closure. Thus, therapists can, when necessary, give clients ideas about general topics that are often relevant in wrapping up a relationship based on efforts toward personal change. As I mentioned earlier, therapists can offer terminating clients the chance to reflect on past efforts and experiences, present functioning and progress, and future goals and plans. In this manner, therapists attempt to get clients to remember, verbalize, and share the most significant components of the time spent together and on related personal development in hopes that such explicit discussion will prompt clients' later recall as needed.

When therapy has worked on problems of drug or alcohol misuse, the therapist at termination is well aware of additional specific topics that need to be addressed. Again one of the therapist's goals is to provide opportunities for clients to articulate whatever they need to say about issues particular to changing their problematic substance use. This includes comparing past and present opinions and feelings about substance use or abstinence, assessing current strengths and challenges for dealing with problems linked to drug or alcohol use, and confirming specific plans for minimizing relapse into later substance use problems. By encouraging the client to voice insights, accomplishments, and action plans regarding the changing role of drugs and alcohol in the client's life, the therapist further equips the terminating client to make more deliberate and better informed choices regarding psychoactive substances.

In addition to creating a context that permits the client to say what he or she needs to say to enhance closure and future potential, the therapist also becomes acutely attuned at termination to impressions the therapist wants to share or messages the therapist aims to leave with the client. In preparation to say farewell, therapists ask themselves what things they want to be sure to communicate to the clients, and what memories and suggestions they hope the clients will take, keep, and use. For clients who have taken on the substantial challenge of reducing problematic substance use, hearing those messages of support and confidence that the therapist believes are too important to be left unsaid before goodbye can help strengthen resolve to maintain efforts and continue progress. For clients terminating with less obvious motivation to change or less clear progress toward goals, the therapist's message of continuing concern, challenge, hope, and support may at least carve out a space in the client's consciousness in which future work on the client's risky substance use is still a possibility. For therapists, huge parts of what makes their work worthwhile are the opportunities at termination to talk about meaningful events in the course of important relationships and to share carefully pondered messages for clients to take with them. The more therapists can structure the termination process to allow clients to distill lessons, insights, and votes of confidence they can use to reduce the risk of future problems with drugs and alcohol, the more effectively therapists wield the powerful tools of therapy to repair damages inflicted by the misuse of psychoactive substances.

Epilogue

Human use and abuse of chemical substances is a hot topic, full of controversies, with impact on numerous sectors of society. The intractable complications linked to addictive and risky misuse of drugs and alcohol make substance abusers a difficult population with which societies must deal. American society is increasingly turning to variations of treatment and therapy in hopes of remedying problems attributed to substance abuse. Although historically substance abuse treatment has been isolated from other mental health therapies, increasing recognition of the utility of integrated approaches is evident. In conducting research for writing this book, I have been impressed and inspired by the number of recent publications, conferences, and clinical programs that are contributing to advancement of the field and development of more effective services.

As mental health practitioners rise to meet the demand for integrated substance abuse treatments, they learn to tease out their own opinions and emotions about substance use issues. They also develop an understanding of how to apply therapeutic interventions to facilitate desirable change in a substance abuser's behavior. Throughout this book, I have tried to emphasize that concerns about clients' substance use can emerge and recur in countless ways across therapy process, creating numerous choice points that therapists need to carefully address. I have highlighted the prevalence of substance use disorders and their relations with many problems brought to therapy in hopes of convincing more therapists and trainees that capacities to assess and treat substance misuse, abuse, and dependence are essential skills. I have also concentrated on how therapists can use their understandings of the tasks and processes of therapy to choose and structure interventions that will in turn encourage clients who misuse psychoactive substances to make better informed choices about their own future behavior, including whether to consume drugs or alcohol.

Wading through the choppy waters of substance abuse treatment usually requires the therapist to create structure for the course of therapy to avoid being submerged. I have offered ideas therapists can use to build structure that gives clients needed information, assurance, and motivation while still maintaining flexibility for responding to the unique mix of personal and cultural factors presented by each client. Flexible structure is also essential for the therapist who wants to help, but may at times feel overwhelmed by the complexities of problems faced by many clients who abuse drugs or alcohol. Work with this population calls for therapists to generate conceptualizations and interventions that give a sense of purpose and direction to therapeutic efforts. At the same time, substance abuse therapists must find ways to respond sensitively and effectively when the client is less than sure about following the therapist's suggestions.

Through the ongoing and interwoven processes of assessment, treatment planning, intervention, and treatment evaluation, therapists detect and respond to patterns indicating the particular meanings that substance use has come to assume for each client. These patterns often reflect themes of asserting one's identity, seeking personal pleasure, expressing interpersonal expectations, and coping with life stressors. As therapists tentatively interpret emerging patterns and test their hypotheses in interactions with clients, they decide on intervention strategies tailored to the client's goals and to the nature of the therapy relationship. Interventions in therapy for substance abuse concerns may involve psychoeducation, relapse prevention, and/or addressing related problems with the client's health, emotional control, communication in relationships, occupation, or legal troubles. The therapist continually adjusts the intervention strategy according to the client's reaction in efforts to maintain or resume a degree of complementarity suitable to the current stage of the therapy process.

Based on my own experience and philosophy, I have emphasized the importance of collaborating with the client to negotiate goals for therapy and strategies for moving toward them. Collaboration can be quite difficult with clients who are ambivalent at best (and hostile at worst) toward suggestions that their substance use habits may need to change to resolve the difficulties that brought them to therapy. Thus, attention to the interpersonal dynamics expressed in therapy transactions is a crucial component of genuine collaborative efforts.

Changing problematic substance use habits is typically a challenging and lengthy process. Yet dedicated, consistent, and well-conceptualized therapeutic approaches utilizing flexible structure and sincere interpersonal responsiveness can make a significant contribution toward dealing with the difficult personal and social problems associated with substance abuse. I hope the reader will share in the reciprocal impact of working with these important issues as the opportunities arise.

References

American Psychiatric Association. (1994). *Diagnostic and statistical manual of mental disorders* (4th ed.). Washington, DC: Author.

American Psychiatric Association. (2000). *Diagnostic and statistical manual of mental disorders* (4th ed., text rev.). Washington, DC: Author.

Anderson, C. (2003, August 18). More U.S. adults serving time. *Arizona Republic*, p. A3.

Annis, H. M., Schober, R., & Kelly, E. (1996). Matching addiction outpatient counseling to client readiness for change: The role of structured relapse prevention counseling. *Experimental & Clinical Psychopharmacology, 4*(1), 37–45.

Anthony, J. C. (1999). Epidemiology of drug dependence. In M. Galanter & H. D. Kleber (Eds.), *Textbook of substance abuse treatment* (2nd ed., pp. 479–561). Washington, DC: American Psychiatric Press.

Baker, T. B., Fiore, M. C., Piper, M. E., McCarthy, D. E., & Majeskie, M. R. (2004). Addiction motivation reformulated: An affective processing model of negative reinforcement. *Psychological Review, 111*, 33–51.

Bandura, A. (1977). *Social learning theory.* Englewood Cliffs, NJ: Prentice-Hall.

Bandura, A. (1997). *Self-efficacy: The exercise of control.* New York: Freeman.

Benson, H. (1975). *The relaxation response.* New York: HarperCollins.

Betz, N. E. (1999). Getting clients to act on their interests: Self-efficacy as a mediator of the implementation of vocational interests. In M. L. Savickas & A. R. Spokane (Eds.), *Vocational interests: Meaning, measurement, and counseling use* (pp. 327–344). Palo Alto, CA: Davies-Black.

Blustein, D. L., & Flum, H. (1999). A self-determination perspective of interests and exploration in career development. In M. L. Savickas & A. R. Spokane (Eds.), *Vocational interests: Meaning, measurement, and counseling use* (pp. 345–368). Palo Alto, CA: Davies-Black.

Bono, J. (1998). Criminalistics—Introduction to controlled substance. In S. B. Karch (Ed.), *Drug abuse handbook* (pp. 1–75). Boca Raton, FL: CRC Press.

Boonstra, H., & Nash, E. (2000). Minors and the right to consent to health care. *The Guttmacher Report on Public Policy, 3,* 1–5.

Bratter, T. E. (1975). The methadone addict and his disintegrating family: A psychotherapeutic failure. *The Counseling Psychologist, 5*(3), 110–125.

Brown, R. L., Leonard, T., Saunders, L. A., & Papasoulioutis, O. (1997). A two-item screening test for alcohol and other drug problems. *The Journal of Family Practice, 44*, 151–160.

Brown, T. G., Seraganian, P., Tremblay, J., & Annis, H. (2002). Matching substance abuse aftercare treatments to client characteristics. *Addictive Behaviors, 27*, 585–604.

Budney, A. J., Higgins, S. T., Radonovich, K. J., & Novey, P. L. (2000). Adding voucher-based incentives to coping skills and motivational enhancement improves outcomes during treatment for marijuana dependence. *Journal of Cousulting and Clinical Psychology, 68*, 1051–1061.

Buelow, G. D., & Buelow, S. A. (1998). *Psychotherapy in chemical dependency treatment*. Pacific Grove, CA: Brooks/Cole.

Cahoon, D. D., & Cosby, C. C. (1972). A learning approach to chronic drug use: Sources of reinforcement. *Behavior Therapy, 3*, 64–71.

Carey, K. B., Bradizza, C. M., Stasiewicz, P. R., & Maisto, S. A. (1999). The case for advanced addictions training in graduate programs. *Behavioral Therapist, 22*, 27–31.

Carroll, K. M. (1996). Relapse prevention as a psychosocial treatment: A review of controlled clinical trials. *Experimental and Clinical Psychopharmacology, 4*, 46–54.

Carroll, K. M., Sinha, R., Nich, C., Babuscio, T., & Rounsaville, B. J. (2002). Contingency management to enhance naltrexone treatment of opioid dependence: A randomized clinical trial of reinforcement magnitude. *Experimental and Clinical Psychopharmacology, 10*, 54–63.

Celluci, T., & Vik, P. (2001). Training for substance abuse treatment among psychologists in a rural state. *Professional Psychology: Research and Practice, 32*, 248–252.

Cheirt, T., Gold, S. N., & Taylor, J. (1994). Substance abuse training in APA-accredited doctoral programs in clinical psychology: A survey. *Professional Psychology: Research and Practice, 25*, 80–84.

Claiborn, C. D., & Lichtenberg, J. W. (1989). Interactional counseling. *The Counseling Psychologist, 17*, 355–453.

Clark, L. A., & Watson, D. (1999). Temperament: A new paradigm for trait psychology. In L. A. Pervin & O. P. John (Eds.), *Handbook of personality: Theory and research* (2nd ed., pp. 399–423). New York: Guilford.

Conrad, C. (1997). *Hemp for health: The medicinal and nutritional uses of cannabis sativa*. Rochester, VT: Healing Arts Press.

Council of National Psychological Associations for the Advancement of Ethnic Minority Interests. (2003). *Psychological treatment of ethnic minority populations*. Washington, DC: The Association of Black Psychologists.

Dailard, C. (2003). New medical records privacy rule: The interface with teen access to confidential care. *The Guttmacher Report on Public Policy, 6*, 6–7.

de Leon, G. (1993). What psychologists can learn from addiction treatment research. *Psychology of Addictive Behaviors, 7*(2), 103–109.

Diaz, J. (1997). *How drugs influence behavior: A neuro-behavioral approach*. Upper Saddle River, NJ: Prentice-Hall.

Dollard, J., & Miller, N. E. (1950). *Personality and psychotherapy: An analysis in terms of learning, thinking, and culture*. New York: McGraw-Hill.

Donovan, D. M., & Marlatt, G. A. (in press). *Assessment of addictive behaviors* (2nd ed.). New York: Guilford.

Doweiko, H. E. (2002). *Concepts of chemical dependency*. Pacific Grove, CA: Brooks/Cole.

Epstein, D. E., Hawkins, W. E., Covi, L., Umbricht, A., & Preston, K. L. (2003). Cognitive behavioral therapy plus contingency management for cocaine use: Findings during treatment and across 12-month follow-up. *Psychology of Addictive Behaviors, 17*, 73–82.

Ershoff, D., Radcliffe, A., & Gregory, M. (1996). The Southern California Kaiser-Permanente Chemical Dependency Recovery Program evaluation: Results of a treatment outcome study in an HMO setting. *Journal of Addictive Diseases, 15*(3), 1–25.

Ewing, J. A. (1984). Detecting alcoholism: The CAGE questionnaire. *Journal of the American Medical Association, 252,* 1905–1907.

Frances, R. J., & Miller, S. I. (Eds.). (1998). *Clinical textbook of addictive disorders* (2nd ed.). New York: Guilford.

Frank, J. D., & Frank, J. B. (1991). *Persuasion and healing: A comparative study of psychotherapy* (3rd ed.). Baltimore: Johns Hopkins University Press.

Freimuth, M. (2002). The unseen diagnosis: Substance use disorder. *Psychotherapy Bulletin, 37,* 26–30.

Galanter, M., & Kleber, H. D. (1999). *Textbook of substance abuse treatment* (2nd ed.). Washington, DC: American Psychiatric Press.

Glidden-Tracey, C. E. (2001, January). *Critical incidents training for the development of multicultural counseling skills.* Presented at the Relevance of Assessment in Culture and Evaluation (RACE) Conference, Tempe, AZ.

Goldstein, A., & Nestler, E. J. (1998). Introduction to special issue on the neurobiology of addiction. *Drug and Alcohol Dependence, 51,* 3–4.

Good, G. E., Thoreson, P., & Shaughnessy, P. (1995). Substance use, confrontation of impaired colleagues, and psychological functioning among counseling psychologists: A national survey. *The Counseling Psychologist, 23*(4), 703–721.

Grilly, D. M. (2002). *Drugs and human behavior* (4th ed.). Boston: Allyn & Bacon.

Harris, K. B., & Miller, W. R. (1990). Behavioral self-control training for problem drinkers: Components of efficacy. *Psychology of Addictive Behaviors, 4,* 82–90.

Hartung, P. J. (1999). Interest assessment using card sorts. In M. L. Savickas & A. R. Spokane (Eds.), *Vocational interests: Meaning, measurement, and counseling use* (pp. 235–252). Palo Alto, CA: Davies-Black.

Higgins, S. T. (1999). Potential contributions of the community reinforcement approach and contingency management to broadening the base of substance abuse treatment. In J. Tucker, D. Donavan, & G. Marlatt (Eds.), *Changing addictive behaviors: Bridging clinical and public health strategies* (pp. 283–306). New York: Guilford.

Higgins, S. T., Wong, C. J., Badger, G. J., Ogden, D. E. H., & Dantona, R. L. (2000). Contingent reinforcement increases cocaine abstinence during outpatient treatment and 1 year of follow-up. *Journal of Consulting and Clinical Psychology, 68,* 64–72.

Holder, H. D., & Blose, J. O. (1992). The reduction of health care costs associated with alcoholism treatment: A 14 year longitudinal study. *Journal of Studies on Alcohol, 53*(4), 293–302.

Hyman, S. (2000, October). *Co-occurring mental and substance use disorders: Challenges for the future.* Keynote address presented at the conference on Behavior, Clinical Neuroscience, Substance Abuse, and Culture, Los Angeles.

Irvin, J. E., Bowers, C. A., Dunn, M. E., & Wang, M. C. (1999). Efficacy of relapse prevention: A meta-analytic review. *Journal of Consulting and Clinical Psychology, 67,* 563–570.

Jellinek, E. M. (1960). *The disease concept of alcoholism.* New Brunswick, NJ: Millhouse.

Kell, B. L., & Mueller, W. J. (1966). *Impact and change: A study of counseling relationships.* Englewood Cliffs, NJ: Prentice-Hall.

Kessler, R. C., McGonagle, K. A., Zhai, S., Nelson, C. B., Hughes, M., Eshleman, S., Wittchen, H., & Kenler, K. S. (1994). Lifetime and 12-month prevalence of *DSM–III–R* psychiatric disorders in the United States: Results from the National Co-morbidity Survey. *Archives of General Psychiatry, 51,* 8–19.

Kiesler, D. J. (1982). Interpersonal theory for personality and psychotherapy. In J. C. Anchin & D. J. Kiesler (Eds.), *Handbook of interpersonal psychotherapy* (pp. 3–24). New York: Pergamon.

Kiesler, D. J. (1996). *Contemporary interpersonal theory and research: Personality, psychopathology, and psychotherapy.* New York: Wiley.

Kilmer, J. R. (2003, October). *Brief interventions with college student drinkers: Reducing alcohol-related harm.* Workshop presented to the Arizona Network of Institutions of Higher Education, Tempe, AZ.

Lent, R. W., Brown, S. D., & Hackett, G. (1994). Toward a unifying social cognitive theory of career and academic interest, choice, and performance. *Journal of Vocational Behavior, 45,* 79–122.

Leshner, A. I. (1997). Introduction to the special issue: The National Institute on Drug Abuse's (NIDA's) Drug Abuse Treatment Outcome Study (DATOS). *Psychology of Addictive Behaviors, 11*(4), 211–215.

Leshner, A. I. (1998). Drug addiction research: Moving toward the twenty-first century. *Drug and Alcohol Dependence, 51,* 5–7.

Lewis, J. A., Dana, R. Q., & Blevins, G. A. (2002). *Substance abuse counseling* (3rd ed.). Pacific Grove, CA: Brooks/Cole.

Lopez, F. (1999). *Confidentiality of patient records for alcohol and other drug treatment.* Technical Assistance Publication (TAP) Series: U.S. Department of Health and Human Services, Substance Abuse and Mental Health Services Administration Center for Substance Abuse Treatment: Rockville, MD.

Mann, J. (1973). *Time-limited psychotherapy.* Cambridge, MA: Harvard University Press.

Marlatt, G. A. (1985a). Relapse prevention: Theoretical rationale and overview of the model. In G. A. Marlatt & J. R. Gordon (Eds.), *Relapse prevention: Maintenance strategies in the treatment of addictive behaviors* (pp. 3–70). New York: Guilford.

Marlatt, G. A. (1985b). Determinants of relapse and skill-training interventions. In G. A. Marlatt & J. R. Gordon (Eds.), *Relapse prevention: Maintenance strategies in the treatment of addictive behaviors* (pp. 71–127). New York: Guilford.

Marlatt, G. A. (1985c). Lifestyle modification. In G. A. Marlatt & J. R. Gordon (Eds.), *Relapse prevention: Maintenance strategies in the treatment of addictive behaviors* (pp. 280–347). New York: Guilford.

Marlatt, G. A. (Ed.). (1998). *Harm reduction: Pragmatic strategies for managing high-risk behaviors.* New York: Guilford.

Marlatt, G. A., & Donovan, D. M. (in press). *Relapse prevention* (2nd ed.). New York: Guilford.

Marlatt, G. A., & Gordon, J. R. (Eds.). (1985). *Relapse prevention: Maintenance strategies in the treatment of addictive behaviors.* New York: Guilford.

Marlatt, G. A., & Tapert, S. F. (1993). Harm reduction: Reducing the risks of addictive behaviors. In J. S. Baer, G. A. Marlatt, & R. J. McMahon (Eds.), *Addictive behaviors across the life span: Prevention, treatment and policy issues* (pp. 243–273). Newbury Park, CA: Sage.

McKim, W. A. (2003). *Drugs and behavior: An introduction to behavioral pharmacology* (5th ed.). Upper Saddle River, NJ: Prentice-Hall.

McLellan, A. T., Kushner, H., Metzger, D., Peters, R., Grissom, G., Pettinati, H., & Argeriou, M. (1992). The fifth edition of the Addiction Severity Index. *Journal of Substance Abuse Treatment, 9*(3), 199–213.

McLellan, A. T., Luborsky, L., Woody, G. E., & O'Brien, C. P. (1980). An improved diagnostic instrument for substance abuse patients: The Addiction Severity Index. *Journal of Nervous and Mental Disorders, 168,* 26–33.

Mee-Lee, D. (2001a, May). *Why integrating mental health and substance abuse is hard and what to do about it.* Workshop presented at the Foundation Associates National Conference on the Future of Integrating Mental Health and Substance Abuse, Las Vegas, NV.

Mee-Lee, D. (2001b, May). *How the new ASAM criteria help integrate mental health and substance abuse.* Workshop presented at the Foundation Associates National Conference on the Future of Integrating Mental Health and Substance Abuse, Las Vegas, NV.

Mee-Lee, D., Shulman, G. D., Fishman, M., Gastfriend, D. R., & Griffith, J. H. (Eds.). (2001). *ASAM patient placement criteria for the treatment of substance-related disorders* (2nd ed., rev., ASAM PPC-2R). Chevy Chase, MD: American Society of Addiction Medicine.

Miller, W. R. (1995). Increasing motivation for change. In R. K. Hester & W. R. Miller (Eds.), *Handbook of alcoholism treatment approaches* (2nd ed., pp. 89–104). New York: Allyn & Bacon.

Miller, W. R., & Brown, S. A. (1997). Why psychologists should treat alcohol and drug problems. *American Psychologist, 52,* 1269–1279.

Miller, W. R., & Hester, R. K. (1980). Treating the problem drinker. In W. R. Miller (Ed.), *The addictive behaviors: Treatment of alcoholism, drug abuse, smoking, and obesity* (pp. 3–13). Elmsford, NY: Pergamon.

Miller, W. R., Meyers, R. J., & Tonigan, J. S. (1999). Engaging the unmotivated in treatment for alcohol problems. *Journal of Consulting and Clinical Psychology, 67*(5), 688–697.

Miller, W. R., & Rollnick, S. (1991). *Motivational interviewing: Preparing people to change addictive behavior.* New York: Guilford.

Miller, W. R., & Rollnick, S. (2002). *Motivational interviewing: Preparing people for change* (2nd ed.). New York: Guilford.

Moos, R. H. (2003). Addictive disorders in context: Principles and puzzles of effective treatment and recovery. *Psychology of Addictive Behavior, 17,* 3–12.

Mukamal, K. J., Conigrave, K. M., Mittleman, M. A., Camargo, C. A., Stampfer, J. J., Willett, W. C., & Rimm, E. B. (2003). Roles of drinking pattern and type of alcohol consumed in coronary heart disease in men. *New England Journal of Medicine, 384,* 109–118.

Olson, C. M., Horan, J. J., & Polansky, J. (1992). Counseling psychology perspectives on the problem of substance abuse. In S. D. Brown & R. W. Lent (Eds.), *Handbook of counseling psychology* (pp. 793–821). New York: Wiley.

O'Malley, P. M., Johnston, L. D., & Bachman, J. G. (1999). Epidemiology of substance use in adolescence. In P. J. Ott, T. E. Tarter, & R. T. Ammerman (Eds.), *Sourcebook on substance abuse: Etiology, epidemiology, assessment and treatment* (pp. 14–31). Boston: Allyn & Bacon.

Onken, L., Carroll, K. M., Rawson, R., Higgins, S. T., & Marlatt, G. A. (2000, August). *Innovations in behavioral therapies for drug addiction.* Symposium presented at the annual meeting of the American Psychological Association, Washington, DC.

Ordorica, P. I., & Nace, E. P. (1998). Alcohol. In R. J. Frances & S. I. Miller (Eds.), *Clinical textbook of addictive disorders* (2nd ed., pp. 91–119). New York: Guilford.

Ott, P., & Tarter, R. (1998). Comprehensive substance abuse evaluation. In R. J. Frances & S. I. Miller (Eds.), *Clinical textbook of addictive disorders* (2nd ed., pp. 35–70). New York: Guilford.

Ott, P. J., Tarter, R. E., & Ammerman, R. T. (Eds.). (1999). *Sourcebook on substance abuse: Etiology, epidemiology, assessment and treatment.* Boston: Allyn & Bacon.

Polcin, D. L. (1992). Issues in the treatment of dual diagnosis clients who have chronic mental illness. *Professional Psychology: Research and Practice, 23*(1), 30–37.

Powell, D. J. (2004). *Clinical supervision in alcohol and drug abuse counseling* (rev. ed.). San Francisco, CA: Jossey-Bass.

Prediger, D. J. (1999). Integrating interests and abilities for career exploration: General considerations. In M. L. Savickas & A. R. Spokane (Eds.), *Vocational interests: Meaning, measurement, and counseling use* (pp. 295–325). Palo Alto, CA: Davies-Black.

Prochaska, J. O., DiClemente, C. C., & Norcross, J. C. (1992). In search of how people change: Application to addiction behavior. *American Psychologist, 47,* 1102–1114.

Prochaska, J. O., & Norcross, J. C. (1994). *Systems of psychotherapy: A transtheoretical analysis* (3rd ed.). Pacific Grove, CA: Brooks/Cole.

Rawson, R. A., Huber, A., McCann, M. J., Shoptaw, S., Farabee, D., Reiber, C., & Ling, W. (2002). A comparison of contingency management and cognitive-behavioral approaches during methadone maintenance for cocaine dependence. *Archives of General Psychiatry, 59,* 817–824.

Rawson, R. A., Obert, J. L., McCann, M. J., & Marinelli-Casey, P. (1993). Relapse prevention strategies in outpatient substance abuse treatment. *Psychology of Addictive Behaviors, 7,* 85–95.

Roche, S. M., & McConkey, K. M. (1990). Absorption: Nature, assessment, and correlates. *Journal of Personality and Social Psychology, 59,* 91–101.

Rollnick, S., & Morgan, M. (1995). Motivational interviewing: Increasing readiness to change. In A. M. Washton (Ed.), *Psychotherapy and substance abuse: A practitioner's handbook* (pp. 179–191). New York: Guilford.

Savickas, M. L. (1999). The psychology of interests. In M. L. Savickas & A. R. Spokane (Eds.), *Vocational interests: Meaning, measurement, and counseling use* (pp. 19–56). Palo Alto, CA: Davies-Black.

Savickas, M. L., & Spokane, A. R. (Eds.). (1999). *Vocational interests: Meaning, measurement, and counseling use.* Palo Alto, CA: Davies-Black.

Selzer, M. (1971). The Michigan Alcoholism Screening Test: The quest for a new diagnostic instrument. *American Journal of Psychiatry, 127,* 1653–1658.

Sobell, M. B., Sobell, L. C., & Sheahan, D. B. (1976). Functional analysis of drinking problems as an aid in developing individual treatment strategies. *Addictive Behaviors, 1,* 127–132.

Sobell, M. B., Wilkinson, D. A., & Sobell, L. C. (1990). Alcohol and drug problems. In A. S. Bellack, M. Herson, & A. E. Kazdin (Eds.), *International handbook of behavior modification* (2nd ed., pp. 415–435). New York: Plenum.

Spokane, A. R., & Decker, A. R. (1999). Expressed and measured interests. In M. L. Savickas & A. R. Spokane (Eds.), *Vocational interests: Meaning, measurement, and counseling use* (pp. 211–233). Palo Alto, CA: Davies-Black.

Straussner, S. L. A. (2001). *Ethnocultural factors in substance abuse treatment.* New York: Guilford.

Substance Abuse and Mental Health Services Administration (SAMHSA). (1999). *Summary of findings from the 1998 National Household Survey on Drug Abuse.* Rockville, MD: U.S. Department of Health and Human Services.

Teyber, E. (2000). *Interpersonal process in psychotherapy: A relational approach* (4th ed.). Belmont, CA: Brooks/Cole.

Thombs, D. T. (1999). *Introduction to addictive behaviors* (2nd ed.). New York: Guilford.

Tidey, J. W., O'Neill, S. C., & Higgins, S. T. (2002). Contingent monetary reinforcement of smoking reductions, with and without transdermal nicotine, in outpatients with schizophrenia. *Experimental and Clinical Psychopharmacology, 10,* 241–247.

Tracey, T. J. (1987). Stage differences in the dependencies of topic initiation and topic following behavior. *Journal of Counseling Psychology, 34,* 123–131.

Tracey, T. J. (1993). An interpersonal stage model of the therapeutic process. *Journal of Counseling Psychology, 40,* 1–14.

Tracey, T. J. G. (1997). The structure of interests and self-efficacy expectations: An expanded examination of the spherical model of interests. *Journal of Counseling Psychology, 44,* 32–43.

Tracey, T. J. G. (2002). Stages of counseling and therapy: An examination of complementarity and the working alliance. In G. S. Tryon (Ed.), *Counseling based on process research: Applying what we know* (pp. 263–297). Boston: Allyn & Bacon.

Tracey, T. J., & Ray, P. B. (1984). The stages of successful time-limited counseling: An interactional examination. *Journal of Counseling Psychology, 31,* 13–27.

Tracey, T. J. G., & Rounds, J. (1996). The spherical representation of vocational interests. *Journal of Vocational Behavior, 48,* 3–41.

Tucker, J. A. (1999). Changing addictive behavior: Historical and contemporary perspectives. In J. A. Tucker, D. M. Donovan, & G. A. Marlatt (Eds.), *Changing addictive behavior: Bridging clinical and public health strategies* (pp. 3–44). New York: Guilford.

Tucker, J. A., Donovan, D. M., & Marlatt, G. A. (Eds.). (1999). *Changing addictive behaviors: Bridging clinical and public health strategies.* New York: Guilford.

Tucker, J. A., & King, M. P. (1999). Resolving alcohol and drug problems: Influences on addictive behavior change and help-seeking processes. In J. A. Tucker, D. M. Donovan, & G. A. Marlatt (Eds.), *Changing addictive behavior: Bridging clinical and public health strategies* (pp. 97–126). New York: Guilford.

Verebey, K., Buchan, B. J., & Turner, C. E. (1998). Laboratory testing. In R. J. Frances & S. I. Miller (Eds.), *Clinical textbook of addictive disorders* (2nd ed., pp. 71–88). New York: Guilford.

Wampold, B. E. (2001). *The great psychotherapy debate*. Mahwah, NJ: Lawrence Erlbaum Associates.

Westermeyer, J. (1998). Historical and social context of psychoactive substance disorders. In R. J. Frances & S. I. Miller (Eds.), *Clinical textbook of addictive disorders* (2nd ed., pp. 14–32). New York: Guilford.

Wise, R. A. (1988). The neurobiology of craving: Implications for the understanding and treatment of addiction. *Journal of Abnormal Psychology, 97,* 118–132.

Wise, R. A. (1998). Drug-activation of brain reward pathways. *Drug and Alcohol Dependence, 51,* 13–22.

Witkiewitz, K., & Marlatt, G. A. (2004). Relapse prevention for alcohol and drug problems: That was Zen, this is Tao. *American Psychologist, 59,* 224–235.

Zytowski, D. G. (1999). How to talk to people about their interest inventory results. In M. L. Savickas & A. R. Spokane (Eds.), *Vocational interests: Meaning, measurement, and counseling use* (pp. 277–293). Palo Alto, CA: Davies-Black.

Template for Assessing a Client's Substance Use

Client's Name _____

Date and Circumstances of Assessment _____

a. Client's Reason for Seeking Assessment _____

_____

_____

_____

_____

_____

b. Substance Use History (Note: AOD is an acronym for Alcohol and Other Drugs)

Category of Drug	First use?	Pattern of use over time?	Frequency of use in past month?	Date/Amount of most recent use?
Alcohol				
Marijuana				

(Continued)

Category of Drug	First use?	Pattern of use over time?	Frequency of use in past month?	Date/Amount of most recent use?
CNS Stimulants or "Uppers" Cocaine, Ritalin, Methamphetamine				

Anxiolytics/Sedatives/Hypnotics or "Downers"
Barbiturates
  Secobarbital/Quaaludes
Benzodiazepines
  Valium (diazepam)
  Xanax (alprazolam)
  Rohypnol				

Opiates or "Painkillers" Heroin/Morphine/Methadone/Oxycodone				
Hallucinogens LSD/PCP/Ecstasy				
Inhalants/aerosols				
Steroids				
Cigarettes				
Have you ever used any of these drugs in combination?				

Therapist's notes _____

_____

_____

_____

c. Physical Consequences	(past/present)	d. Psychological Symptoms (past/present/AOD cause?)		
Headaches	/	Concentration difficulties[e]	/	/
Nausea[a,f,g]	/	Memory loss/lapses	/	/
Nosebleeds	/	Disorganized thinking	/	/
Tolerance[a,b,c,d,e,f,g]	/	Hallucinations[a,d,g]	/	/
Sweating[a,f,g]	/	Bad dreams[b,c]	/	/
Increased appetite[b,c,e]	/	Flashbacks[d]	/	/
Fatigue[b,c]	/	Irritability[e]	/	/
Vomiting[a,f,g]	/	Anxiety[a,e,g]	/	/
Using to avoid withdrawal symptoms	/	Restlessness[e]	/	/
Rapid pulse rate[a,g]	/	Low mood[b,c,e,f]	/	/
Decreased heart rate[e]	/	Depression	/	/
Chronic cough	/	Mood swings	/	/
Hand tremors[a,g]	/	Sedation	/	/
Insomnia[e,f,g]/hypersomnia[a,b,c]	/	Suicidal thoughts	/	/
Hangovers	/	Suicidal gestures	/	/
Blackouts	/	Anger[e]	/	/
Passing out	/	Paranoia[b,c,d]	/	/
Psychomotor agitation[a,b,c,g]	/	Homicidal thoughts	/	/
Psychomotor retardation[b,c]	/	Violent behaviors	/	/
Seizures[a,g]	/	Inability to care for self	/	/
Muscle aches[f]	/	Other _____	/	/
Lacrimation/rhinorrhea[f]	/			
Diarrhea[f]	/			
Yawning[f]	/			
Fever[f]	/			

Superscripts indicate the category of substance with which each symptom is associated in the *DSM–IV*: [a]alcohol, [b]amphetamine, [c]cocaine, [d]hallucinogens, [e]nicotine, [f]opioids, [g]sedative/hypnotic/anxiolytics.

Therapist's notes _____

_____

_____

_____

_____

_____

_____

_____

_____

_____

e. *Medical concerns*

  Past
    Problem(s)?

    Medications?
    (prescription or OTC)

  Current

    Problem(s)?

    Medications?
    (prescription or OTC)

    (for women) Are you Pregnant?

f. *Treatment history*

  Outpatient therapy (incidence/outcomes)
    For substance use?

    For mental health concerns?

    Other?

    Were providers aware of your AOD use?

  Inpatient treatment/hospitalization (incidence/outcomes)
    For substance use?

    For mental health concerns?

    Other?

    Were providers aware of your AOD use?

  (If Pregnant) Are you receiving prenatal care?

g. *Environmental factors*

  Residential situation
    Anyone else living with you?

    Anyone else in your residence an alcohol or other drug (AOD) user?

    Is your living situation safe?

  Social support system
    Whom do you count on for support?

    Anyone in your social network an AOD user?

    Has your AOD use interfered with any of your relationships with people?

Family and Developmental History
Messages received growing up about AOD use?

Anyone in your family an AOD user?

Has your AOD use affected your family? How so?

Any mental health concerns in your family?

Significant events during childhood?

Educational/Vocational factors
Relevant history (if student, indicate status: Full-time/Part-time)

Has your AOD use interfered with any of your school/work obligations or goals?

Financial factors
How much would you estimate you spend on alcohol and/or drugs per week?

Has your AOD use contributed to any financial problems?

Therapist's notes _____

_____

_____

_____

_____

_____

_____

_____

Transportation factors
  How did you get here today?

  Do you have a valid driver's license?

  Do you have access to a car or other vehicle?

  Have you ever driven under the influence of alcohol or drugs?

  If so, how many times in the past year?

Legal concerns
  Ever been arrested?

  Number of times/reasons?

  Charges/Disposition?

Therapist's notes _____
_____
_____
_____
_____

h. Motivation for treatment

Do you think you have a drug or alcohol problem?

Do you plan to stop or reduce your AOD use?

If yes, how confident are you that you will be able to do so?

Do you think you need treatment?

Has anyone urged or required you to get an assessment or treatment? Who?

Do you have any questions about AOD assessment and/or treatment?

Therapist's notes _____

_____

_____

_____

_____

_____

| Therapist's signature | Date | Supervisor's signature (if required) | Date |

Stress Management Worksheet

Your Name:

REDUCE STRESS
by making wise choices

Instructions: Place a mark on each line below that best describes your response to each question about the following stress management techniques. Different questions may be more relevant to you at different times in your own process of learning to better manage stress in your life.

Stress Management Techniques	How often do you use each technique in your current daily life?	How often did you use each technique while you were using drugs or alcohol?	Would you like to use this technique more often in the future?	Has using this technique created changes in your ability to control your stress level?
Listen to your body	Never — Always	Never — Always	No — Yes	No — Yes
Have a personal place	Never — Always	Never — Always	No — Yes	No — Yes
Reach out to others	Never — Always	Never — Always	No — Yes	No — Yes
Share your secrets	Never — Always	Never — Always	No — Yes	No — Yes
Laugh at yourself	Never — Always	Never — Always	No — Yes	No — Yes
Be assertive	Never — Always	Never — Always	No — Yes	No — Yes
Leave time for fun	Never — Always	Never — Always	No — Yes	No — Yes
Confront your fears	Never — Always	Never — Always	No — Yes	No — Yes
Exercise	Never — Always	Never — Always	No — Yes	No — Yes
Schedule wisely	Never — Always	Never — Always	No — Yes	No — Yes
Get straight financially	Never — Always	Never — Always	No — Yes	No — Yes
Practice relaxation and/or meditation	Never — Always	Never — Always	No — Yes	No — Yes
	Consider discussing responses with therapist		**Worksheet developed by C. Glidden-Tracey**	

291

Sample Termination Letter

[return address]

[client's address]

[Date]

Dear [client],

I hope this letter finds you well. I am writing because I have been unable to reach you directly by phone, having tried three times to call you since you missed your last two scheduled therapy sessions. I am uncertain of your intent to continue the work we have begun together, so I request that you contact me to confirm your plans. I invite you to come to at least one more session so we can discuss our options and, if your decision is to end therapy, we can wrap up our work. I feel we have made some important strides toward the goals we formulated, and I hope you will decide to continue in therapy. Whatever you decide, I wish you the very best.

I ask that you contact me by [date] if you wish to schedule a session. If I have not heard from you by that date, I will assume that you are no longer interested in therapy, and I will close your file in order to make this timeslot available for a client on our waiting list. Also, if I do not hear from you, I will send a letter to your probation officer verifying the dates and number of sessions that you did attend. This action would be based on the consent you signed on [date] requesting that I release information to your probation officer verifying your attendance.

I am glad to have had the opportunity to work with you. I hope to speak with you again; but in any case, good luck with your future endeavors.

Please feel free to contact me at [contact information] with any questions or if you are interested in additional services.

Sincerely,

[therapist's name and title]

Author Index

Subject Index